Cornelius O'Berien

Philosophy of the Bible Vindicated

Cornelius O`Berien

Philosophy of the Bible Vindicated

ISBN/EAN: 9783744660679

Printed in Europe, USA, Canada, Australia, Japan

Cover: Foto ©Lupo / pixelio.de

More available books at **www.hansebooks.com**

PHILOSOPHY

OF

THE BIBLE VINDICATED,

BY

REV. C. O'BRIEN, D. D.

CHARLOTTETOWN, P. E. I.:
BREMNER BROTHERS, PRINTERS, QUEEN ST.
1876.

Entered according to Act of Parliament, in the year one thousand eight hundred and seventy-six, by CORNELIUS O'BRIEN, D. D., in the office of the Minister of Agriculture and Statistics of the Dominion of Canada.

PREFACE.

IN the Holy Bible we have truths of the natural and supernatural order; we have historic, philosophic, theologic, and other truths. Being destined for all time, and for the good of mankind, its teachings can never be antiquated, neither can they ever run counter with the real interests of man. Inspired by an Infinite Wisdom its words are not empty sounds, but are replete with sublime meaning; its assertions are not vague and contradictory, but precise and harmonious throughout. Ages will bring no change to the truth of its message; scholars will never exhaust the treasury of its lore. Learned believers will reverently investigate its history and its claims to our obedience, not because they have any doubt, but to give a "reason for the faith that is in them," and its light will shine the more brightly: learned unbelievers will assail first one, then another of its truths, vainly calling to their aid some particular branch of knowledge, but each development of science will only tend to cast a more brilliant ray—if that were possible—of evidence around its eternal verities. In the following pages the Author has endeavoured to present, in a compendious form, the Philosophic truths of the Bible, and to prove them as concisely as possible. Only such truths as can be known by the light of human reason are here subjected to treatment. Historic truths, and those which could only be known by revelation, fall not within the scope of this roughly sketched treatise.

In this age of crude theories and disjointed systems that are launched upon the stream of literature, in a wild confusion not unlike the shifting visions of a diseased brain, it may not be amiss to offer to the consideration of the public a system of Philosophy the oldest, the most coherent, the most ennobling that this world has ever seen. The christian philosopher is not haunted by the ambition of "founding" a new school of philosophy: he may, indeed, be the founder of a new method of treatment, but substantially all his conclusions are found in the Bible. Briefly outlined the christian system of philosophy is this: "there exists an infinite, necessary, intelligent Being who, of his own free will, created all contingent things; these he rules by his providence and cares for in his love. Man is the lord of visible creation; he is the work of the Most High, and is endowed with freedom of will and an immortal soul. A law has been imposed upon him by his Creator; by its observance he can merit reward, by its transgression he will incur condign punishment. Viewing man historically the moral necessity of a revelation is made manifest; God can reveal, he has, in fact, revealed. Miracles are possible, and they are one of the evidences of revelation. No one truth can contradict another, hence between reason and revelation there can be no real contradiction." Many other questions bearing on these points fill up the grand system of biblic philosophy. It is one of great importance; it has direct bearing on social life; its exposition and defence constitute a noble work.

Two things have long appeared certain to the Author—first, that the science of Metaphysics is not so dry, difficult, and obscure as it is generally thought: secondly, that the spread of irreligion is greatly facilitated by an almost general ignorance of the elementary principles of this science. The very mention of metaphysics sends a shudder through the frames of many persons. They look upon it as a something misty and obscure; they fancy that it is a sort of scientific nightmare which broods gloomily over the brain of the anxious student. Others do not dread it to such an extent; still, they consider it an unprofitable study. To them it is a virgin forest, filled with gnarled old trunks that defy alike the axe of the husbandman, and the eating tooth of time. They cannot penetrate its mazy depths, they say: a tangled undergrowth of hard definitions intervenes between themselves and the knotty trees of Substance, Existence, Creation, and other giant trunks that grow in the vast wood-land of metaphysics. Perhaps they have ventured to peer timidly into its leafy groves; and then started back with a feeling akin to that experienced by children, when they hurry away from a dense wood, terrified by the echo of their own footfalls. Others again, will ignorantly declaim against this science without knowing more about it than its name. That the spread of irreligion is facilitated by an ignorance of metaphysics, is evident. The person who has mastered the elements of this science can refute materialism: he can prove that the soul is not matter; that it is a something distinct and different from the body; that the will is free, consequently that we are responsible for our actions. He can refute, in a word, all those false philosophic principles which are opposed to Biblic Revelation; he can prove that between Revelation and true science there can be no opposition. Man is probably, no more prone to evil now, than what he formerly was; but man, both professors and scholars, are more superficial in their attainments. Herein it seems, lies the explanation of this widespread infidelity. "Professors" who now are extolled as prodigies of learning, would, had their lot been cast in the oft reviled "middle ages," have been considered noisy school-boys. No respectable university, or college, would have allowed them to occupy a chair.

Now the Author was, and is, firmly persuaded that metaphysics could be made more popular; the science though abstract is not abstruse. Like every other human science it has been overshadowed by professional mystery; professional jargon and jugglery are the twin dragons that guard the entrance to every human science. If you overcome the former by patient study, you are still in danger of being kept away from the enchanted castle by the misleading tricks of the latter. The prince of philosophers, St. Thomas, has shown us that a profound subject may be treated in a clear manner. Truth is always clear in itself; hence natural truths can be made quite clear to every person of ordinary intelligence. It is only when the path of truth is left, or when a writer strives to explain something inexplicable by human reason, that confusion and obscurity arise. Whole pages are filled with misty propositions, jagged reasonings, and contradictory assertions about the simplest truth. A few words is often enough about a question which will be agitated in newspapers and reviews for months. To endeavour to popularize the elements of metaphysics, and thus to oppose, in some degree, a barrier to the spread of irreligious theories, was the object of the writer. This work is not intended for a class-book; it is rather intended as a book in the reading of which any intelligent person may find profit. Hence the style is not dry and strictly philosophic. The wish of the Author was to clothe the great truths of metaphysics which bear immediately on religion, in language which might be clear, and not devoid of attraction. How far he has succeeded the public will judge. Even if his work be pronounced a failure, he will not forego the belief that such a thing is possible, and if taken in hands by a more competent writer, would be productive of great good. The age is busy and restless; large volumes or long chapters are not, as a general rule, read. Hence brevity joined with perspicuity has been chiefly kept in view. Of a set purpose, an outspoken, or what some may call an arrogant tone, has, in many places, been adopted. When error is continually brawling in a dogmatic manner the defenders of truth ought not to put their propositions forward apologetically.

The Author desires to publicly express his obligations to the Rev. Azade J. Trudelle, of Hope River, formerly his professor, who kindly read the manuscript, and made some valuable suggestions. Had circumstances permitted the adoption of them all, the work would be much more worthy of public favour.

Even when desirous of keeping the right path, the human mind may err in its train of reasonings; or it may advance propositions that are at variance with the truth. Almighty God has instituted, as we believe, a church which is the depository and guardian of revelation. Between natural and revealed truths there can be no contradiction; the latter being known with infallible certainty have an indeclinable right to the consent of our intellect. Whatever is opposed to them must, of necessity, be false. Hence if there be in these pages aught that is opposed to the teachings of that church we repudiate, condemn, and hold it for not written, and wish our readers to do the same. The cause of true knowledge can never be promoted by rebellion against the truth.

Indian River, Feast of the Assumption, 1876.

CONTENTS.

PART FIRST.—NATURAL THEOLOGY.

CHAPTER I.—OUR STARTING POINT.

Two errors, Rationalism and Scepticism, to be avoided—We know some truths, but our intelligence is limited—We start from certainty, or from three grand truths. . . . . PAGE 1

CHAPTER II.—FUNDAMENTAL TRUTHS.

Our existence, our ability to know with certainty, and the principle of contradiction are called Fundamental Truths—These do not require proof, they are presupposed—Subjective and objective truths—Apprehension and comprehension. 4

CHAPTER III.—SOURCES OF CERTAINTY.

Inner consciousness—Evidence—Universal consent in that which intimately interests each individual—Testimony of trustworthy witnesses—Each faculty has its legitimate object. 7

CHAPTER IV.—THE SUBJECT *I*.

The existence of the subject *I* cannot be doubted—A sure basis of philosophy—Precision of terminology required—Substances and accidents—Simple, compound, and spiritual substances—Necessary substance—possible things. 9

CHAPTER V.—CAUSA CAUSARUM, OR THE FIRST SUBSTANCE.

Nobility of this subject—Current of modern thought seems to run backward—Absurdity of a denial of God—What we mean by God—What some mean by that name. 12

CHAPTER VI.—THE EXISTENCE OF GOD.

The subject *I* is certain that it is limited and dependent—Each one must admit the existence either of effects or phenomena—A first action, or a first cause must be admitted; this must be from itself—The infinite a simple act—Numbers always finite—Reasoning from abstract principles must be admitted—German transcendentalists—A mixed mode of reasoning. 16

x   CONTENTS.

CHAPTER VII.—THE INTELLIGENCE AND WILL OF GOD.

Attempts to deny a personal God—God has the plenitude of being, and of knowledge—He acted freely; hence he has will.   .   .   .   PAGE 22

CHAPTER VIII.—GOD AS LEARNT FROM THE PHYSICAL ORDER.

Beauties of visible creation—Absurdity of supposing an unintelligent cause—Absurdity of supposing matter with its properties as a sufficient explanation of the physical order—Physical laws not always constant in their development.   26

CHAPTER IX.—UNIVERSAL BELIEF IN THE EXISTENCE OF A GOD.

Belief in the existence of a God constant and universal—Its cause is the evidence of reason—Ignorance of physical laws not the cause of this belief—The greatest minds believe in a personal God—His ruling power always acknowledged.   34

CHAPTER X.—RECAPITULATORY.

Solidity of our position—How the subject *I* rose to a knowledge of God's existence—Attributes of God—His infinity.   38

CHAPTER XI.—PANTHEISM.

What it is—It is very insidious—Reasons why—Its various systems—Their common fundamental principle—Confusion of destinction with *diversity* exposed—Various ways in which one thing may be contained in another—Absolute and relative perfections—Admission of finite perfections not derogatory to the infinite—Plurality of substances—Pernicious effects of pantheism.   41

CHAPTER XII.—REALITY OF THE PHYSICAL WORLD.

Real and ideal defined—Every substance a reality—Every substance a force—Notion of existence—Perception really in us—Object of perception must be a reality—Nature of the physical world—Two erroneous systems on this head confuted—True system evident.   50

CHAPTER XIII.—CREATION.

The ways of error various—Consistency of a true system—Creation defined—Finite substances created by God—Created things not eternal—Time and creation coeval—Unchangeability of God's essence not effected by creation—Conservatism—Only God can annihilate—Action of created things. 59

CHAPTER XIV.—PROVIDENCE.

Providence defined—Proved from various heads—It is easily reconciled with all physical and moral facts.   68

CHAPTER XV.—END OF CREATION.

God had an end in view in creating—It is the external manifestation of his perfections—How this is obtained despite the malice of men and devils   73

PART SECOND.—PSYCHOLOGY.

CHAPTER I.—NATURE OF THE SUBJECT I.

Know thyself—What is meant by the soul—Its continued indentity with itself—Substance and accident defined—Sensations explained—How excited—Monads—Essence of things unchangeable—Inertia an absence of a self-determining power—Three classes of monads. . . PAGE 77

CHAPTER II.—SIMPLICITY OF THE SOUL.

Haters of human dignity—Their theory—Ours—Simplicity of the soul demonstrated from its perception of a square—Objection of materialists answered—Self-determining power of the soul proves its simplicity—So does comparsion of ideas. 87

CHAPTER III.—SPIRITUALITY OF THE SOUL.

Spirituality defined—It is no figment of the schools—Traces of this idea found among all nations—Fundamentally it is as old as our race; its present precision due to christianity—Spirituality of soul demonstrated from actions of intellect and will. 95

CHAPTER IV.—ESSENCE AND ORIGIN OF THE SOUL.

We have a clear idea of the soul—Limitation of knowledge no proof of its total absence—Various false theories regarding origin of the soul refuted—Its true origin assigned. 100

CHAPTER V.—FACULTIES OF THE SOUL.

Two grand faculties, intelligence and will—What memory is—Imagination—Intelligence and will not distinct from the soul—Perception—Ideas—Knowledge, how acquired—Difference between an idea and its perception—Cause and origin of ideas—Theories regarding them—The soul must always have some knowledge—Two ideas, at least, coeval with the existence of the soul 105

CHAPTER VI.—THE WILL.

Two-fold tendency in man—Animal tendencies must be guided by reason—All desire happiness—Liberty of the will explained—Physical and moral liberty, what they mean—Power of erring not necessary to true liberty—Definition. 113

CHAPTER VII.—LIBERTY OF THE WILL.

It is proved, 1*st, from our inner consciousness*—2*nd, from the nature of finite goods*—3*rd, from the notion of reason*—4*th, from the manner of acting of all mankind*—5*th, from the absurdities which would follow in the contrary sentence.* 117

CHAPTER VIII.—UNION OF THE SOUL AND BODY.

The whole individual man considered—Union of soul and body, physical and substantial—Importance of previous chapters—Facts of psychology reconciled with those of physiology—Reciprocal action between soul and body—The soul the vivifier of the body—Organic sanity a *condition* for healthy intellectual action, not its cause—Sleep, disease, death—perfectibility of our intellectual powers. . . . . . . PAGE 123

CHAPTER IX.—IMMORTALITY OF THE SOUL.

Importance of this subject in a social and moral point of view—Degrading effects of materialism—Idea of immortality—The soul can exist and act separated from the body—No created force, no natural process can destroy the soul—God wishes it to be immortal, as proved from his wisdom and justice—Man's nature considered in itself, and in its relation to society proves the immortality of the soul—Universal belief of mankind, and individual feeling evince the same truth. 133

CHAPTER X.—CAUSE OF EVIL IN THE WORLD.

Evil a negative of good—metaphysical, physical, and moral evil—Only moral evil considered—Absurdity of the manichean system: its insufficiency even if admitted—Abuse of human liberty the cause of moral evil—God's concurrence in human actions explained—Only good the effect of God's action. 142

CHAPTER XI.—KNOWLEDGE OF GOD, AND LIBERTY OF MAN'S WILL.

God's knowledge ever infinite, ever the same: man's acquired by degrees—Future free actions of man known to God—This knowledge does not effect their freedom—Man does not do them because God knows them, but God knows them because man is about to do them. 147

CHAPTER XII.—FUTURE PUNISHMENT.

Ignorance and presumption of those who deride the teachings of christianity—Selfism, or animalism strong at denial—Naturally a law has been imposed on man—Its observers and transgressors cannot obtain the same after-state—Deprivation of the enjoyment of the supreme good part of the punishment of the impious—Bitterness of this punishment—God is just as well as merciful; mercy reigns here, justice will preside in the next life. 151

CHAPTER XIII.—PSYCHOLOGICAL PHENOMENA.

Life—Laws of propagation of sentient things—Vital principle always created by God—Examination of some phenomena that seem to prove that one soul can act on another even in life—Certain class of dreams. 158

CHAPTER XIV.—PRINCIPLE OF LIFE IN THE BRUTE CREATION.

Degrading tendency of the theory of evolution—Brutes have various sensations and distinct sensible perceptions—The subject of these is physically simple, and created by God—Essential difference between the human soul and the vital principle of brutes—Absolute impossibility of the latter developing into the former—Instinct no degree of intelligence—Essential difference between them as seen from the power of reasoning and articulate speech in man—Neither actively nor potentially is reason in brutes—Cruelty to brutes considered—Man's prerogatives regarding brutes. 164

CHAPTER XV.—DARWINISM.

Hankerers after notoriety—Darwinism subversive of the common consent of mankind, of morality, and of reason—What it is—Authorities cited by Mr. Darwin prove nothing in his favor—His appeal to the reader—He discourses with wonderful self-complacency on "changed conditions" and "organism," but tells us nothing new—Some of his difficulties answered —"Inherited qualities" explained—He rambles and relates, but does not argue very closely—His conclusion that "all species may be from four or five," or perhaps fewer, subjected to examination—It is illogical, it is opposed to facts—Progressive development, if it exists, is the natural effect of innate causes, hence each generation ought to show a change; but this is not so—Metaphysical argument against his theory—Species—Plan and order of creation not difficult to understand—Mosaic history of creation cannot be refuted—Darwin and posterity. . . . . PAGE 179

PART THIRD.—QUESTIONS HAVING AN INTIMATE CONNECTION WITH ONTOLOGY.

CHAPTER I.—TIME, ETERNITY, SPACE.

Time a succession of events—It exists relatively to the finite, not to the infinite—Eternity not made up of years—It is relative to the infinite—Space, popular notion of it—Extension a relative property—It is a relation of one finite being to another—It is a phenomenon arising from our limitation of essence—St. Thomas felt the truth of this theory—Its harmony with catholic dogma—neither time nor extension for the infinite. . . . 197

CHAPTER II.—CERTITUDE.

We can be certain of some things—First principle of certitude is the intellect perceiving—St. Thomas and St. Augustine quoted—Difference between this doctrine and rationalism—It is philosophic and in harmony with sound theology. 205

CHAPTER III.—RELIGION.

Religious tendency of some kind ever exhibited by the human race—What we mean by religion—Its connection with metaphysics. . . . 210

CHAPTER IV.—REVELATION.

Harmony of the Sciences—Revelation defined—It is possible—Its acceptance no degredation to reason. 213

CHAPTER V.—NECESSITY OF REVELATION.

Literary imposters—Historic view of mankind—Great depravity of man, as a general rule, before Christ—Morally speaking, revelation was necessary to emancipate mankind from their degrading errors. . . . 219

CHAPTER IV.—MIRACLES.

Difference in proceedings of the true and false philosopher—universal belief in miracles—What they are—No natural law abrogated or suspended —Sublimation of natural forces possible—Miracles not to remedy an oversight of the Creator; they entered into the plan of creation. . . 224

CHAPTER VII.—EXISTENCE OF MIRACLES.

They were always looked upon as a test of a divine mission—Scientific proof of miracles can be obtained even from the testimony of the ignorant—Canons on this point—Miracles did not cease with the apostolic times—Prophecy: it is a miracle in the intellectual order—Its possibility and scientific proof. . . . . PAGE 234

CHAPTER VIII.—A DIVINE REVELATION HAS BEEN MADE.

Authenticity of the scriptures assummed—General belief, in early times, of the coming of a Redeemer—Historic fact of the coming of the one who claimed to be son of God—How his works prove this—Intellectual benefits from his teaching—Its expansion and duration. 242

CHAPTER IX.—RELIGIOUS INDIFFERENCE.

Scientific fops—Their vagaries—Right idea of modern and free thought—An internal as well as an external order—Religious indifference a sign of mental decay—Why we ought to accept revelation. 247

CHAPTER X.—HOW TO SEEK REVELATION.

Faith often vilified—Dangers to youth from an infidel atmosphere—Method to be followed in seeking revelation—Not a method of logical induction, but one from motives of credibility—Miracles as motives—Unity and perpetuity of a system of revelation. 252

CHAPTER XI.—FAITH AND REASON.

Contradictions of pretended scientists—Manufactured fame—Faith does not enslave reason, it ennobles it—No real contradiction between truths revealed, and true conclusions of science—A German egg story—Assent to revealed truths most reasonable—Two natural ways of acquiring truth—Faith must be intolerant of error, reason perfectible, faith unchangeable. 258

CHAPTER XII.—FAITH IN ITS RELATION TO THE BODY POLITIC.

Man is sociable by nature—God wishes civil society—God the source of all power—True sense of the "divine right" of kings—difference between conferring power and determining its organ—Responsibilities of rulers—A king may forfeit his right to rule—Who is to judge his offence?—Two divinely constituted orders in the world—Origin of collisions between church and state—Gregory VII and Pius IX—War of hell against the church—Education—Man can fully discharge all his obligations both to church and state. 269

CHAPTER XIII.—THE RESURRECTION OF THE BODY.

Growth and decay in the vegetable kingdom—Cheering hope of the resurrection—Its possibility—No suspension or abrogation of nature's laws is verified in the resurrection—Difficulty met—Two reasons that tend to prove that our bodies will rise again—Burial and cremation. . . . 286

ERRATA.

Page 24, second paragraph, eighteenth line, for "we elected," read "he elected."

Page 145, second paragraph, fourth line, for "exacted by God," read "required of God."

PHILOSOPHY OF THE BIBLE
VINDICATED.

CHAPTER I.

OUR STARTING POINT.

IN order that our investigations, in any branch of human science, may be useful, we must have constantly before our eyes the great truth that human intelligence is incapable of comprehending everything. There are two errors which, like Charybdis and Scylla, render dangerous the course along which the metaphysician has to steer. Some, degrading reason by maintaining that it is incapable of acquiring truth, have been drawn into the vortex of scepticism: others, extolling it too much by asserting that it is capable of discovering and comprehending all truth, have been lost in the whirl-pool of rationalism. Each of these errors is dangerous; each of them is an insult to human reason. The followers of the first must admit that we know at least one thing with certainty, viz.: *that we know nothing*: the followers of the second insult reason by disregarding its teachings. Our intelligence tells us that we are limited beings; consequently our capacity must be limited: it proves, moreover, that there is an unlimited and infinite Being, and as a logical consequence, it tells us that our limited capacity cannot fully comprehend that unlimited Being, that infinite Truth. Those simple observations are, of themselves, quite sufficient to overthrow the bulwarks of scepticism and rationalism. Once that the rampart has fallen the minarets and turrets of ornamental rhteoric will offer but a feeble resistance to the blows of truth. Any intelligent school-boy who retains these observations in his memory can confute the most gloomy sceptic, or the most inflated rationalist.

The two false extremes, scepticism and rationalism, prove conclusively two things : first, that we can know some truths, secondly, that our intelligence is limited and liable to err in its logical deductions. The sceptic and the rationalist must both admit at least one certainty ; they must, likewise, admit that they cannot both be right ; hence the human intellect is liable to err in deducing its conclusions.

The middle course, then, between these rugged promontories of error, is safe. It is the course which Catholic Philosophers, guided by faith as a compass, and enlightened by the teachings of Divine Revelation, have ever sailed. Faith does not destroy reason ; it ennobles it ; it opens up a broader field for the speculations of the intellect. Once we are certain that a thing is so, we can detect reasons for its being so which perhaps, we would never have detected. Hence we cannot be a thorough Philosopher without being first a sound Theologian ; hence, too, the fact that infidelity cannot produce one worthy of the name of Philosopher. Let it be understood from the outset that we deny the title of Philosopher to the founders of schools of error. 'Tis a sad thing to hear a man called a Philosopher who has spent the talents God gave him, in obscuring the light ; 'tis sadder still to hear this done by Christians. The man who, as a general rule, blunders in the art he professes to follow, is not called a tradesman, but a botcher: why, then, call meaningless scribblers Philosophers. They are literary fungi.

We start in our metaphysical investigations from certainty, or if you will, from three grand truths—viz: our own existence; our ability to know with certainty some truth; and that a thing cannot both be and not be, under the same respect, at the same time. Unless these be presupposed you can have no science. Science is the *" knowledge of things by means of their ultimate causes;"* knowledge is such that its contradictory cannot be true. If, therefore, we do not suppose the existence of the intelligent subject *I*, we cannot have knowledge, or anything else; equally we cannot have it unless we have an aptitude for knowing with certainty; and equally we cannot have it unless the principle of contradiction be admitted. Therefore these three truths are the basis of all philosophic science—the starting point of all metaphysical investigations.

CHAPTER II.

FUNDAMENTAL TRUTHS.

THE great philosophers of the past called the three truths, mentioned in the preceding chapter, *fundamental* truths. Our own existence was called the *first fact:* our ability to know with certainty, the *first principle;* and the axiom, " the same thing cannot both be and not be, under the same respect, at the same time" the *principle of contradiction.* We shall call them by the same names : the human mind has strayed long enough from the right path in metaphysics, let us humbly endeavour to return to it.

These three truths do not require proof; because, as we have seen, they must be presupposed in every scientific research. A truth is proved, or demonstrated by a principle more clearly perceived than itself. Hence it follows that everything cannot be proved, because there are some things so clearly perceived that nothing can be more so. These things can be simply declared, not demonstrated. Amongst this class of things come the fundamental truths. So self-evident are they, that to attempt to demonstrate them would be as ridiculous as to hold up a rush taper to show the daylight. The man who attempts to deny his own existence is not to be reasoned with ; a kindly keeper is required : or if he be considered sane, a rude shake might possibly awaken him to the fact that he both exists and feels. He who denies the first principle, affirms it, for he maintains that he is sure at least, of one thing, viz,—of knowing nothing. The one who denies the principle of contradiction likewise affirms it, because he must invoke it to support his denial; since, then, these truths are self-evident and cannot be denied, or called in doubt without evident absurdity, they are rightly termed fundamental, and are to be admitted by every sane mind.

Truth may be considered *subjectively*, inasmuch as it is an apprehension of the intelligent subject; or *objectively*, that is, in the object itself. Considered objectively, "whatever is is true in as much as it is," or, it is the conformity of the object to the archetypal idea in the divine mind, about which more will be said hereafter. Subjective truth is the conformity of our idea of an object to that object itself. If we apprehend it as it is, we have truth concerning it. It is here to be observed that there is a vast difference between apprehending, and comprehending. To apprehend, it is sufficient to be cognizant of the existence of an object and of its characteristics: to comprehend, it is necessary to know of the existence of the object, and all its properties. If there be even one only property which we cannot explain, or which is beyond the range of our intellect, we do not fully comprehend the object. Hence we apprehend numberless things; we comprehend but few. Facts we have in abundance, and hence information is not scarce: the why of facts is rarely known, and hence knowledge is very limited. The commonest facts of every-day life are often insoluble mysteries; and still, strange to say, men who cannot solve even these, pretend to explain learnedly the most sublime truths. A moment's reflection ought to convince anyone that our intelligence, whilst on the one hand it knows, and can know much, on the other is limited; and that there are a thousand and one truths above its grasp—far beyond its province.

Until we have mastered this fact, or acquired this humility of intellect, it is useless to begin scientific researches. We would only lose our time and muddle our brains, by straining after the impossible.

CHAPTER III.

SOURCES OF CERTAINTY.

WE have seen that we can be certain of some things; it may be well to say a few words on some of the chief sources of certainty.

1st.—Our inner consciousness, or the intelligent subject *I*, modified in a certain way, and testifying to its modification. It is self-evident, that this is a source of certainty regarding the intimate affections of the sentient subject. No one can persuade a man that he feels warm so long as his inner consciousness testifies that he feels cold. The same may be said of the various affections of the subject *I*.

2nd.—*Evidence* or the apprehension, by the intellect, of a necessary connection between a subject and its predicate. The perfection of the intelligence is the acquisition of truth; hence it must be fitted to acquire it. But it could not be fitted to acquire it, were it possible that it could err when it calmly and deliberately apprehends a necessary connection between a subject and its predicate. No means of correcting such an error could be found; consequently the mind would be unfitted for the acquiring of certainty.

3rd.—*Universal consent* in a thing which intimately interests each individual. This universal consent means that in all ages, under every variety of circumstances, mankind have agreed in recognizing as true, something which intimately concerns each and all. The reason is, that a constant and universal effect, such as this would be, requires a constant and universal cause. But, humanly speaking, there can be no constant and universal cause, except the evidence of reason. Passion, prejudice, fear, education, every other cause imaginable, is local and variable. The evidence of reason only will remain unchanging and unchangeable in sunshine, or in gloom; in poverty, or in wealth. When the truth admitted by this universal consent, ought to act rather as a restraint on the passions and pleasures of mankind, than as an incentive to their indulgence, the more forcibly does this consent strike us as a source of certainty.

4th.—The testimony of persons worthy of faith. Persons are worthy of faith when it is known that they have a knowledge of what they testify, and a desire to speak truly. As this source of certainty pertains more to history, than to metaphysics we shall merely mention it here.

Our external senses: sight, touch, &c., are in a certain degree, sources of certainty regarding their legitimate objects. They enable us to shun many dangers, but they are not fitted, nor intended for the acquisition of metaphysical truth. The eye of the chemist will serve him in discovering the physical properties of bodies; but once he presumes to cast it beyond its legitimate bounds, and to sweep with it the vast horizon of metaphysics, he can no longer rely on its fidelity. The gross errors of Huxley, Darwin, and Tyndall, have originated in a disregard of the principle known to every tyro in logic that each faculty is a faithful witness only in regard to its legitimate objects.

CHAPTER IV.

THE SUBJECT *I*.

ALMOST every truth has been denied, or called in doubt, by some one who called himself a philosopher. Cicero tells us there is nothing so absurd but what has been maintained, at some time, by some would-be follower of wisdom. This great truth should make us intellectually humble and cautious. There is one truth, however, which no one can seriously deny, or doubt—that is, his own existence. Whether he considers himself as thinking truly or falsely, as feeling real or imaginary sensations, he must still admit the fact, I think, I feel. He may call everything else in doubt; he may view the world with the eye of a cynic; he may deny the existence of God; of right and wrong, but turn as he will, deny what he may, the one great truth, I feel, I think, will force itself continually upon him. St. Augustine, the greatest human mind after Solomon, indicates this truth as a most sure basis of philosophy, (L. de liber. arb.) Des Cartes, amongst moderns, took his cue from that great Doctor of the Church. Now this *I* which feels, thinks, and wishes, and whose existence no one denies, will be called by us the intelligent subject *I*, or the soul. Precision of terminology is the cream of science. Sophists, and dealers in false scientific coins, delight in obscurity of language, and indefiniteness of terms. With them obscure phraseology holds the place of a military ambuscade; and want of precision the place of grape-shot. A forest of difficulties can be hewn down by a few sharp defining strokes. Well, this intelligent subject I exists. More than this, it testifies to the existence in itself, of various affections, some pleasing, others disagreeable. It, likewise, testifies that these affections are often produced by something which is not itself; something of whose existence it is as certain as what it is of its own; but whose actions it cannot control, or modify. Hence the inner consciousness of the subject I makes us certain of the existence of numberless other things, distinct, and different from itself, and from one another. We thus arrive at the firm conviction that we are but one of an immense multitude of beings, which surround us on all sides. Some of these we apprehend as essentially similar to ourselves; others as essentially different. We accurately distinguish between the affections which are in us and caused by ourselves, and those which are, indeed, in us but not caused by us. Hence the certainty of the existence of objects which form no part of our being, of which we are not modifications, and which are not modifications of us. The inevitable conclusion, then, from inner consciousness and evidence is, *that we, many beings like ourselves, and many unlike exist.* Another conclusion from these sources of certainty is, that we are limited in our being, restricted in our capacity, and subject to modifications during our existence.

Now we call *substance* that which exists by itself, not requiring another in which to adhere, as in a subject. From this it follows that we know ourselves, and many other things to be substances. The modifications, or affections, which we advert in ourselves, and apprehend in others, we call accidents. These require, humanly speaking, a subject in which to adhere.

A substance is physically simple when it has no parts into which it can be divided: it is physically compound when it can be divided into parts. A substance is spiritual when it is simple and endowed with intelligence and will, and can exercise these independently of corporeal organs. That substances physically simple exist is easily proved. Compound substances exist; therefore simple ones exist. The antecedent will not be denied; we are certain of the existence of beings distinct from ourselves, and which can be divided into parts. This being granted, the consequence, therefore simple ones exist, is as inevitable as the following: a brick house exists; therefore each particular brick of which it is composed exists. In a word, composition presupposes simplicity. If we have a compound, its component parts must exist. Therefore there are some physically simple substances.

A substance is said to be necessary, or to exist *necessarily*, when it depends from no preceding cause, but contains in itself the reason of its own existence; otherwise it is contingent.

A thing is *possible* when the notes which form its conception are not mutually destructive: otherwise it is impossible; or, what is the same, it is an absurdity.

CHAPTER V.

CAUSA CAUSARUM, OR THE FIRST SUBSTANCE.

THE human reason is never more nobly employed than in vindicating the honour of its Creator. The genius which discovers, and evolves the physical laws by which the planets are guided in their orbits; or, which demonstrates some intricate proposition, is hailed, and justly too, as engaged in a noble pursuit. But much more noble is the study of that intellect which rises in its investigations far beyond the most distant stars,—transcends in its sublime flight the various orbs which whirl through the azure, passes the innumerable orders and grades of created things, and their physical laws, and fixes its attention on Him from whom all these depend. If it be accounted great wisdom to know something of the motions of the solar system, how much more wisdom must it not be to know something of the great Author of that system? And if it be a noble science to investigate the secondary causes which are continually at work in nature, how much more noble will it not be to learn something of the First Cause of all—the great " Causa Causarum " recognized by Socrates, Plato and Cicero.

One might have thought that our boasted " progress" had been such as to render unnecessary a formal proof of the existence of a First Cause—of a Creator. One might have reasoned thus: if the greatest minds of antiquity, with all their disadvantages, clearly perceived that an intelligent cause must have been at work in the ordering of the world, surely the great minds of to-day, with all their advantages, must be firmly convinced on this point. And so, indeed, all great minds are quite certain of the existence of an intelligent first cause. But there are some minds which pretend to be great, and which make a huge parade of unmeaning bombast, in order to be considered learned, which endeavour to deny that First Cause. It would seem as if that most irregular of streams, the "current of modern thought," as it is euphoniously termed by those who sail adown its tide, had bent backward its course and run, up hill, to the dim ages of the past. Certain it is that the scientific barque, in which many who claim to be advanced thinkers paddle their dangerous way along, is composed of the fragments, and the most shattered ones too, of the old sophistical punts broken centuries ago by the blows of Aristotle, Socrates and Plato. During their pleasure trip *up* the "current of modern thought," our thinkers discovered these stranded and condemned boats; wishing probably, to appear singular, they attempted to make wrecks sea-worthy by painting them anew. The brilliant colouring of their word-painting dazzled the eyes of a few who cheered, as the professors sailed along: the heads of the poor professors became dizzy at the sound of the applause; they claimed as their own the ship which they had merely varnished.

Seriously, it is hard to imagine how anyone, laying pretentious to sanity, could deny the existence of that, without which, he himself would be an absurdity—viz: an effect without a cause. We can see only one reasonable explanation of this mental aberration. We do not wish to accuse the teachers of philsophic error, or any one else of moral delinquencies, but we must say that the practical conclusion from any theory which denies either an avenging God, or the liberty of the will, or the immortality of the soul, or the eternity of punishment, is—do *as you please, so long as you escape the clutches of the civil law.* The human mind is naturally logical; it may not see, nor care to see, the error in the premises; but it will clearly perceive that, taking any of these systems as its guide, the individual who kills his own mother, or debauches his own sister, may be just as easy in mind, and quite as respectable, as the son who toils for the support of his parent, or braves dangers for the honour of his sister. In a few years they will be both in the dust; their constituent atoms floating in the "infinite azure of the past," and no more! The cultivated mind revolts at this infamous conclusion: even those who uphold the false theories above named, would scarcely dare defend, in any respectable company, these deductions. Still, they are severely logical; they are as cogent as any geometrical demonstration. Now, it is evident that when the logical consequence of any premises is absurd, the premises themselves must be faulty. Hence none of these systems can be correct. But the race of men who compose the communists, will eagerly lend ear to such doctrines. It just suits them.

The good man, be he learned or illiterate, rejoices to believe that there exists a Being, immense, eternal, incomprehensible, supreme and perfect, that does not depend from any cause, but contains in itself the reason of its existence. It is an *Ens a se*, a self-existing Being. They believe this Being to be endowed with intelligence and will: its intelligence designed all the glorious works we see, and the laws which govern them; and its free will created them. This Being is one, simple, infinite act, knowing no change— gaining no knowledge because always infinitely wise—losing no power, because always the source of action. This Being exercises a watchful Providence over all its works; it will punish the transgressor, and reward the doer of its will. It is called God; and we rejoice to call it Father. Right reason can demonstrate the existence of such a being, with the above-mentioned attributes. 'Tis the noblest work of the metaphysician to prove this. Those who boast so much about following reason would do well to attend to the arguments which will be set forth in the next chapter. If they will only grasp the logical outcome of arguments from reason, they will be thoroughly convinced that there is a God, such as we have described.

There are few, perhaps none, who seek the appellation of learned, who deny the existence of some higher force than that of matter. But many will only admit a God after their own fashion. With some He is a power, but a blind one, and one that necessarily acts; with others, He is intelligent, but otiose: He made the world, perhaps, but does not look after it: He is a kind of absentee landlord, only less attentive; the latter will sometimes (alas! very often) evict his poor tenants, whereas the former will never punish them. Now, all this talk about "nature," and other such names, by which certain writers seek to elude the arguments in favour of the existence of God, is mere chaff thrown into the eyes of the unthinking. Either this "nature" is such a being as we have described God to be, or it is not. If it is, then it is the christians' God, and Catholic Philosophy is right: if it is not, it cannot be the First Cause, so they are only acting absurdly by having recourse to it. They must either build on the same foundation with us, or they cannot build at all, unless they have become adepts in that peculiar branch of architecture which devotes itself to the building of "castles in the air."

CHAPTER VI.

THE EXISTENCE OF GOD.

WE defined above what we mean by God; but we will prove, by parts, His attributes. We will first prove the existence of a substance which is the First Cause, the primary actor, from which depend all visible things.

We have shown that each one is intimately convinced of the fact—*I exist*. The intelligent *subject I*, not only knows its own existence as a certainty, but it, likewise, knows with equal certainty, that it is dependent and limited. If it asks itself the questions: what am I? whence came I? The answer will inevitably be: I am limited, subject to change, dependent. I am an effect produced by some cause. But suppose for a moment some one should say: I exist independent of any cause. Then you must have in yourself the reason of your existence; you exist by necessity of your nature; consequently you must have always existed, such as you are now. No one, outside of a mad-house, has ever asserted that he has always existed such as he now is: hence he cannot exist by necessity of nature; he must be contingent, or in other words dependent. Moreover we are convinced, as shown previously, that numberless things exist: we see things daily springing up which were not before. Now no matter what may be the peculiar system of so-called philosophy which any one may follow, he must admit either

THE EXISTENCE OF GOD. 17

effects or phenomena. The Egotist and Idealist must admit the thinking subject and its modifications: the Sceptic, the vicissitudes of phenomena; the Materialist, matter; Kant and Hume, effects. Each one is, therefore, intimately convinced that there are, at least, various vicissitudes of phenomena,—various actions of which one is determined by another. Now in this motion of things; in this succession of cause and effect, there must be a first action or cause. Produce the chain as long as you will, you must eventually hang it to an immoveable something which nothing precedes. There must be a first action in these phenomena, or a first cause amid the various causes and effects. To escape this argument, there is but one way, and 'tis this: *to suppose a long chain made up of links but without a first one.* If any one can persuade oneself that this way is reasonable, one will certainly be clear of the difficulty, but in no other way can one hope to escape admitting a first action, or cause. If A is from B, and B from C, and C from D, and so on, no matter how many links you imagine, there must be the first one, Z. Being the first it cannot be from a preceding one; it must be from itself.

It may here be remarked that infinite is that, greater than which nothing can be conceived. Nothing can be added to Infinity, nothing can be taken from it. It is not made up of any amount of finite things; if it were, something could be always added to it. The infinite must, therefore, be a simple act. Numbers are always finite: so is a series of units no matter how long you may imagine it; for it will be composed of one, two, three, &c. It is as absurd, then, to talk of an infinite number, as what it is to suppose the long chain without a first link. No one, therefore, can have recourse to an infinite series of successive phenomena, or of causes and effects. No matter how many the successions may have been up to the present moment, they must be finite, because they can be numbered by one, two, three, four, &c. Let the intelligent *subject I* turn whichsoever way it will, in explaining the phenomena, or effects, of whose existence it is certain, it must eventually come to a first action, or cause; otherwise it must swallow one of two absurdities—either a succession of phenomena without a first, or a series of dependent effects without a first independent cause. The pagan poet saw the absurdity of this conclusion and said: "the last link of the chain must be fastened to the foot of Jupiter." And Young: "can one link depend and not the whole?" The conclusion from the above is simple and inevitable: there exists a first actor or cause. We have shown that this consequence must be arrived at, no matter what theory one may embrace: either phenomena or effects must be admitted. Either of these being admitted, the above conclusion must be admitted; otherwise, the mind is diseased. There can be no argument with the man who holds a series of phenomena without a first one, or a chain of dependent effects and causes without an independent cause.

Now this first actor must be from itself; being first it cannot be from a preceding one. It must, therefore, exist by necessity of its nature: it is entirely independent of any other, whilst all others depend from it. It must have always existed, because its essence always necessarily included existence. It must be unchangeable, because whatever it has, it has by necessity of nature. It must be infinite, because it could not be limited by any other, being independent; nor by itself, because it did not deliberate on its mode of existence before existing; and moreover it is by necessity of nature.

In order to leave no room for sophistry, we will here observe that reasoning from abstract principles must be admitted. A certain modern English author, following in the steps of some thick-headed sceptic, rejects metaphysics. One can well imagine a common debauchee unwilling to recognize anything more refined, or subtle, than gross physical sensations. His course of life clouds his intellect, and renders him altogether unfit for scientific pursuits. But how a cultivated mind, such as, no doubt, the author in question thinks his to be, could reject metaphysics, one knows not how to explain. Certain it is that some foolishly deny reasoning from abstract principles; everything must be *a posteriori*. Now all mathematical science is founded in the evidence of conceptions, or abstract principles; and each individual who has attained the use of reason, even the most illiterate, knows certain calculations with numbers, and, by a kind of natural Geometry, measures angles, lines, and surfaces. Therefore each individual is intimately convinced of the truth of conclusions derived from abstract principles. When, then, he finds himself modified by external causes, and beholds the vicissitudes of things, and their mutual dependence, he arrives at the certainty that there must be a first absolute, and independent action from which the others depend.

Finally, to meet the objections of the disciples of the transcendental German school, who, lulled into a semi-somniferous state, by lager beer and strong cigars, talk misty things which they call transcendental, we will put our argument into another shape. Really, a sensible man ought not to take notice of the hazy, verbose German transcendentalists. The unwary too often take obscurity of expression for sublimity of ideas, and for depth of research: hence the applause of the German "Philosophers." It was the boast of one German "founder of a school," Hegel, that only one person understood him, and not even that one understood him. We suspect that he was the individual himself: and it is quite credible that he did not understand himself. If he did he could, most certainly, so express himself as to enable others to get, at least, a faint inkling of his meaning. So much for our estimation of German transcendentalists.

Kant asserted that abstract notions showed only the agreement of ideas, and did not prove, with certainty, the actual existence of any object. Moreover, although he admitted the existence of God, he maintained that reason could not prove the fact. Balmes has justly observed that Kant's "critique of pure Reason" is the death of reason.

To rebut the above subtilty of Kant, and other kindred ones, we put our argument into another form. Something exists: therefore an *Ens a se* exists. It is evident that this is not purely an argument *a priori;* it is not from purely abstract notions. It is a mixed mode of reasoning. The antecedent asserts a fact admitted by all—viz: something exists; at least *I* exist, whether *I* be a phenomenon or an effect: then from the existence of this something the reason deduces the existence of a necessary Being, an *Ens a se.* It proceeds by the inexorable logic of evidence. Something exists: this something is either a necessary being, or it is not. If the former, then there exists a necessary being, and our first step is secure: if the latter, this something not existing by necessity of nature, must have been produced by something else, which we will call B. The question arises, is B a necessary being? If it be, then it is the substance whose existence we seek to prove: if not it must be from C. Thus we fall into a series of dependent effects and causes, and must, as shown above, admit a first independent cause, or swallow the long suspended chain, that has no first suspended link.

From the foregoing it is evident that there is no refuge for the atheist, save in a maze of absurdities. Any boy of ordinary intelligence can confute the most subtle atheist, idealist, or any other follower of the *genus* error, as regards the existence of a first and independent cause. A phenomenon, or an effect exists. Therefore there exists a primary actor. Of no truth can the dispassionate mind be more thoroughly convinced. To reject it we must "kill reason," because we must make our very reason an absurdity.

Lastly the subject *I*, as shown before, is firmly convinced that it is not infinite; that it exercises no control over many external things. Hence the necessary being, whose existence the intelligent subject *I* deduces from the existence of phenomena, or effects, is not the *I* itself, but something altogether distinct from, and independent of it. It would be either a piece of satire or pride, or sheer madness, to pretend that everything is comprised in the subject *I*. That something distinct from the thinking subject exists, is as clear to the mind as its own existence; equally clear to it is the fact that it is not the primary cause of that something. Therefore outside of itself the great primary actor is to be sought.

CHAPTER VII.

THE INTELLIGENCE AND WILL OF GOD.

IT might seem superfluous to many to hold a polemic dissertation on the Intelligence and Will of God. Our wish, however, is to prove by the light of reason, every assertion we make. We trust that these metaphysical disquisitions, so far as they go, will be complete. Infidelity threatens destruction to the human race. In its mad career it spares nothing. It sends ahead its loathsome precursor—impiety. Hearts must be first depraved before intellects can embrace absurdities. A soul unspotted by sin could never be induced to deny its Creator. The impious systems of a revived paganism that, like noxious weeds, spring up thick and fast, are the sickly products of souls deprived of the light of grace. Were it possible, then, to prove that God is but a blind force, free rein could be given to our basest passions. Hence the efforts to destroy the idea of a personal God. 'Tis the old, old cry of the wicked; it was raised in the time of David—God does not understand: *non intelligit Deus.* It has come down the path-way of ages, and has been taken up and screeched in chorus by modern infidels. Being driven, by the force of evidence, to admit some primary actor, who must be independent and supreme, they vainly seek to have him shorn of intelligence. We wish to expose the fallacy of their theories; to vindicate the glory of our Creator; to supply arms by which each reader may successfully combat their errors. Hence our intention of contesting each inch of ground. We know that right is on our side, and we are confident of success.

We have proved the existence of a Being which exists by necessity of nature—which is independent of everything else, and which is the first cause of all. Whatever this being has, it has by the necessity of nature, and consequently it can never have, at any time, anything which it had not always. With it there can be no change; for it there was no yesterday, neither will it have a to-morrow. It simply *is*. The definition which that Being gave of itself, as recorded by Moses, is the self-same as that which right reason must give it—I am what I am—or, in another place —"*who is*, sent thee." Yes; this is God; He who is. Being necessary, He is, as we saw, infinite; consequently, He has the plenitude of being. "I am what I am." To prove intelligence in God we can first use an argument *a priori*. God is infinite; therefore perfect. This is self-evident; for the infinite is that to which nothing can be added; but something can be added to the imperfect—viz: the perfection it lacks. Hence, since God is infinite He must be perfect. Now intelligence is, undoubtedly, a very great perfection: consequently it must be in God. Intelligence is a simple perfection; it does not include the idea of any defect. Reason supposes a defect—viz: the necessity of deducing conclusions regarding things less clearly known, from ones more known. Hence in God there is intelligence, but no necessity of reasoning. He knows in the same manner as He exists, that is—by necessity of nature. The manner of acting follows the manner of existing. In God existence is by necessity; so is knowledge: the essence of God necessarily includes existence; so it, likewise, includes knowledge. The essence is infinite; so is the knowledge. The infinite must be a simple act. There cannot be in it any parts, otherwise it could be added to, and subtracted from. Hence in the infinite there is no real distinction between the essence and its attributes. God having the plenitude of being must have the plenitude of knowledge. Everything knowable must be known to Him; and this knowledge is not acquired by parts, nor by deducing conclusions; but it is all in one simple act, eternal and unchangeable. All this is clear from the fact of His being infinitely perfect.

But the deriders of metaphysics may call this too subtile. One would suppose that no reasoning could be too fine spun for the "great minds" of our great age. If their intellectual powers be such as they boast them to be, they ought to delight in abstruse logical investigations. But since the mud, to which they so viciously cleave, unfits them for a lofty mental flight, we will give other proofs. God is as shown above the first cause. Either he acted freely in producing the phenomena, or effects which exist, or he did not. If he were necessitated in acting, then everything exists by necessity. Now that which exists by necessity must be unchangeable, because whatever it has, it has necessarily, and consequently must have the same always. But the subject *I* testifies that it, and all visible things are subject to modifications. We know to-day something which we did not know yesterday. Therefore we do not exist by necessity of nature, therefore the primary cause acted freely in producing us. We elected to act; but election supposes an act of intelligence, and freedom of will. Hence from the nature of the subject *I* and other phenomena, it is conclusively proved that God has intelligence and freedom of will. We only exist because he freely elected to give us existence. This argument is founded in the essence of contingent things;

the reason is led on to its conclusion by the force of evidence. Pantheism, be it real, ideal, or emanistic is completely destroyed by this reasoning. It is to be hoped that this argument is not too "subtle," or "scholastic," for the "great minds" which follow the "current of modern thought."

CHAPTER VIII.

GOD AS LEARNT FROM THE PHYSICAL ORDER.

THE cultured mind will, already, have found sufficient proof of the existence of a personal God, such as christians believe to exist. But all minds are not cultured; and some are so much cultured that they seem to have run to seed. Amongst these latter must be classed the gushing writer who, in well-written prose, rejects metaphysics. The hey-day of his intellect must be with the "years beyond the deluge;" no flowers, no matter how brilliant their hues, can attract his gaze. Hard, dry seeds, much akin to acorns, are the only pleasures of his imagination. 'Tis a sad lot, yet, the usual one reserved for those whom pride has drawn from the path of truth.

For the unlettered, then, as well as for the lovers of physical nature, we will trace the footsteps of God in the universe. Physics, being a less sublime science than metaphysics, is more adapted to the understanding of those who care only to sport a moth-like existence of a day. It would be useless to enumerate here the beauties and order of visible things. Each one sees them for oneself. If he is a scholar he can read the glowing pages of Cicero, of Virgil, of Young, or of every writer of note, whether ancient or modern. On no one subject has so much been written, as on the wonderful beauty and order of the universe. On no subject has there been so much unanimity of sentiment. The writer of centuries ago,—the writer of to-day,—the writer in the east, as well as in the west, have all proclaimed aloud the same fact, that beauty, harmony, regularity, prevail in the physical order. If one is not a scholar, one has only to step forth into the fields and watch the plants and flowers springing up, producing useful fruits, or delighting the eye, and then forming a seed from which another similar plant will, in due season, shoot forth. He will remember that the seasons come round with unfailing regularity; no matter how great the heat may be to-day he is sure that a cool season will soon come to refresh the parched earth; no matter how deep the snow may lie on his well-tilled fields he is certain that it will melt, and leave the ground fresh and vigorous, in time for the next crop. Let him then raise his eyes to the heavens and he will see the glorious sun continually returning to cheer us with his light, and to fertilize the fields with his heat. When he sees it sinking, in a blaze of glory, to rest, no fear of its never again appearing disturbs him. He is certain that in a few hours it will return, and he makes his calculations for work or pleasure, accordingly. By night, he sees the heavens studded with innumerable stars, and from observations he has learnt that he can determine the hours of night by the relative positions of some of them. He knows with certainty the phases of the moon, and he, likewise, knows, though ignorant of astronomy, that the moon and the planets have their appointed course; they whirl rapidly around; cross each other's path; draw near, pursue, recede, but never come in contact. If a man be learned in the physical sciences he has great cause for wonder. He learns that in all the changes, whether effected by light, heat, or electricity, no one particle is ever made, or destroyed. He finds the atmosphere to be a vast store-house, in which are treasured up the atoms of decayed matter, to become, in time, the elements of other bodies. A continual round of production and decay is going on; well-regulated laws are observed in all physical phenomena. Now, let a man be what he may, he must admit the fact of the existence and regularity of physical phenomena, such as we have described. The question at once arises: is there any author of these? If so, who, and what is he? A man who desires knowledge, must not be content to know the mere fact of the existence of a thing; he must endeavour to learn as much as possible, its cause. The questions asked above will naturally rise in the mind of any one who considers the phenomena described. Is there any author of these? No one in his senses, will say that there is no cause, or author of these striking effects. He may quibble about the nature of that cause, but he must admit that there is some primary actor; otherwise he has a series of phenomena without a first one; a chain of dependent effects without a cause. The first question must be answered affirmatively, yes, there is an author, or a first actor. Who, and what is he? We will not give in detail, the various erroneous answers to this question. We will say; the author is either intelligent, or he is not. The atheists whether they be materialists, pantheists, or any other *ists*, say that the author is not intelligent. They labour, in various ways, to obscure the truth; still, shorn of their stupidity and verbosity, their theories are reduced to this; the author of the physical order is not an intelligent cause. Let youthful readers bear this well in mind. Let them not be deceived by high-sounding terms, or brilliant expressions. The whole question must be reduced to logical terms: either the cause is intelligent, or it is not. If it is intelligent it must be something distinct from the phenomena; for no one, it is to be supposed, is so demented as to attribute intelligence to physical phenomena. In the hypothesis, then, that the cause is intelligent, it must be the infinite God of whom we spoke; because the author of the phenomena must be independent, and must exist by necessity of nature, not being from any other cause; and consequently must be infinite. They who take the other horn of the dilemma are tossed into the regions of absurdity. They must say the author is not intelligent. Can any man believe that laws, to understand which great human intellects have labored, have come from an unintelligent lawgiver? But let us pursue them more cogently. Your author is chance. But, pray, who and what is this chance? Is it intelligent? If so, you admit an intelligent author of the physical order. If it is not, it is nothing: wriggle as you may, if chance is unintelligent it is a mere nothing, a blind for the unwary: it can be nothing more than that you mean phenomena are the productions of a lottery, a game of hazard. If the right ticket happens to be extracted from the box, the sun will rise to-morrow; provided always, that thousands of other tickets are so extracted that each planet will keep its course, and not come in collision with the earth. And for thousands upon thousands of days this game of lottery has been going on, and thousands upon thousands of just the right sort of tickets are coming out, from amongst millions upon millions of ones which might just as well be extracted! Can any absurdity be greater than this? Yet, reduced to its last analysis, such is the theory of chance. Such the stuff which the would-be doughty champions of reason ask us to believe. Place even fifteen numbers into a box, and it is a moral certainty that you will not extract the same number three consecutive times. But what if you had millions of numbers in the box, and had to extract, in the same order, the same hundred numbers, a hundred times? Bah! it is sickening to have to write against such nonsense!

But some will say, you mis-represent our theory: we do not believe in chance, as the author, any more than you: we explain physical phenomena by supposing matter with its properties, and physical laws of attraction, repulsion, &c. This theory has, at first sight, an appearance of learning, and saves its advocates from being immediately laughed at, as bogus lottery agents. In reality, however, it is founded in the old game of chance. Modern atheists saw the absurdity of the *casus* of the ancients, and abandoned it; the ship was leaky, so they fled; but the boat into which they leaped, though more gaudily painted, is not a whit more sea-worthy. Let us overhaul it. They suppose matter with its physical properties. Not a bad supposition to begin with; but it has just this grievous fault—it is only a supposition. Let us make the supposition that we ask them how came this matter with its properties? Is it from chance? They answer indignantly, no; we do not admit chance as an author. Very good; is it from itself? If it is, you admit an *Ens a se* a substance that exists by necessity of nature, and, consequently an infinite one. But, as shown above, the infinite must be simple: hence it is not matter which is always compound. Therefore if you say that the elements are from themselves, you admit not one, but millions of necessary beings, each infinite, each intelligent, each unchangeable. This absurdity is just as great as chance. If you say that matter is not from itself it must be from another, from, say, B. If B is from itself we come to our infinite substance God; if not he is from C, and climbing up the genealogical stem we must finally come to the parent Z. No other preceding him, he must be from himself, and is, therefore, God. Hence when we analyze this learned supposition, its supposers must either be content to herd with the ancient chance men, or they must admit a personal God.

Not to be too hard on the enlightened thinkers let us leave unquestioned their gratuitous supposition; let us for a moment, suppose that matter exists with its various properties and laws: not even then could this well-ordered universe arise, without an intelligent cause to dispose, in certain places, certain quantities of matter. If the elements of matter existed independently of God, they would exist by necessity of nature: all their properties and actions would be essential and, as a consequence, unchangeable. The position they first occupied, and the actions they first produced, would be necessary, and therefore should always remain the same. The order and collocation which were in the beginning, would have to continue until the end. Now the science of geology evidently demonstrates that many changes have taken place, and are still going on. This could not be, if matter and its properties are to be supposed as existing and acting independently of any supreme cause. If even one part of matter, if even one element of a body should change its site, the whole physical order, with one fell swoop, would fall into chaos, unless there be an intelligent cause that foresaw this change of site, and provided an opportune remedy. It is evident that we can change the relative position of whole masses, and, still, the harmony of nature is undisturbed.

Again; from no other collocation of elements than the actul one, could this physical order arise, if it be purely the production of matter and its properties. Now it is self-evident that the number of possible collocations which the particles of the world could have is many millions. Must it not have been a most happy *chance* which brought about the present one? As Cicero said when refuting this same absurd theory, it is just as credible to suppose that by tossing in the air a number of types they would form, on reaching the ground, the annals of Ennius, as to suppose that this well-ordered globe could be the result of elements possessed of certain physical properties. Would any upholder of this system believe that his elaborate essays could be formed by tossing in the air all the type and plants of every printing office in London. Yet, it is more credible that this should take place than that all the beauties, wonders, and harmony of nature should arise merely from matter and its forces.

Finally, it is admitted that various circumstances, such as difference of temperature, relation of site and a thousand others exercise a modifying effect on matter and its properties. How is it, then, that in man, beast, bird and fish, the eye, for instance, always occupies the same site, in the same race. Why does it not frequently appear on the top of the head, or the arm, back, or neck? The embryo is, certainly, subject to various causes which must modify the properties of matter, still the eye appears in millions of men, for thousands of years, in the same place, and that place, too, the safest and most useful. It must, indeed, be a consistent chance that does all this. Take any one, of the thousand and one phenomena of every-day life, which occur with equal regularity, though under very different circumstances, and you will find how vain it is to attempt to explain them by merely supposing matter with its forces. But if you suppose an infinite intelligence that gave each element its peculiar properties, and foresaw all possible contingences, and so disposed matter as to meet them, and which prepared a ready compensation for each change, or loss, then, and then only, can the physical order be explained. All difficulties vanish; the mind may be overcome at the depth of the wisdom of that cause, but it is intimately convinced that only such wisdom could produce such effects.

We can here add a fact which must be known to those who are versed in physics—viz: that physical laws are not always constant, or regular in their development. One example is sufficient: it is a law that the intensity of electricity in a galvanic pile increases with the number of pairs of zinc, copper and cloth saturated in diluted sulphuric acid. This law holds good for a limited number of pairs; finally a certain intensity is reached and, add as many pairs as you will, that intensity will not increase. Moreover you can so alter the condition of the surrounding atmosphere as to come to this stopping point, sooner or later. Many other laws are subject to like anomalies. We know the explanation of this phenomenon, still, it does not destroy the fact that physical laws are not necessarily alike, at all times, in their evolution. Hence it is unscientific to suppose that the various phenomena could occur with such regularity, even though matter and its properties existed independently of God. From this the reader will see how cautious he ought to be, in accepting the dicta of certain scientists, who talk about nature and its laws. The physical order loudly proclaims an Infinite Intelligence.

CHAPTER IX.

UNIVERSAL BELIEF IN THE EXISTENCE OF A GOD.

IF we turn down the pages of history; if we read the annals of any nation, or listen to the tradition of any tribe, we find that all men, at all times, have agreed in admitting the existence of a being superior to themselves; a being whom they ought to adore. Those who have pretended to disbelieve in a God are so few that they are, in the moral order, what monstrosities are in the physical. No one for a moment considers that the monstrosities which, from time to time, come into existence, destroy certain physiological laws; neither can any one pretend that the few atheists, who reject reason for a time, destroy the universal belief in a God. Of course, many and great are the errors regarding the nature and attributes of God; but the fact remains firm that all men have been intimately convinced that there exists a being far superior to themselves. No sceptic has attempted to seriously question this universal consent. Epicurus admitted it; Kant, although he alleged that reason could not prove the existence of God, said that we ought to hold his existence by reason of this fact. It is scarcely necessary to transcribe the words of Plutarch against Colotes; he says: "If you roam over the earth you may find cities without walls, letters, kings, palaces, wealth, and monies; cities ignorant of gymnasiums and theatres; but a city without temples and gods, which does not use prayers, oaths and oracles, which does not offer sacrifice to procure favors, and which does not strive to ward off evils by religious rites, no one ever' saw. I think it easier to found a city without ground for it, than for a city to be founded and stand, if the idea of a God be destroyed." Plutarch would have been confirmed in this belief had he lived in the days of Petroleum and Paris. Now, the Philosopher ought to seek the reason of this universal belief. It is constant and universal; therefore its cause is constant and universal; were it not, the effect would be sometimes existing without any cause. No other constant and universal cause can be assigned except the evidence of reason, the voice of nature heard by all who attain the use of reason. Even the blasphemies which come from the mouth of the impious attest their belief. These imprecations are the ravings of a soul naturally Christian, We have said that no other cause, save the evidence of reason can be assigned. All others are either limited, or variable. Priest-craft, or any other craft, is not sufficient; it might succeed with some, and in some places, and for a time; but it could not be constant and universal. Prejudices vary; ignorance is lessened; what is advantageous to one is disadvantageous to another. Thus we can go through the various causes assigned for this fact, and we will find them all inadequate. The voice of nature alone, always the same, whether by the Ganges, or the Amazon, can explain this universal consent.

The great stronghold of modern atheists, who consider that the acme of knowledge is circumscribed by the narrow limits of their brain, is the ignorance of the people regarding physical laws. This ignorance, they say, explains the universal phenomenon. Of course, all was darkness in the world until the particular atheist who makes this assertion, honored this mundane sphere by being born in it. This intolerable pride is so senseless that we would not notice it, only we wish to guard young readers against an error into which they may easily fall, if they read infidel books, or newspapers. Reading continually the stale stock-phrases, of "modern thought," and "progress of the age," on the one hand, and "mediæval ignorance," on the other, they may think that only the illiterate believe in the christians' God; and that only the atheists are learned. Now the case is just the reverse. The most learned in nature's laws were, and are, the firmest believers in God as ruler of the universe. Liebnitz, Newton, Linæus, Bonnet and a host of others in the past; Secchi and others whom each reader can name for himself in the present. The atheists cannot point to a man in their ranks, or who ever belonged to them, that enjoys any solid reputation as a scholar, or a scientist. A few of them enjoy a manufactured fame, which lasts for a day: but none of them has ever attained that enduring glory which bespeaks great genius. When they will have their names as indelibly stamped on the pages of their respective country's history, and as intimately linked with its scientific glory, as the great names above, then will it be time enough for them to prate about "mediæval ignorance." So far as the ages of the world have run out, all the genius, all the true nobility of the human race has been on the side which defends a Supreme Ruler; on the other, has been the bloated Epicurean, the depraved libertine, and the self-conceited theorist. This may sound harsh, but it is the stern fact as proved by history. If any one can persuade oneself that half-a-dozen professors, who can write sufficiently well to varnish over their gross blunders, comprise the intelligence of the human race, the reader, while pitying his delusion, must surely laugh at his folly.

Finally, the voice of nature, speaking through man, not only proclaims the existence of a God, but, also, his ruling power. Supplications and sacrifices for rain, or fair weather, thanksgivings for plentiful crops, all tend to prove the same thing,—belief in the ruling power of God. They must have been convinced that the physical laws were subject to him; that by an act of his will he could intervene in an extraordinary manner. Men have believed, and sad experience has taught us moderns, that human society cannot exist without a recognition of God. There can be no society without the recognition and observance of moral precepts. Take away these and you have a den of thieves, a vast brothel of iniquity. Now the idea of a moral law, or obligation, necessarily supposes a lawgiver, and a vindicator of that law. Hence human society absolutely requires a belief in God. Since, therefore, all men, at all times, have believed in a God, and since without this belief society is impossible, it is the insanity of absurdity to doubt the existence of God. We will here observe that very many of the traditions of the human race, though disfigured by fables, if considered in their substantial part, will be seen to point to this same universal belief in a God, and even to a primitive revelation.

CHAPTER X.

RECAPITULATORY.

TAKING for our starting point the three fundamental truths, I exist, I can know with certainty, and the principle of contradiction, we established ourselves on a solid foundation. Our camp was so well fortified that no assault could make a breach in its walls. Any blow aimed at either of those three truths, only redounds on the aggressor. By denying, or doubting, either of them, he proves it. Hence the impregnability of our position. From this safe retreat we made an attack on the lines of atheism; we went forth armed with some certainties, and from these deduced, by the evidence of reason, others. The intelligent subject *I* did not remain shut up in itself; its reason wants a wider field in which to seek for truth. The subject *I* equally convinced of its own, as of others' existence, sought enlightenment. It wished to know who, and what, is the primary actor of the wonderful phenomena it contemplates. Strong in the conviction of its ability to know with certainty, it began its investigations. It soon discovered that there cannot be a series of phenomena without a first; or a chain of effects and causes without a primary cause. In either case this primary actor must exist by necessity of nature; its very idea supposes it. If it is the first, then it is from no other; therefore by necessity of nature. Thus the subject *I* arrived at the conviction that there exists a necessary Being, independent of others, and from whom all else depends. Proceeding in its investigations it saw that since mundane objects are contingent, the necessary Being must have produced them freely; but free action supposes intelligence. Therefore it became convinced that this necessary Being is endowed with intelligence and free will. The subject *I* has thus, by the light of its reason, arrived at the knowledge of a personal God. It confirmed this knowledge from the physical order, and from the universal consent of man. The feeble shots fired by the atheists were easily turned aside. Their only refuge was in submission, or in a labyrinth of absurdity. Chance, chance! 'Twas the "abyss crying to the abyss." The subject *I* having vindicated the dignity of its reason, finds a sense of joy and relief. The wonders of nature are no longer matters of perplexity; it knows them to be the productions of an infinite Intelligence.

Turning again to this necessary Being it finds it eternal, supreme, perfect. There can not be two infinite substances; the very idea is self-destructive. Hence God must be one substance, and that substance must be simple. It can have no parts, otherwise it could be increased, or decreased. Whatever property is in the infinite, must be infinite, because it is nothing more than the essence considered under a certain respect. Being a necessary substance all its properties are necessary; hence it is unchangeable; its properties being unchangeable and infinite it must once, together, and always know and will, whatever it knows and wills. God is thus a simple act, having the plenitude of being, and the fulness of wisdom. Whatever is knowable must be known to him in that one act. He comprehends himself, because his intelligence is infinite; he cannot be comprehended by anything else, because everything not God is finite and of limited capacity. Being intelligent, he established an order; being good, he desires its observance; being wise, he provided means for this purpose; being perfect, he must hate the transgressor; being powerful, he will punish him.

God being infinite, he must comprehend everything. He is more intimately present to each thing than what that thing is to itself. Still, he is not diffused in parts through matter, because he is simple; but by reason of his infinity everything which exists must exist in Him, although distinct from Him. He is the infinite reality; outside of Him there is nothing; we are living and moving in the ocean of his infinity, but are always distinct and diverse from Him. This infinity of God, not rightly understood, has been the occasion, to some, of propagating a pernicious error which we will refute in the next chapter. The subject I is lost in wonder contemplating such a Being, it cannot comprehend it; but it sees how beautiful and consonant to reason is all this,

CHAPTER XI.

PANTHEISM.

PANTHEISM is only masked atheism; its advocates pursue various paths, but the final conclusion from their principles must inevitably be, there is no God. This erroneous system is very insidious, and its effects are most disastrous. It speaks often of God, and with pretended veneration; in fact, its champions are, according to themselves, the only true zealots of God's infinite perfection. Hence its danger, especially to those who are not much versed in metaphysics. It is pernicious in its consequences, in as much as, it destroys the liberty, and consequently, the responsibility, of human action; and makes right and wrong equally the necessary result of the action of the infinite. It is thus more impious, perhaps, than open atheism, and quite as absurd. It is a horrible blasphemy to deny the existence of God; but, in our opinion, it is still worse to admit the existence of an infinitely perfect Being, and then to attribute to him all manner of iniquity. But such, stripped of its pious mask, is the outcome of pantheism. As we before observed, to deny a personal God is the great object of those who have reason to fear him. Not being able to succeed by open atheism, because the natural conviction of man was, of itself, sufficient to refute that absurdity, the impious became all at once seized with a great admiration of the infinity of God, and made God everything, that they might succeed in making him nothing. The reader must always remember that the God mentioned by the pantheist, is not the God of the christians. Our God is, as we have shown, an infinite, necessary Being, supreme, perfect, and endowed with intelligence and liberty of action; the God of the pantheist is an aggregation of contradictions: he is infinite, but likewise finite, because the phenomena we see are God; he is perfect, but likewise imperfect, because the efficacious cause of sin; he is intelligent, because he is man's intellect, but he is likewise unintelligent, because he is a stone. It is scarcely credible that any sane man ever seriously maintained such absurdities; unless, indeed, God permitted one who denied him with his mouth, to become so blinded, as to be given over to a reprobate sense. 'Tis a sad proof of mental aberration that Spinoza, the modern champion, or perhaps, even the author, of the system, has been applauded as the vindicator of the infinite perfection, and as a rigorous logician! Why, the school boy, who in his first logical essay would be guilty of such gross contradiction, would most surely be doomed to lose his first holiday, and obliged to write five hundred times—Idem non potest simul esse et non esse—the same thing cannot both be and not be at the same time. Yet, such is the itch with some to drug themselves of Christian truth, that they will gulph down anything against it, even though reason be choked in the attempt.

Perhaps some may think we are manufacturing accusations against the men who speak so religiously about the Infinite. If so they are deceived. We will advance nothing which we are not prepared to substantiate. A slight knowledge of metaphysics, and a little logic, are all that is required to prove our charges. Our object is to warn the youthful reader of the pretty veil, which conceals the hideous features; and then to lift that veil and show pantheism to be a stupid monster, the offspring of ignorance and conceit.

Pantheism, like all errors, has been split up into various systems. The principal ones are Realistic, Idealistic and Emanastic. It is not our purpose to refute these singly. Indeed, we think that christian writers commit a blunder, when they lose their time in writing an elaborate refutation of every erroneous conclusion, from some false premises. There are some men whom you can never convince; their intellect is a tangled wilderness, and their heart a parched mountain ridge. You may labor to cultivate the one, or to clear the other, but your efforts will be vain, unless the dews from heaven irrigate the soil. Any man who will defend conclusions which necessarily follow from a principle that is proved to be false, is, it would seem, one of these inconvincible men. Hence we will content ourselves with demonstrating the fallacy of the pantheistic principle; observing that all pantheists, of whatever hue, start from the same proposition—there is but one substance, and that infinite. Spinoza strives hard to prove this; so do all subsequent pantheists. The fundamental error in their mental wanderings consists in confounding *distinction* with *diversity*. Two things perfectly alike in all their properties are not *diverse*, but they are *distinct*, one is not the other. Two things, with qualities unlike, are both diverse and distinct. Anyone sees the vast difference between diversity and distinction. Now the reader will, perhaps, hardly believe that the *great(!)* logician Spinoza ignorantly confounded these two. But here are his words: "There cannot be but one substance. If there were many, they should be known by means of different attributes, and then they would have nothing in common." Therefore, according to this beautiful piece of reasoning, there is no such thing as numeric difference: if A and B are two apples alike in size, color, flavor, &c., A is B. This is in philosophy, what communism is in society —your house is mine. Thus at the onset we discover the flaw in Spinoza's argument. His train of reasoning is founded on the supposition that there is no such thing as numeric distinction; this supposition is shown to be false; hence the airy fabric falls in ruin. The pantheist must first prove that two objects, without any diversity of properties, are not distinct. This he can never do, consequently he has no starting point. He is like Archimedes, he has no fulcrum on which to rest his lever; consequently he cannot move the heavens and the earth.

The next oracular proposition of the Dutch Apollo is equally absurd: "Two substances of different attributes would have nothing in common, and one could not be the cause of the other; for, to be its cause it should contain it in its essence and produce effects on it." Here we find that this boasted genius had no higher idea of the way in which an effect could be contained in its cause, than the grovelling material one of water in a basin, or a chick in the shell. Certainly if there is no water in the cup I cannot pour any out of it; but there is a more elevated idea of cause and effect. The intricate piece of machinery was not in the mechanic, but did he not produce it? Try to persuade a man that some piece of work which he has just performed, was not done by him; you will say, it has different attributes from you, therefore it was not in you; consequently you did not make it. The veriest boor would laugh at you and say: " true it, as it is, was not in me, but there was in me the *power* of producing it." By this simple observation, which the most ignorant workman would make, the great difficulty would be solved. Truly the sublime genius of the pantheist borders on the ridiculous.

The two errors exposed above are the result of ignorance of the nature of the Infinite. God is infinitely perfect; consequently every perfection which is found in a finite being must be in God in some manner. The pantheist is right when he says that in God is found every perfection which is in the creature; but he errs regarding the manner in which it is in him. There are three ways by which one thing may be contained in another: 1st—Materially, or formally, as water in a basin: 2nd—Eminently, that is, in a greater degree, or a more noble manner, as the power of a governor in the king: 3rd—Virtually, that is, when the cause has the power of producing the effect; thus, the engine is contained in its manufacturer. Again; perfections are either absolute, or relative. In the conception of the former there is no idea of a defect included; the perfection is absolute: in the conception of relative perfections there is included the idea of a defect which limits them, and makes them perfections only in a sense relative to something else. Thus, intelligence is an absolute perfection, though it is not necessarily infinite, because it simply includes the idea of understanding; reason, or reasoning, is only a relative perfection, because it supposes the necessity of deduction and argues a defect in the possessor, viz: a limitation of understanding. Now we say that the perfections of finite beings are contained in the Infinite in some one of these three ways. Simple perfections are contained in him formally; relative ones, either eminently, or virtually. Hence the number and variety of finite perfections in created beings, do not derogate from the infinite perfection of God. They serve rather as a means of giving us some dim inkling of what must be his glory, since he contains each and all of them, in a greater degree, and in a more sublime manner. Spinoza, seeing only one way in which a thing could be contained in its cause, viz: in a formal manner, thought it derogatory to the Infinite to admit any perfection distinct from his. The foolish objection,—if you add the perfection of the finite to the infinite you increase the latter—arises from not understanding the various ways by which an effect may be contained in its cause. Suppose Parliament were to pass a law conferring the power of a governor on her Majesty, what would the Queen say to Mr. Disraeli when he would inform her of the loyal act? Something, most probably, like what Queen Elizabeth is reported to have said to the "men of Coventry,"—"Good lack! what fools you be, have I not already that power, aye, and a much greater one. 'Twas I who, out of the plenitude of my sovereign power, gave jurisdiction to the governor; mine was not decreased by the act; neither can it be increased by its revocation." This response would bring to the blushing Premier's mind the old axiom: qui potest plus, potest et minus, in eodem genere. Now apply this to the Infinite: out of the fulness of his perfection he bestowed certain limited perfections on creatures. Was his perfection decreased by the act? Evidently not, even as the imparting of knowledge to others does not diminish our own store. Would his perfection be increased were you to add to it the perfection of the creature? Certainly not, for he has already that same perfection in an infinitely greater degree. From this it is evident that we can explain in a reasonable manner the existence of finite and infinite perfections, and can show how the admission of finite ones in no way derogates from the infinite; on the other hand, Spinoza and his followers are driven to admit contradictory properties in God, and thus destroy him. There are certainly finite perfections; but these, they say, are in the infinite in a formal manner. Therefore the infinite is also finite! These properties make God a contradiction, or in other words, destroy him. Therefore pantheism, reduced to its last terms, is atheism. **Have we not proved some of our charges?**

We might here end the question, because we have proved the absurdity of the suppositions on which pantheism, as a system, is built up. But we will pursue the subject still further. Is there but one substance? The subject I being consulted answers unhesitatingly, there are many distinct substances. At least, there are two, I and not I. My inner consciousness testifies clearly to the fact that there exists something which is not I, nor a part of me, nor a modification of me. If there are not, at least, two distinct substances, there is none at all; for to the subject I essentially pertains the judgment, A is not B. If in reality A is B then there is a perpetual opposition between the idea and the reality, or rather there would be no reality being always and necessarily false. Hence there would be no substance at all. But we have seen that the subject I must be admitted; therefore, also, the not I or another distinct substance. If there can be two, there is no reason why there cannot be a thousand and one: now the subject I is persuaded that there are many. Therefore, in fact, many distinct substances exist.

This is still further confirmed by our relations with kindred subjects. In the pantheistic systems, A is B, consequently Hegel is Newton, and Jones is Brown. Now the subject I reasons thus: if I am Jones I must know everything that Jones knows; but experience teaches me that I do not know many things known to him; therefore I cannot be Jones. We would wish to see an answer, in form, to this reasoning. High-sounding phrases will not avail in syllogistic argumentation; mysterious words will not do. The question is: is Brown the same substance as Jones, yes, or no? If he is, his feelings, ideas and knowledge must be identical with those of Jones. But they certainly are not; therefore they must be distinct substances. Therefore every shade of pantheism is false. This latter argument ought to have some force in

Germany now. The "transcendental" German may say, perhaps, with impunity, that Bismarck is pious William, or Bismarck is God; but woe betide him if he should say Bismarck is Kullmann, or Kullmann is a modification, or an emanation, or an idea of Bismarck! The dungeons of the empire would soon rejoice at the reception of another occupant! Why the coarsest taunt that the coarse mind of Bismarck could invent against the "Ultramontanes," that is, the Catholic party, was to assert that Kullmann belonged to them. Evidently he disowned all connection with that individual. Hence if there be any disciple of Hegel in the Fatherland, he had better be on his guard: let him not comprise in his lucid system of the I being the not I, two such—well, pious pilgrims, as Bismarck and Kullmann.

Finally, pantheism is most pernicious in its effects on society. Everything being either a necessary modification, or an emanation, or a manifestation of the infinite, it follows that God is the author of every impiety. If we are not responsible agents, our actions are necessary; if I kill my neighbor it is only a necessary manifestation of the infinite: if I burn his house with petroleum, it is only a necessary phenomenon of the infinite. And thus we might go through the sickening catalogue of vices, and find in them nothing reprehensible; they would be all necessary manifestions of the infinite. The very demons would disown such blasphemy. Order, physical or moral; duty, charity, heroism, all are destroyed by this infernal system, because all become necessary phenomena. Such, gentle reader, is the logical outcome of pantheism; such the conclusions from that system that begins with hypocritical professions of veneration for the majesty of the Infinite. We need not be surprised at this; ignorance of the elements of metaphysics, and self-conceit, could scarcely produce aught else. Those who, perhaps, never read a line of scholastic philosophy sneer at it; they start out in their investigations with confused ideas, and with the fixed purpose to destroy, if they can, christianity. What wonder that such as these should fall into the most stupid errors? What wonder if they make a god of their own? 'Tis their interest to do so; but to quote Bruyere: there does not exist a sober, temperate, chaste, just man that denies the existence of God.

CHAPTER XII.

THE REALITY OF THE PHYSICAL WORLD.

REAL is a term generally used by metaphysicians in opposition to ideal. A thing is said to be ideal, or to exist ideally, when it exists merely in the mind of the subject *I*, thus a golden mountain exists ideally. It is to be observed that nothing can have an ideal existence the notes of which are contradictory. Thus a round square cannot have an ideal existence, because the properties of rotundity and squareness are mutually destructive in the same subject. Such things are said to be impossible, absurd, or simply nothing. When there is no repugnance in the notes of a thing, it is possible, although it never existed really, and, perhaps, never will. A thing is said to be real, or to exist really, when its notes do not involve a contradiction, and when it, moreover, has an existence outside of the mind of the subject *I*. In order to avoid all cavilling about terms, we mean by real existence a substance in act; a being whose existence is as actual as is that of the subject *I*. Hence, with us, substantial and real, in regard to existence, are convertible terms. Every substance is a reality; every reality is a substance. Again; a substance is a force, that is, every substance has necessarily action. The manner in which different substances act, is different, but each and all have a proper action. The notion of existence needs no explanation; there is nothing more clearly known than the first fact, I exist, I am. Let the subject I imagine a not I that has the same certainty as itself, so that the not I may say with equal conviction, I exist, I am; it will thus have as clear a perception of what the existence of a thing outside of itself is, as it is possible to have. Many rail against the "subtilities of the schools," but it is open to doubt if ever the most subtle school-man, engaged in a more otiose question than is that of seeking to elaborately explain the meaning of existence. The most clear-headed philosopher has no more correct, or perspicuous idea of what it is, than has the peasant. The certainty of both is equal in measure, degree, and kind; neither of them can find a stronger asseveration than—I am as certain of it as I am that I exist.

Now it is a fact which no skeptic, or idealist attempts to deny, that the subject I has a conviction that it perceives various things which it calls trees, stones, grass, horses, &c., and the aggregation of those it calls the physical world, the universe, creation. This conviction is not fleeting; from the cradle to the tomb it perseveres in the subject I. We cannot divest ourselves of it; the sceptic, or idealist, may say that there is no reality corresponding to our perception, still he must and does admit that the perception is really in us. Now it is self-evident that a mere negation cannot be perceived; I perceive a nothing, is equivalent to saying, I have no perception at all. The fact of our having the perception of the physical world being admitted by all—and it having been shown that whatever we perceive must be a something, it inevitably follows that the object of our perceptions must be a reality. You may differ as to the nature of that reality; you may deny that it has the properties attributed to it; you may say that it is produced by God, or by the intrinsic power of the subject I; but you can never deny the reality of the object of our perceptions. We thus, at once, distinguish between the *nature* and the *reality* of the physical world. Its reality, in the sense explained, that is, in as much as the object of our perception must be a something, cannot be questioned. You may just as well deny the existence of the subject *I* as deny its perception; you may just as well deny its perception as assert that the object of its perception is a nothing. Hence the only controversy can be about the nature of the admitted reality. Philosophy seeks the knowledge of things through their causes; we are not content to know a fact, we desire to know its why. What, then, is the object, what the cause of this universal and constant perception? For our part we think the question is easily answered; we do not consider ourselves as possessing what is termed genius, still, we must confess to a feeling of surprise that those, who are considered as having had that mental quality, should have fallen into absurdities, when endeavoring to answer this question. Perhaps the very simplicity of the answer may be the reason that genius did not perceive it. Possibly genius is, in the mental order, what aristocracy is in the social; it only takes notice of elevated notions, and consequently, like its social counterpart, sometimes proves itself ridiculous. Or it may be that a wish to air some original idea may have caused authors, of undoubted attainments, to theorize when they ought to philosophize. Be this as it may, the strange fact remains that some have attributed the sensations which we experience, and which are commonly thought to be produced by external finite agents, to the immediate action of God; others to an intrinsic and necessary force of the subject *I*. All other erroneous systems on this head, can be reduced to one of these two. Let us first analyze these systems, then we will give the correct one. The authors of the first system recognize, at least, two distinct substances, God and the subject *I*. They are not, therefore, pantheists nor atheists. They admit the multiplicity of substances; why stop at two? Evidently, according to them, there is no contradiction in admitting thousands of distinct substances. So far all right. But why attribute to God actions which can, from their own principle of the multiplicity of substances, be otherwise accounted for? It is unphilosophic to have recourse to the Infinite to explain phenomena that can be explained otherwise. It savors of that pagan superstition which depicts Jupiter with a gleaming thunderbolt in his hand. We do not deny but what God could, and, perhaps, sometimes does, excite in us sensations which would be produced by the object to which we refer them. But these are exceptional cases; and moreover, there is always a means of knowing with certainty, that the object is only apparently, not really present. Theology supplies an example in the B. Eucharist. Now what we contend is this: the subject *I* can know with certainty, as already proved; its object is truth; the acquisition of knowledge is a part of its perfection. It must, then, have a natural aptitude for truth, and a natural tendency to it, as well as a means of detecting error. Now the subject *I* is borne by a natural and invincible tendency to attribute some of its sensations to external and finite objects as the true cause of them. The farmer casts a seed into the ground, he sees it growing, he cuts it, shells it, grinds it, finally eats it. During the progress of these various actions the subject *I* by a natural and invincible tendency attributes the various sensations of feeling, sight, weariness in cutting and threshing, and refreshment in eating, not directly to God, but to a finite substance. If he be in error, his error is invincible: if he be in error, nature has led him into that error: and nature must be hourly leading millions into invincible error ; or to put it stronger ; God, the infinite truth, for those who defend this system believe in God, is not only permitting us to fall into error, but is drawing us at every moment into it. The aptitude of the mind for truth ; the ability of detecting error, are both destroyed, and the subject I becomes the sport of a continual and necessary delusion. Let it not be said that this delusion can be dispelled ; the few writers, who labor to build up this system, cannot be said to destroy the universal conviction of mankind. Moreover, before their time there was no escape from the error ; millions of intellects, during thousands of years, were hourly led into necessary error. Who will believe it? Again ; as we before observed, if there be a perpetual conflict between the idea and the perception, the subject I becomes a continual falsity, or a nonentity. But if we suppose God to be the immediate cause of our sensations, this perpetual conflict would be verified., Therefore, this system would deny what it admits, viz. : the existence of the subject I. Finally, the mind is intimately convinced that many sensations may be produced in itself at pleasure. I will to stretch out my hand and I feel the table ; I will to close my eyes and the lovely scenery fades. Now if the sensations are caused directly by God how can a simple act of my will prevent their reception?

The second false system is very absurd and only merits mention in order to show the reader how cautious we ought to be, and what humility of intellect we ought to have. All the sensations are produced by an intrinsic and necessary force of the soul. Such is the system. Now we have some sensations which we suffer against our will ; we wish to avoid them, but we cannot ; we are certain that the thing which produces them is not the subject I. No one could convince the wretch stretched on the rack that it was the same subject I that both felt and inflicted the pain. 'Tis the old story, the not I is the I: Kullmann is Bismarck.

These two systems being exploded, it remains for us to explain the true one: 'tis simple, logical, harmonious, worthy of the majesty of God, and consonant to human reason. We proved against the pantheists that, at least, two substances really distinct exist. But not only does the subject I pronounce infallibly that it is not the not I, but it with equal certainty says B is not C, C is not D. It may be unable to enumerate all the points of distinction, but it knows enough of them to be certain that they are distinct and diverse. In its communication with other intelligent subjects, the mind not only discovers its own distinction from them, but, likewise, their distinction from one another. During the course of its life it finds phenomena susceptible of modification at will; that which it calls a rock will always present the same appearance, and produce identical sensations, unless the subject I choses to seize what it calls a sledge, and effect therewith modifications on it. 'Twould be romancing to the moon to say that these appearances, which respond to my will, have no real cause outside of myself, or are produced by God, who suits his action to my caprice. Bear always in mind that we are metaphysically certain of the existence of, at least, two substances; hence plurality of substance is, not only not contradictory, but actually exists. Again, we are metaphysically certain that the finite I acts, consequently, that it is capable of causing a sensation, provided there be any object on which to act. Moreover, by communication, we become metaphysically certain that there is a not I which is finite like ourselves, because it does not know something which we know. Therefore we have the infinite, and, at least, two finite substances. We can thus proceed, by the evidence of reason, and prove that many finite substances exist. Their existence becomes as certain as our own. Now a substance is a force; or if it please better, a substance must have action; therefore, it can produce sensations. Therefore the various sensations we experience are produced by finite substances; and our natural and invincible tendency to attribute sensations to finite beings is reconcilable with our aptitude for truth. In this system everything is coherent; God is the primary cause; finite substances secondary ones. The essential notion of a substance, viz.: force, just fits in; we prove various substances to exist; their essential notion implies action, and action is here attributed to them. The greatness and wisdon of God shines more resplendently; his dignity is better consulted. The subject I is no longer a continually deluded being; its chain of reasonings harmonizes with its natural propensity. To explain the phenomena of daily life we have no need to recur to absurdities; we have proved the possibility of this system; reason finds it in harmony with its natural tendency. The system which attributes phenomena to any intrinsic force in the soul, was shown absurd; the other, if not proved actually absurd, is shown to be most improbable, unphilosophic, and even injurious to God. We thus see that the universal belief is, in this case, more reasonable than the fantastic imaginings of philosophic minds in their moments of aberration.

The physical order, then, is real; there are thousands of substances distinct from us; by reason of their essential property, force, they act and produce the phenomena which make up the physical world. These substances are finite and contingent, for they are subject to modifications; they depend from the Infinite, and are only secondary causes. But if we seek still further and ask: when I perceive a stone, what is it? It is an aggregate of simple substances having such relation to one another that they form a whole, which is, consequently, compound; and properly called matter. Each one of the simple elements, of which the stone is composed, has its force and acts on the organs of vision : each element, having a different relation to us, acts differently, or in a different direction, and hence we distinguish right and left, up and down, in the stone. Each simple element of the stone· retains its individuality, so to speak ; though the relation of the elements to one another is such, as to cause them to exercise a mutual action from which results adhesion, and a compound whole ; still no element is, as it were, swallowed up. It is scarcely correct to say " compound substance ;" substance is essentially simple. A certain relation of a number of simple substances produces what is called a compound substance ; but this composition does not affect the essence of the substance ; it only betokens an external relation. The components must be prior to the compounds ; just as the individual soldiers must be prior to the brigade. Hence materialism involves a radical contradiction, and argues ignorance of the most obvious principles. To sum up: many finite substances exist ; substance essentially supposes action : in reality it acts. A certain relation of various simple substances produces what is called matter, or compound substances. These necessarily have action : if we have a certain relation to them they act on us and produce sensations. From experience we find that certain portions of matter produce identical sensations, hence we classify them under one head, calling them stones, &c. When but a few substances make up a compound whole we may feel the action of the compound although we do not see it ; thus the odor from the flowers, although invisible, produces a sensation. The reason may be, the imperfect sensibility of the visual organs. There is no doubt but the odor, being composed of various simple substances, acts on our organs of sight ; but its components being few in number, their action is weak, and makes no noticeable impression on the eye.

Were the sensibility of our organs very much increased, we could see various things which are now invisible. Although, therefore, a thing is invisible, it does not at all follow that it is not acting on our eye ; it is like a gentle tap on the knocker, a real action, but one too weak to produce the desired effect. Another reason may be assigned : the combination of forces in the invisible odor being that of only a few, the relation which each one has to us may be so nearly identical, that we cannot distinguish a diversity of direction, or cannot collocate them to the right, or left. Our system gives a rational proof of the reality of the physical world, and a satisfactory explanation of its phenomena.

CHAPTER XIII.

CREATION.

THE ways of error are many and strange; they are like the wakes made by ships traversing an unknown sea. As the noble barque passes proudly on, a glittering trail appears; the passengers gaze on it with silent delight; they watch the curling and rippling of the disturbed water with deep interest. Innumerable prisms are formed which divide, reflect, refract the rays of light in so many different ways that the most fantastic and, at times, gorgeous colorings illume the track. It would seem to the gazer that an illuminated pathway was formed along which he might, at least, return to his starting point if he could not reach his destination. But lo! a few moments elapse; the swaying of the watery elements ceases; the fleeting prisms dissolve; the illumination dies out, and the erst glittering trail becomes confounded with the great mass of dull, sluggish brine. Other vessels will cross that track and not observe it; the same barque that formed it, seeing breakers ahead, will turn about and cross and re-cross it a dozen of times, while the man at the wheel imagines that he is steering back along the original course. Thus the propagators and defenders of false systems, exploring the vast field of metaphysics, will present a theory clad with beautiful expressions, and decked with all the glory of ornamental rhetoric. Its outward beauty excites the sympathy of the hearer; he imagines it the truest "evolution of modern thought;" surely this brilliant system is the way of truth. If, however, he be a man of thought, and follow the deductions of this system—listen to its explanations of the daily phenomena we witness, he will see how inconsistent it is; how it has to destroy to-day what it labored to build up yesterday. It is as uncertain a guide to itself and others, as is the wake of the ship to the 'nighted mariner. On the other hand, a true system of philosophy is always consistent; it may appear plain, even commonplace, because truth is more simple than error, but its explanation of one phenomenon will not contradict its explanation of others. It may not, always, be able to make us comprehend everything of which it treats; but this will arise rather from our limited capacity than from any defect of the system. The beacon, placed near a point of danger, does not tell the sailor whether it be a reef, a shoal, or a whirlpool, that is to be avoided; it merely tells of certain shipwreck if he ventures to approach. So a true system of philosophy can always warn us from following paths that end in absurdity, even though it may not be able to prove, with metaphysical certainty, that the opposite is the right road. The same succeeds with the geometrician. A *reductio ad absurdum* demonstration is just as convincing, just as certain, as a direct one. It is unfair, therefore, to require from the metaphysician a direct proof of everything; one of two contradictory propositions must be true; if one be shown absurd the other must be right. So with contradictory systems. The man who really desires truth will keep these things in view, and not waste his time in meaningless cavils.

We have proved the existence of various substances, and the reality of the physical world. But the mind is not yet satisfied. It seeks more truth; it asks: whence are these substances? The answer to this question involves the explanation of the word placed at the head of this chapter, Creation. Creation, or the act of creating, is a free act of the Infinite, willing that substances, which before were only possible, exist. As shown above the notion of existence is clear enough, as is, also, that of non-existence; hence the conception of creation can offer no difficulty. Imagine nothing but God existing; he wills the subject I to exist, and straightway I am. This is creation: *nothing* is not the material out of which I was formed; it simply indicates a negative terminus from which God's action began. There was nothing but God; he willed, and the subject I rejoices in existence. In philosophy production differs from creation: the former supposes the pre-existence of the material out of which the article is made. Thus, a chair is produced, not created, by the mechanic. It is only a new form of old material. In creation both form and substance are new. God being absolutely simple in essence it follows that, in the event of his creating, he did not make the things out of part of himself, nor out of anything else, because we suppose nothing but God existing: hence a transit was made from nothing to something. The will of God was the efficient cause of our existence. We have an imperfect image of this in ourselves: an act of our will becomes the cause of various emotions; what was merely possible is made, by an act of the will, real. A true transit is made from nothing to something.

Having explained the notion of creation, a notion which is clear and involves no contradiction, we answer the question: whence are the various finite substances? by replying, they were created by God. Those who admit the plurality of substances, and that is nearly everyone, materialists included, cannot, with even an attempt at reasoning, deny this. Either these various substances are all necessary beings, or they are not. If the former, then we would have many infinite beings; because a thing which exists by necessity of nature must be, as proved before, infinite. But plurality of infinite beings is a repugnant idea; each would have all power, and at the same time it would not be all powerful, for it would not have power over its brother infinite. Therefore, plurality of infinite beings is repugnant; therefore, likewise, plurality of necessary beings is repugnant. Therefore there can be but one necessary substance; all the others are contingent, or dependent on some other for their existence. We thus fall on the other horn of the dilemma, viz: they are not all necessary beings: consequently they are the effects of a primary cause; A may have been produced by B, B by C, but the last one Z, must be the direct effect of the Infinite. Nothing existing except the Infinite, he being simple, and being the efficient cause of Z, he must have created it. Once you admit the plurality of substances, you must admit the contingency of all of them except one; contingent substances being admitted, creation is necessarily supposed. The trite axiom, as clear as $2 \times 2 = 4$, is not more severely correct, is not one whit clearer, than the argument in favor of creation. It is difficult to imagine what fascination so overclouds any intellect as to make it reject this self-evident reasoning. Unless it be a pride similar to that of Lucifer, who thought to make himself like unto the Most High, one cannot see what else it is. Were we not created, of course we would be necessary beings, and consequently, infinite. Tom, Dick, and Harry, each being infinite, each being supreme, Tom would be superior to Dick, Dick superior to Tom, and Harry superior to Tom and Dick. If they should happen to come in collision, the feline tribe of Kilkenny could no longer be cited as the most unflinching warriors on record. They, at least, saved their tails; but Harry, Tom, and Dick would knock one another into nothing!

The pantheist, whose principle is that there is only one substance, has some show of reason when he combats creation. No one else has. But, with the pantheist, it is only a show of reason, not reason itself. We proved, conclusively, that the fundamental principle of Pantheism is false; we demonstrated the existence of various substances. If at least two do not exist, none exists, because if the not I is the I then the I is a perpetual contradiction, a nothing. There being two, one must be created as shown above. If you admit the creation of Jones, one does not find any philosophic reason for denying the same to Smith. To sum up: those who admit the plurality of substances must either admit the creation of all of them save one, or must fall into the absurdity of admitting a plurality of infinites. Those who admit only one substance are first to be instructed in the most elementary principles of logic, for example, the principle of contradiction; then they are to be led into the camp of metaphysics and taught the proper definition of substance; after which they may be able to grasp the evidence of the arguments adduced to prove the plurality of substances. Only gross ignorance, or a headstrong spirit, could keep a man a pantheist after that very elementary training. The intelligent reader will find sufficient proofs in this, and preceding chapters, to enable him to prove the fact of creation to any man of sane mind.

From the fact that creation is an act of the free will of the Infinite, for finite beings being contingent there was no necessity of creating them, it follows that created things are not eternal. You may make them millions upon millions of years old, still, the free action of the Infinite was prior to them; consequently they are not eternal. Again, the very notion of a created eternal is repugnant. Contingency necessarily involves the idea of a beginning, however remote; they were not; God willed, and they were. Eternal matter is as full of meaning as a round square.

It would be long and profitless to enumerate the various grotesque theories of the ancients, regarding the origin of the universe. They were not pantheists, however. Blinded though they were by the debasing superstitions of paganism, they still retained a sufficient glimmering of reason's lamp to enable them to acquire the obvious truth that the *I* and the not *I* were substantially distinct. Generally they admitted the eternity of matter, but even in this error, their greatest minds were far superior in logical acumen to our modern materialists. They had an Infinite God, the supreme ruler of all, and the vindicator of his law. Plato, Socrates, or Cicero, would have laughed to scorn the gross idea of the materialist, who recognizes nought in creation save what is matter.

Time and creation are coeval; so soon as the first finite being passed into existence, time began, not before. We have said that God once, always and forever wills what he wills. Hence the act of creation, considered in God, does not include the idea of change. It was once, always and forever willed by him. By that act things passed into existence and assumed extrinsic relations to God; but intrinsically the infinite substance suffered no mutation. Daily things might come into existence, and still no change would take place in the essence of God; new external relations would be formed, but no inward mutation; for in the one act is included everything that he will ever create. Suppose a man lecturing to twenty persons; he has an extrinsic relation to each of them by reason of his voice acting on their organs of hearing. If another man should enter, the speaker will assume an outward relation which he had not previously, but no inward change is effected. The voice that fell on the ears of twenty now falls on those of twenty-one, but it is the same voice, and will remain the same, even though new listeners arrive each moment. This may help to give us some imperfect idea of the unchangeability of God, while new substances come into existence. Only God can create, because the act requires an infinite power. From not to be, to existence, is the greatest possible transit; only an infinite power could effect that. In this, physical science gives its testimony. Its first principle is that by no chemical means can one particle of matter be made, or destroyed. Changes on existing matter may be effected, but no creation, no annihilation. 'Tis necessarily so; 'tis happy for us that it is so. We are not at the mercy of friends, or foes. Could each one create, the earth, instead of being a well-regulated warehouse, would soon become a disordered lumber-room, each one creating as fancy might dictate.

It is to be observed that in contingent things there is no more necessary connection between the successive moments of their duration than what there was between their creation, and the first moment of their existence. Being contingent, there is never any necessity of existence in their essence; consequently, in the same manner that they require an act of God to bring them into existence, in like manner they require his continual action to preserve them in it. This act is called conservation, but it is in God, identical with the act of creation; or it is the perpetual continuance of the creative act. From this it follows that a positive act is not required, on the part of God, in order to annihilate; he need only suspend the creative act. Since annihilation supposes a suspension of God's act, it follows that only God can annihilate. How beautiful and coherent is the system of truth! How satisfactorily it can explain abstruse things! It never contradicts itself: but each development unfolds some new charm,—offers some new satisfaction to the mind. No obscurity, no groping in the dark: starting from certainty, it walks straight on, acquiring fresh light and new vigor at each step. Truth after truth is added to the store; it follows the golden chain that links each to the other and all to God. The needle does not point as unerringly to the pole as does right reason, when investigating the physical world, point to God.

It is worthy of note that the account given by Moses, of the creation, is just what right reason and geological research find it to be. Moses is, we think, the only ancient philosopher who speaks of creation. Is this fact not strong presumptive evidence of inspiration?

When we call God the Creator, and primary cause of the physical order, we do not exclude the action of created things. On the contrary, we hold that every substance acts, in some way or other. God created innumerable monads; he endowed them with various properties; essentially they had action. His infinite wisdom designed an ordered universe in which planets should revolve, plants grow, seasons succeed each other, &c.: but this sublime machinery was to be kept in motion in virtue of the various properties given to created things. Strata were to be formed—minerals to coalesce—fossils to accumulate, during lapsing centuries, through the action of created things. Hence what are called "physical laws," are the foreseen and intended results of the properties given by God to the substances he created. Certain conditions being verified, certain results must follow. Had God wished he could have given different properties to the monads; different physical laws would have been the result; he might have given a repellent, instead of an attractive property, to two balls of lead. In a word, all created things being contingent, their creation and accidental properties depend from the free will of God. God, then, designed the physical order; its sublime regularity and beauty would prove it; he gave such properties to the monads, and provided such ready compensations, in case of disturbances effected through the action of free agents, that that order will persevere so long as he has decreed it to endure, and no longer. The action being from him, he can at any moment revoke it: he can, if he deem it expedient, suspend the usual effect of any, or all, of the physical laws. The physical world, with its code of laws, is, on a sublime scale, what an intricate piece of machinery is on a small one. The mechanic designs in his mind a watch; he sees that such wheels indented in such a manner, are necessary, and he prepares them. He disposes them in proper positions; the spring moves, the machinery is set in motion. 'Tis what he foresaw and intended. By a slight alteration he could make the wheel turn to the left instead of the right. Unlike God, he cannot provide a compensation for disturbances, and the machinery must eventually stop.

CHAPTER XIV.

PROVIDENCE.

IT is generally supposed that an author thinks more of his literary productions, than what others think of them. It is not at all likely that a writer would tear out the leaves from his own book, in order to have something in which to wrap up an ounce of snuff, or a tallow candle. The grocer, however, would not hesitate to do it. In this connection I shall never forget the impression made upon my mind, by an incident of which I was an eye-witness. Some companions and myself called at a grocery, in a little town in Italy. We were getting edibles for a lunch of which we would partake, on the bank of a beautiful lake near by. One of the necessary articles of an Italian *merenda* is *presciutto*, ham. We asked for ham, and the burly grocer weighed out the required quantity. He must have been an aristocratic grocer, for he did not use common brown wrapping paper. Several large volumes were lying on the shelves; he tore some leaves out of the largest one and rolled our ham carefully enough in it. We asked him why he tore the book; he replied that he intended using them all for a like purpose; they came cheaper than wrapping paper. On looking at the leaves in which our *presciutto* was infolded, judge of our surprise to find them to be from the unfortunate Passaglia's great work, "De Immaculata Conceptione,"

How vain appeared the aspirations of an author after fame, if his works were to receive such usuage as this! Yet, without doubt, the productions of other great writers have, at times, suffered similar treatment. Their authors, however, will treasure them up; dust them carefully; arrange them neatly. Every intelligent workman, if his works prove good, likes and cares for them. Now God is, as we showed above, the creator of the physical order; we and every visible thing are the works of his hand. The natural conclusion is, he loves and cares for us: the contrary would be as unnatural as it is false. God was free to create; having resolved to operate he must have intended his work for some purpose, otherwise he would be a foolish God: being all-powerful he is able to attain the desired end. Hence the wisdom of God absolutely requires that he should dispose and direct all things so as to obtain the end desired. This disposition and direction is called *Providence;* therefore the providence of God is to be admitted. So self-evident is this fact that few, very few, either ancient or modern, ever doubted of it. The epicureans did, for the gross reason that God being happy in himself, would not mar that happiness by troubling himself with mundane affairs. Some moderns deny it; possibly in order to give free rein to their passions. As was before remarked, every means is tried in order to destroy the idea of an avenging God. Not being able to deny his existence, they seek to make him blind; he created, they say, but he cares no more about us; he has left us to ourselves; he will not require an account of our actions. The impious said the same in David's time—non requiret Deus. Of course we do not deny the liberty of action enjoyed by man; we do not say that he does always what would be most pleasing to God; far from it; but we say that God created the world for a purpose; he disposed and directed it to that end; and he will have that end despite the malice of men and devils. We do not say that every event is directly brought about by God; but we say that every event was foreseen by him, and that he so disposed things as to make each event finally subservient to the great intended end. To deny this would be to deny the intelligence of God in not knowing the future: or his power in not being able to attain the desired end by reason of created obstacles. From this there is no escape.

We proved the existence of God from the duration and regularity of the physical order; we detected his foot-prints on all sides. Therefore we proved his Providence. Again, the universal belief of man can be invoked. The history of every nation has no fact so prominently brought into view, as its belief in a God, and in his providence. Sacrifices for rain, before battle, before bargains; prayers and offerings were made at all times by the pagans. The Jewish and Christian religion directly teach the providence of God. We have thus the whole of mankind with a few exceptions, so few that they no more destroy the universal testimony, than do the solar specks impede the glorious sunlight. These latter swim in an ocean of brightness but remain opaque, an expressive image of that human intelligence which is blind to the existence and providence of God, though bathed in a sea of evidence. Whether, then, we consider the wisdom and power of God, or the physical order, or the history of the human race, we must be convinced that God did not create his works and then abandon them; but that he disposes and directs them to the end for which he brought them into existence.

It seems altogether credible that many of those learned in physical science, who deny the Providence of God, do so from not rightly understanding what sound metaphysics teaches on this head. They imagine that we take all action from physical things; that we attribute every phenomenon, that is a little unusual, to the immediate action of God. Now we condemn the foolish theory of "*occasionalism*," or a destroying of secondary causes; we contend, and what is more we prove, that every substance is essentially active, and that, generally speaking, physical phenomena are the results of the action of physical things. We combat, and we think, successfully, the superstitious idea of recurring to the Divinity for an explanation of these phenomena, as a general rule. At the same time we contend that these effects were foreseen and intended by God; that he gave action to created things to produce these effects, and that he provides, daily and hourly, a ready compensation for all incidental disturbances, so that the physical order may continue until he shall please to permit a final catastrophe. This is his providence as regards the physical world. No man of science, unless he wishes to deny God, can deny this. It is as idle to talk about the absolute immutability of the properties of a contingent being, as what it is to talk about its necessity. The properties of a being are co-extensive with its nature; the nature being finite, contingent and, consequently, dependent, the properties must be the same. Moveover, we gave an example to prove that physical laws are not regular in their development, and are influenced by various circumstances. Therefore there must have been an intelligence that foresaw and provided for all these varieties of circumstances, in order that the harmony of nature might not be destroyed. The man who fails to see this is but a tyro in the science of nature. Those who make a study of physical things become enamoured of the order, beauty and harmony therein discovered. They behold crystals following, in their formation, certain fixed laws; the salts of the earth's surface producing, by chemical action, the various minerals we prize; the thermoelectric currents of the earth, caused by the unequal heating of its surface, directing the course of the magnetic needle. All these phenomena, produced by physical action, enrapture them; they too often rest satisfied with the contemplation of these facts, and never ask themselves the question: "but whence these salts, and whence their action?" We do not deny the truths revealed by chemistry; we accept them, and only find in them new cause of wonder at the wisdom and power of the Most High—new proof of the existence and providence of God. Let the chemist hold to all the certain conclusions of his science; but let him, at the same time, remember that other sciences have their truths; so that, while holding fast to his own, he may endeavor to learn the truths of metaphysics. It would be a professional craze for a man to imagine that there were truths in no other profession except in his own. Now the truth of one science can never be opposed to the truth of another. The sensible man will accept them all, knowing that there can be no real contradiction between them, although there may be an apparent one. Sound metaphysics, while invincibly proving the existence of God, the fact of creation and providence, easily and clearly reconciles these truths with the wondrous order and action of physical things. In fact, metaphysical truths are necessary to explain the physical ones. Now the lover of chemistry, who rejects the demonstrations of metaphysics, can give no reasonable explanation of the origin of the phenomena he so much admires. He has only a choice between two absurdities—the necessity of contingent things, or the action of that mysterious old rogue, Chance. We should all be eclectics in the sense in which St. Clement of Alexandria was one, viz: in seeking truth wherever it is; but not in the sense of some who pretend to reconcile contradictory propositions.

CHAPTER XV.

THE END OF CREATION.

WE showed that God, being an intelligent operator, must have had some end in view in creating. Whenever we perform an action deliberately, we always have an object in doing it. Perhaps the action may be really disadvantageous to us, still we apprehend it under a respect in which we imagine that it will benefit us. We may do it to satisfy a hatred, to obtain wealth, fame, or favor with God; but at all times, and in the case of all, there is an object in the performance of every deliberate action. The more sensible the man is, the more reasonable will be the object; the more capable and reasonable he is, the greater it will be. From this consideration we arrive at the certainty that God, who deliberately created, must have had an end in view. Now God being infinitely wise and perfect must have intended an end worthy of himself; otherwise he would be imperfect. The man who does an action unbecoming one in his sphere of life, is said to disgrace himself—to have acted foolishly. Man, being finite, may perform an action, and intend something unworthy of his dignity, but with God it cannot be thus. Infinite in wisdom, his action must have an end worthy of that wisdom. But it is self-evident that there is nothing worthy of God, except God himself: hence we must conclude that the end intended by God, in creating, must be the external manifestation of his infinite perfections, his glory, wisdom, power. We say "external manifestation," because millions of worlds can add nothing to his intrinsic glory; it is already infinite; but by creation it is outwardly expressed. This was the end in view, and well is it attained in creation; the heavens, indeed, relate the glory of God; the streams and rivulets murmur his praises; the innumerable flowers that bloom bespeak his beauty; the whole physical order proclaims his wisdom and power. It is quite evident that the whole irrational creation constantly glorifies God: but what about man, the high-priest of nature? Some may doubt whether God attains the intended end in his regard. The absolute end of man's creation is God's glory; but there is another conditional end of man which more immediately concerns man himself: it is to glorify God by good deeds in life, and to receive eternal happiness in heaven. This latter end is, we say, conditional, dependent on the free will of man assisted by the grace of God. If man glorifies God by virtuous actions, he will attain his final and personal end; if he does not, he will lose his personal end, but the absolute end intended by God will be gained despite man's malice. God can be glorified externally by manifestations of his infinite goodness, or by manifestations of his infinite justice. If man be virtuous, God is glorified in his goodness; if he be impious, God will be glorified in his justice by condemning him. To man only will there be a loss if he be wicked to him only; the gain if virtuous: in either case God will have his glory. Hence the absolute end intended by God in creating will be always attained. Moreover the very passions and crimes of man will be made subservient to God's glory. The Almighty does not wish sin; he hates and will punish it; but if, abusing his free will, man should commit crimes, God will know how to bring glory to himself out of them. Examples may make this interesting point clearer. God did not wish the Jews to crucify the Saviour; they did it, nevertheless, and from that act came the glory of the triumph over sin and death. God did not wish the oppression of Erin; she was oppressed, nevertheless, and out of that oppression God drew the glory of having his faith spread over Australia, America, Africa. God does not wish the impious conduct of the tyrant Bismarck; but of his own perverse will, Bismarck rages against our holy church, and God is glorified in the constancy of the persecuted, who renew before a world, grown old in iniquities, the heroism of early christianity. Thus we might bring to examination every historic fact, and see how out of the malice of man God drew glory to himself. When the day of final reckoning will have come we will see all this more clearly. In the meantime the light of reason is sufficient to enable us to discover the end of creation, and to prove to us that nought can frustrate the designs of the Omnipotent. The faint heart, or the mind not given to meditation, is often assailed with a doubt of God's providence; but we should reflect that God is a general provider, not a particular one. The order of his providence is not that the just should always prosper here; they may sometimes, or they may not. God gave faculties to man; by the exercise of these, by the concurrence of various circumstances, riches, for instance, may be acquired. The impious sets all his faculties to work to gain money, by lawful, or unlawful means. Were God to step in at all times and by his immediate action to frustrate the schemes of that man, he would be destroying the order established by himself. Out of the injustice of that wretch he will finally have his glory; but being eternal, he can be patient. Again, there is none so bad but has, at some time, done a good action. Each good action will get its reward; the impious get that reward here in worldly comforts, fame and wealth. In a word, the providence of God is a general law; he never sanctions evil, he only permits it; but out of it he will draw good. The impious man who is attentive to business often succeeds, because God does not wish to disturb the order of his providence by making attention to business and industry unsuccessful. All this, however, only proves that the book of accounts is not closed by death.

PART SECOND.

PSYCHOLOGY.

PSYCHOLOGY is a science which treats of the nature and attributes of the human soul. It holds the second rank in metaphysics. No words are required to impress upon any thoughtful mind the importance of this branch of knowledge. It is a pity that its study is so much neglected. Persons quite capable of writing with ease and elegance in various languages—persons brilliant in drawing-rooms, or eloquent on platforms, are often found to be profoundly ignorant of the nature of their own soul. They have a shadowy idea that it is a something, and there their knowledge of it ends. This universal ignorance, on this point, is very favorable to the growth of errors regarding religion and social duties. It is our humble wish to excite an interest in this science; to make its study as easy and pleasing as the nature of the subject will allow. Truth and perspicuity are to be consulted; hence inelegancies of diction may abound, but, we trust, obscurity will be rare.

CHAPTER I.

NATURE OF THE SUBJECT *I*.

HITHERTO we were content with the fact of our own existence; we started from the fundamental fact, I am, I exist. The principle which was conscious of its own existence we called the subject *I*, so as to leave no room for misunderstanding, or sophistry. No one, be he pantheist, idealist, or materialist, could attack us, for we simply confined ourselves to the admitted fact, I am, I think. Taking our own existence for a basis we showed that two other facts were to be admitted, viz: the aptitude of the subject *I* to acquire certainty, and the principle of contradiction. The former, it may be observed, is presupposed in the fact that we are certain of existing; the latter is supposed by denying, or doubting it. Our position, thus, became such that no sane man would dream of assailing it: on all sides it was impregnable. From the evidence of reason we demonstrated the existence of a supreme being that exists by necessity of nature, and who is, consequently, infinite, perfect, the creator and ruler of the physical world. Each of these truths was shown to be as certain as the existence of the subject *I*; in fact, once that a finite being, such as we know ourselves to be, exists, there must exist the infinite from which it depends. The absurdities of pantheism, egoism, and epicureanism, were fully exposed: although we did not occupy ourselves with the various phases of these erroneous systems, we clearly proved that their fundamental principles were false; that being demonstrated, no mind open to conviction would defend their conclusions how specious soever they might appear. So many truths being acquired respecting things extrinsic to the subject I, it now behooves us to turn our attention inwardly and, from the I itself, to learn what it is.

An ancient philosopher is said to have given expression to the sentiment—know thyself—and to have considered it a most important knowledge. And truly it is most important. What would it avail us to know the history of nations, the deeds of renowned leaders, the changes of empires, the huge mass of celestial bodies with their wonderful order, and celerity of motion, if we were ignorant of our own nature,— our condition, our origin and our end? Hence it is a study worthy of man to endeavor to know himself, both in a moral and metaphysical sense. It is not, however, an easy matter for man to know himself; he is according to the Greeks, a " mikrokosmos," or a little world, inasmuch as his structure exhibits, in a small mass, the greatest marvels of visible creation. In the christian system of philosophy there are, in man, two distinct and diverse substances so united as to act reciprocally, and to constitute one individual, Peter. At present we will not speak of that gross material part which we feel and see. Few, if any, deny its existence. We have said that each one is conscious of the fact of his own existence; I am, I exist, I think, I will, I feel. The subject, or principle, which has this consciousness, was, hitherto, called by us the subject $I;$ we now say that this is what we call the human soul. Therefore, in the sense explained, the soul exists. If any materialist should ever glance over these pages, let him not, as he comes to this, accuse us of " petitionem principii," of supposing what is to be proved. He will not find here a stumble in logic. We have not, as yet, said whether the soul be simple, or compound, distinct or not from the body: we merely explain what we mean by the soul, viz: the subject *I*, the principle that is conscious of feeling, willing, understanding. In this sense, neither he, nor any one else can deny the soul to exist. Step by step we will proceed; inch by inch we will dislodge the materialists from their fancied strongholds, by the inexorable force of reasoning; little by little they must surrender, or be scattered in wild dismay, like a flock of bats whirling blindly away from the presence of a blazing light.

The principle, then, of intelligence and will, and which we call the soul, exists. What is it? What is its nature? This is the question to be answered in this chapter. If the soul reflects a moment on itself it becomes conscious that it is the one same principle that thinks, feels and knows. It does not say: I think, but another I knows: it is quite certain that it is the one same I that does both. Moreover, it is certain that although it has various and changing affections, still, the subject of these is always identical. I am the same I that think to-day, as thought yesterday, or a year ago. I am one and the same; my feelings, thoughts and wishes succeed one another in rapid succession, but still *I*, the subject of these, remain unchanged. I am, as it were, the stationary screen on which the fleeting images of a magic lantern appear and vanish, and are quickly followed by others. The old man tottering under the weight of eighty years, recognizes himself as the same one who, at seven, chased butterflies in midsummer. Therefore the soul is always one and the same. This identity of the soul with itself will help to give a clear idea of what a substance is as opposed to accidents. Substance is usually defined: "*That which exists by itself not requiring another in which to adhere as its subject.*" An accident does not exist by itself but requires another in which to adhere; thus size or shape is an accident. The accidents may change, but the substance remains the same. From this it is evident that the soul is a substance, and the various sensations and emotions we experience are accidents, or modifications of the soul. These latter do not exist by themselves; they require the soul as a subject in which to adhere. Take a piece of soft wax; you can fashion it with the hand in any way you please; now you make it round, now oblong, now square. These different shapes are accidents, or modifications of the wax; but during all these passages from shape to shape, there was something permanent, something which the hand did not destroy, though it destroyed the shapes. That something was the substance of the wax. Thus in the soul the principle that is always identical with itself proves the soul to be a substance, and its varying emotions accidents.

Again, as we before observed, action, of some kind, is essential to a substance, and only a substance can have action. In our sense, then, whatever acts is a substance. Now it is evident that the soul acts; our inner consciousness testifies that the soul can, and does produce various actions: therefore the soul is a substance. We have said that whatever acts is a substance; it might be objected that color, for instance, is an accident, but it apparently acts on our visual organs. To this we reply. that color is only a sensation excited in the soul by reason of the action of some compound substance; according to the various relations of the parts of the colored object to one another, various colors are produced. The ray of light which falls on the object is divided, and reflected to the eye. A certain disposition of parts will reflect one of the prismatic colors, another disposition, a different one, or a combination of several. Thus the relative positions of the parts of matter, acting on the ray of light before it is reflected to the eye, is the reason that matter excites in the soul the sensation of this or that color. By steeping wool in certain solutions a change is effected in the previous relations of its parts, and it excites in the soul a different sensation; we say its hue is changed. In a word, what are called the " properties of bodies" are the sensations excited in the soul by the action of the substance. These properties are beacons to warn us of a resistance to our passage.

It is now evident that only a substance can excite a sensation; sensation is the result of action on the soul; only substances can act. Therefore only they can excite sensations. Now since we continually have sensations of various kinds, and since we are certain that many of them are not produced by our own soul, we are certain that some substance, besides ourselves, exists. But we proved before that the infinite substance does not excite these sensations; therefore we are certain that many, very many substances exist. From the uniformity of sensations produced by some objects, we deduce uniformity of action on their part; from uniformity of action we conclude similarity of substance, and thus classify certain objects under one generic term of stones, metals, wood.

If it be still further inquired after the nature of substance, we must remind the seeker that we do not see *intuitively* the nature of things: we judge of objects only by their properties, or the effects produced by them on our soul. When the chemist analyzes a portion of matter, he learns more about it than what he knew before; still, his knowledge has been acquired by means of his senses. If the test has been made by fire, the fire only served to set free certain ingredients, under the form of vapor. He could, thus, judge better of the remaining ingredients. If he resorted to mixing, the effect of the object under trial, was seen to resemble, or to differ from the effect produced on the mixture by another object; hence he could deduce the similarity, or diversity of the two objects. In a word, tests, of any kind, are only scientific spectacles; they enable the operator to observe properties that would otherwise have escaped notice. The judgment of the greatest chemist, like that of the most ignorant, is only from the sensation produced in his soul by the object under examination.

For our own part we would say that a substance is a force; if that is not sufficient, we can only say we know no more about it. God is the great reality, the great force; being good, and desirous of diffusing his bounty, he created innumerable forces, or substances; these, having no physical parts, may be, called, with Liebnitz, *monads*. Each monad imitates in some way the Divine Essence; some imitate it in a greater, others in a lesser, degree. Each has something in common with the other, and also, with God; they all have, at least, action. These monads, being contingent, can only have such properties as God chooses to give them; in other words, they were made to imitate his essence in a certain way, and they must always retain that imitation. To deny this would be to attribute to them an infinite power, viz: the power of creating; for if you say that they essentially imitate God in a greater degree than what they formerly did, they must have created themselves anew. We must distinguish between an essential and an accidental resemblance: take two rough boards and smooth and paint one of them. The one so treated may be made to bear a resemblance to a marble slab; accidentally it does, but essentially it no more resembles marble than what the rough one does. In a word, essence being that by which a thing is what it is, it follows that the essence of anything is absolutely unchangeable. Now the essential properties of a thing, that is, the properties without which a thing cannot be imagined, are proportioned to the essence, grounded in it, and consequently, absolutely unchangeable. Hence it is evident that the peculiar essential force given to a monad, at its creation, must remain essentially unchanged, so long as that monad exists. We have here, as will be shown in another place, a metaphysical principle that proves the absolute repugnance of the Darwinian theory of development from the monkey to the man.

It may be thought that we are making a mere gratuitous supposition regarding the existence of monads. Supposition is an article in which the true philosopher does not deal; he leaves that unprofitable branch of speculation to philosophic quacks, such as Hegel, Kant, Darwin and *id genus omne*. Facts are our wares, and their demonstration our advertisement. We have proved the existence of various substances; all admit compound ones such as stones, wood and iron. It was shown before that a compound thing presupposes the parts of which it is compounded. Just as the whole house presupposes the existence of each brick, so each brick presupposes the existence of the parts of which it is made up. It is true that some imagined divisibility of matter to proceed indefinitely; but this, probably, arose from following with the eye each successive division. Take a brick: it is a finite object and necessarily made up of a finite number of parts; we do not mean *atoms*, for these are compound, also, but a certain determined number of simple parts must be in that compound object. Now we cannot by any chemical means completely disintegrate the brick, consequently, physically speaking, we are baffled in the division. But our reason says, the parts being finite in number if I go on taking away one part at a time, I must finally arrive at the last one. If there are but ten buckets of water in the well I cannot draw twelve therefrom : if the number of parts is definite, the division must end. If, therefore, we use our reason, and not our senses, we inevitably find that a compound substance is made up of many simple ones ; these are what we call monads ; therefore monads exist. Since monads exist, and are simple, they must have come into existence by creation ; because it is evident from their physical simplicity that they are not the result of a process of formation ; they are not from themselves, because they are finite ; therefore they were created by God, and each has, and must always retain, such essential properties only as were bestowed upon it by the creator. Hence simple substances exist ; but all substances essentially have action ; therefore simple substances act. Materialists must be pressed hard on this point. Though these simple substances do not fall under the notice of our senses, they are not to be looked upon as mere nothings ; possibly if our senses were more acute we might experience their action. In any case, they have action as an essential requirement.

In order to avoid misconception we must explain a term which is often taken in a wrong sense, viz : *inertia.* Inertia does not mean an absence of all action ; nor does it mean a state of rest : it simply implies an indifference in the object to either rest or motion ; consequently, it bespeaks the absence of a self-determining power. Put a stone in motion ; it is inert ; put it at rest, it is inert, because it would keep forever either of these states unless some extrinsic cause should intervene. But whether in motion, or at rest, the stone, though inert, was acting.

There are, then, monads created by God and endowed with such properties that by their various relations they might, generally speaking, produce all visible objects and phenomena. Reason can discover three classes, at least, of monads in visible creation. The essential difference between these classes consists in the monads of each class imitating the divine essence in a different degree. The difference being thus essential, a monad of one class can never be developed into one of a higher, nor can it degenerate into one of a lower. The simple substances that are the components of matter, constitute the lowest class of monads. They have action but not self-determining power. The principle of life and feeling in the brute creation comprises a higher class; in addition to action they have sensation and life. The subject *I* of each man, the principle that knows and wills, or human souls make up the highest class. These have action, life, self-determining power, intelligence and free will. This is the nature of the soul.

I do not know whether all of the foregoing reasoning will appear as evident to the reader as it does to myself. In any case we have proved the soul to be a substance, an active being: moreover we clearly showed the possibility of simple substances, that is, such as have no physical parts. We will now undertake to prove that the soul is a simple substance. No one can say *a priori* that it is absurd; because simple substances can exist and act. Our proofs will show it to be a metaphysical certainty.

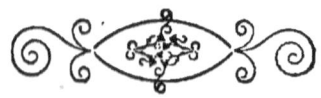

CHAPTER II.

SIMPLICITY OF THE SOUL.

IT is generally supposed that man inclines to pride; that he will rather seek to exalt than to degrade himself. He boasts of his ancestry if, perchance, any of them may have been distinguished; sometimes even when they have not been distinguished but only notorious for their rascality. "Blue blood" is a weakness that runs pretty well through the veins of the human family. By one of these huge delusions under which a people labor at times, the United States are supposed to be the very paradise of democrats, or rather, the nursery of kings; for every man of them thinks himself a sovereign. Let the foreigner, who is simple enough to cherish this idea, land in America and proclaim himself poor, sprung of obscure parents, but still equal, socially, to the bulls and bears of Wall street. A crowd of boys might proclaim him a "brick"—a policeman would call him a "flat" and warn him to beware of "sharks," while a raw native might say "that's the lingo." But the aristocratic circle would simply ignore him. If we turn our gaze backward and look up the stream of time, we will see that some of the great ones of antiquity were not satisfied with having a long human pedigree, they aimed still higher, and boasted descent from the gods. These facts go to prove that man seeks to exalt himself by dignity of origin. Some thought that this arose from an inward consciousness of a dignity that strove to vindicate itself. Be this as it may, it is pretty evident that the generality of mankind are not indifferent to the glory of ancestry. Latterly some notable exceptions have appeared on the stage. They seem to hate, with a bitter hate, the dignity of human origin and of our present state. We are, they say, but ingenious pieces of mechanism, set in motion in some strange way. Our feelings, thoughts and wishes,—all our noble aspirations—our heroic resolves—our most sublime conceptions, that which we call our soul, all these are but the unsubstantial quiverings of the human mechanism. The machinery will run for a time, and then,—that which thought, loved, felt, longed for bliss will be no more; the broken machinery will fall to dust, and everlasting nothing will be man's only doom. It must be admitted that this theory is not calculated to flatter human pride, nor to conduce to generous actions. Humiliating though it is, it is not the offspring of humble parents; it is an excrescence rather of human pride; or the figment of guilty minds. A man imagines himself learned; he hankers after notoriety; he cannot obtain it by following the beaten track, for his genius is not sufficient to give new expression to old truths. He delves in his own brain; the mine is not very rich, but he strikes upon a crude idea. In the clothing of this with expression he carefully interweaves threads of pure gold; a jumbled mass of truth and falsehood is the result. The uncautious note only the glittering of the dress, they do not see the utter worthlessness of the idea. The operator becomes noted; sometimes he knows well that he is only obtaining applause under false pretences; sometimes he persuades himself he is right, either from pride, or from a wish that there was no hereafter, as he has reason to fear it.

Some again who see the wondrous structure of the body, its great adaptability to its end, and not properly understanding what sound metaphysics teaches about the soul, and its union with the body, fall into error. If any such should read these pages, we ask him, as he values true knowledge, to read the whole of the treatise on the soul before throwing the book aside. If he will do this he will see how easily the truths of psychology are reconciled with physiological facts.

It would be a desolate task to enumerate the various opinions broached regarding the nature of the soul. Our point is to demonstrate that it is something distinct and diverse from the body; that it is not the fibres, brain, nor any part of matter, but that it is a simple substance, endowed with various faculties, having a union with the body, but not confused with it; and consequently, that the dissolution of the body does not involve the destruction of the soul. We already proved that it must be a substance, for the subject *I* certainly acts. The emotions, thoughts and wishes of each of us must be in a subject, not in airy nothingness; this subject must be a substance, because an accident in an accident is repugnant. The soul being a substance, it must be either simple or compound; there is no medium. If it is admitted to be simple, then our task is ended; if not it must be compound. Now let us examine closely and we will find that it is absolutely impossible for the soul to be a compound substance, that is, one made up of physical parts.

Each one is conscious of having the idea of a square, for instance: this object presents itself to us with its parts so arranged that we distinguish four sides; each particle of the surface is acting on the soul; the one at the right side is not identical with the one at the left; each has its own action, and each is acting on the soul through the medium of the visual organs. If now you say the soul is compound, it must be made up of a certain number of parts, say ten. Since we perceive the square, either there is a perception of the square in each of the ten parts, or a part of it in each part, or the whole of it in one of the ten parts. One of these three hypotheses must be chosen, no other is possible. If you take the first one, viz: that the perception of the whole square is in each part, you grant more than we want; for each of these parts being supposed simple, you give ten simple subjects of perception; we only ask one. But our intimate sense clearly testifies that the subject of perception is only one; only one *I* perceives, not ten. If you take the second, viz: that there is only a part of the perception in each part, it follows that since each part is distinct, there would be no one subject in us that perceived a whole square; each one perceived a tenth of it. Now it cannot be said that these partial perceptions might coalesce and form one. For apart from the fact that perception is an action that remains in its subject, there is the same difficulty. If they coalesce they must unite in one part; is that part simple? If so you grant the simple soul. Is it compound? If so, then the same argument returns; either the united perceptions are all in one simple part or not. If the former, we have the soul; if the latter, then again no one part has a full perception. Thus you would be running round forever in a circle. The same argument, the same difficulty continually remains; you would never have a subject in man that perceived the square, unless it were devoid of physical parts. There remains only the third hypothesis, viz: that the whole perception is only in one part: this part being simple, you admit a simple subject of perception. This would be the soul; the other parts would be, at most, organs of perception. From this argument it is self-evident that only a simple subject could perceive a square; since we perceive a square it follows that the subject *I* is simple; but it is, also, a substance: therefore the soul is a simple substance.

This argument may be illustrated by remarking that a compound substance can only have a representation of a thing by parts on parts. Place a square block before a mirror; there will be seen a representation of the square, but only a part of it on each part of the glass. Suppose each particle of glass as conscious. No one part of it would be conscious of the representation of the whole square : it would only know its own part. The same would be the case were the soul compound.

From this it is quite clear that it is absolutely impossible for matter to perceive. Materialists say we do not know all the properties of matter, consequently we are unable to say whether or no, it can perceive. This is a specious objection and apt to mislead the unthinking. To refute it, however, it is enough to remark that it is one thing to know all the properties of an object, and another to know what properties are repugnant to it. In order to know the latter, it is not necessary to know the former. I do not know all the properties of Jones, but I feel quite certain that he cannot " leap over the moon." I do not know all the properties of a delicately constructed sewing machine, but I am certain that it is absolutely impossible, physically speaking, for it to sew two metal plates together. Thus this oft-repeated objection is only a miserable sophism founded in a false supposition. If we know only one property of an object we have a metaphysical certainty that that object cannot possess another property which is contradictory to the first one : of matter we know that it has parts; we have shown the impossibility of perception of a square, unless in one simple part : therefore we have a metaphysical certainty that matter cannot perceive.

Another proof can be drawn from the self-determining power of the soul. All admit that matter is inert; it is, in fact, the characteristic of matter : it is one of Newton's three laws regarding gravitation. No one attempts to gainsay it. Now we are intimately conscious that our soul is not inert; the subject *I* can modify itself whenever it pleases. Quicker than lightning it can turn its attention from one object to another; with one glance it can survey an extended landscape, attending to mountain, valley, trees, rock and lake. More than this; it can determine the body to motion; it wills to write, and straightway the muscles of the arm are set to work; the joints of arm, hand, fingers,—all are in rapid play; it changes its will and these cease their motion. The man who would deny this determination to motion to be an effect produced by the soul must be mentally deranged. Therefore the soul is not inert; it has a self-determining power; as a consequence it is not matter, or in other words, it is not a compound substance: it must, therefore, be a simple substance, as there is no medium. This argument is as decisive as the first one, and its force is, perhaps, more easily understood. It is idle to look for an explanation of this effect in the brain, or in any part of the system. The subject *I*, or the soul, that wills to write, must be a something; either it must be a simple substance, or a certain portion of the human frame. If the latter, it would be inert, and incapable of modifying itself. Even if we supposed the absurdity that a certain portion of our body was the subject *I*, how could it act in this manner? Each particle must be endowed with a determining power; how then would unity of action invariably result? One would contract the muscle to the right, another to the left, another midway, and so on. Imagine a crowd of men together; they begin to move; would it be possible that they should all go in the same direction, even once, unless there were one master mind that ruled and directed their course? Certainly not; how if they were moving hundreds of times a day? The same must be in the human system; there must be one simple substance endowed with superior qualities, with determining power. Only in this way could there be harmony of action in man. Imagine a person climbing a dangerous cliff as the only means of escape from death. The eyes are eagerly seeking a root, or branch that may afford support; the hands convulsively clutch it; the feet nervously press against the rock to get some slight support from its uneven surface; every joint is quivering, every fibre is vibrating, every muscle is strained—all, all these actions are conspiring to the one end; one is subordinate to the other, and all work harmoniously. Can any rational being convince himself that the subject *I* which is all the time conscious of the danger and difficulties of the situation, which sees the means of escape, and directs the action of the whole frame-work of man, is nought but a sensation of the brain, a nervous phenomenon, or a mass of matter?

Again; the soul compares two ideas and judges concerning them. This operation can only take place in a subject which is physically simple. In fact; either the two ideas co-exist formally in the soul; or one of them exists with a remembrance of the other; or the remembrance of both exists. One of these three hypotheses must be verified, otherwise there could be no comparison instituted. Therefore, in the act of comparing, there are two distinct, and widely different representations in the soul, at the same point of time. Now this could not be possible were the soul physically compound; the parts of the one would become confused with the parts of the other; neither would be true; an ideal monstrosity, so to speak, would be the result. If you say that one representation would be in one part of the subject, the other in another part, you do not escape the difficulty. In that supposition there could be no' comparison; each part of the soul would have its own idea, but could not compare it with the one in another part; no more than Peter can compare an idea of his own with one that is in the mind of John. Both ideas must be in the self-same subject, at the same moment, otherwise comparison is impossible. If our ideas and affections are but physiological phenemona, but the quivering of the fibres, it would be the height of madness to talk of comparision. As well might you suppose that a bell could compare its various sounds, as that man could compare his ideas, unless you admit in the latter a substance physically simple and intelligent, which is the subject of all ideas and sensations, and which, by reason of its self-determining power, can excite feelings formerly had, and compare them with the present ones. This is so self-evident that it is hard to imagine that a rational being could seriously impugn it.

Finally; the subject I is, as we before observed, identical with itself, from the first moment of its earthly course to the last. Now all material things are undergoing continual change; few, if any, of the particles of our bodies are identical with those we called ours ten years ago. Several times during the allotted three score and ten our corporeal elements are renewed, but our soul remains always the same. Were it physically compound it would, undoubtedly, be subject to the same change.

From the foregoing arguments it will be seen that our soul whose existence, as an intelligent and sentient subject, all must admit, is a substance physically simple, distinct and different from the body, and consequently, that the dissolution of the latter does not necessarily include the destruction of the former. Moreover, material substances are absolutely incapable of thought, because the whole idea must be in an indivisible unity. Parts physically distinct can conspire to produce one external action; but they can never conspire to produce an internal one; if they could all their forces would have to be transfused into one of the parts.

CHAPTER III.

SPIRITUALITY OF THE SOUL.

PERHAPS no philosophic truth so commends itself to the feelings of our nature as the one we are going to demonstrate. We all feel this truth; we all are glad to feel it. We recognize in ourselves a nobility and dignity superior to that in other visible things. We admire the delicacy and wonderful structure of our body, still we are intimately convinced that there is something in us more wonderful still; something which is not necessarily dependent on this tangible organism in the exercise of its powers, although united to it. This conviction more or less plainly shadowed forth in conversation, points to the spirituality of the soul. We call a spiritual substance a simple substance endowed with will and intelligence, and capable of exercising these independently of corporeal organs. Our soul, as shown above, is the subject of will and intelligence; it is, also, a simple substance; consequently if we prove that it can exercise its faculties independent of sensorial organs it will be spiritual. The spirituality of the soul is no figment of the scholastics, as certain ones, who only lack the one thing to be learned, viz: knowledge, pretend. The idea is traceable in the philosophy of every nation, from Moses to our own time. Its dress may be as varied as the costumes at a masquerade; but as surely as a human being is enshrouded in each of these fantastic masks, just so surely is the idea of the spirituality of the soul, hidden under all the ridiculous expressions about *genii*, the Elysian fields, Thor, Manitou, and all the gods and goddesses that ever obtained a niche in Rome's great Pantheon. The legends generally ran, that these had formerly been men renowned during life, and changed into gods. The conviction of these people, then, was that death did not destroy all of man—*non omnis moriar* —but that a something of him triumphed over the wreck of the body and thought and willed, although hidden from mortal gaze. It is true that often they made the soul a body of more refined mould, still there remains the fundamental idea of a distinction and diversity between the soul and body, and of the life of the soul after its separation from its grosser companion. No nation, or tribe, ever yet confounded the soul with the body in such a manner, as to deny to the former the power of acting independently of the latter. They were considerably in advance of our modern pagans. They made the soul of the nature of fire, or air, or thrice ·efined matter. Now we maintain that this is an idea of ）irituality in the embryo. The light of the christian reli- ˙on illumed men's minds; their thoughts turned into purer annels; they ceased to be the " animal man," of which . Paul speaks, and became more spiritualized. Hence ;ir philosophy became clearer; their expressions more ;cise ; their ideas more refined. Hence they proved that soul cannot be matter, not even the most subtle; it ;t be physically simple; at the same time they held with ancients that it can and does act independently of the ）real organs. Fundamentally the idea of spirituality is l as the human race; the precision it now enjoys is the of christianity. It is mere trickery to quibble about ⅃inology once your adversary has plainly stated the sense he attaches to it. A vast deal of philosophic precision is due to scholastic philosophy, and its trenchant form of argumentation—the syllogism.

It is a philosophic axiom that the "manner of acting follows the manner of existing," or a thing acts in accordance with its nature. Hence sensible organs can only be affected by sensible things. That which is entirely above and beyond the range of physical nature cannot, it is evident, be conceived by a subject whose perceptions are entirely dependent on corporeal organs. The thick plate of an iron-clad ship of war is not more impervious to an arrow that what our organs of sense are to the conveyance of purely intellectual ideas. Now we have ideas that are altogether outside the sphere of sensible things; we have abstract notions; we apprehend perfections, relations, and dependencies; we contemplate virtue and truth. In a word, our intelligence rises far above all material things, and reasons about truths which have no material property. Were our intellect but the slave of organic instruments, were it but the tremor of our nervous system, or a mere sensation of the brain, it could not have even one abstract idea; it could not deduce conclusions; it would be insensible to heroic actions; to glory, fame, or the judgment of posterity. If, therefore, we wish to have a rational explanation of our intellectual operations, and of the feelings which sway many of our noblest actions, we must recognize in our soul the ability to exercise its intelligence independently of sensible organs.

If we consider the actions of our will we shall perceive, even more clearly, the spirituality of the soul. Corporeal organs, like mechanical arrangements, act necessarily and in a uniform manner, provided the conditions of action be fulfilled. Our eye must see, if open in the light; our ear must hear sound that strikes on it—all our senses must be affected by external objects under certain conditions. Moreover our senses, by reason of their sensitive tendency, seek to avoid that which causes them pain. The eye instinctively closes in a glaring light—our hands are nervously withdrawn from objects which are too hot, or too cold. Now any one can prove for oneself that our will can resist this sensitive tendency. Despite the sufferings caused by keeping our hand in freezing water, we can keep it there. Our sense of feeling craves to be released, but our will can lord it over the sensation and hold it captive. Do you suppose that Scævola did not experience bitter pain while holding his hand in the camp-fire of Porsenna? Aye, surely he did, and all his sensations rose in rebellion and demanded its withdrawal; but his will was inflexible; it acted not only not in accordance with his sensations, but in direct opposition to them. Therefore the will must be capable of being exercised independently of corporeal organs. Take the actions of every day life. How many continually repel the suggestions of the sense; some through love of virtue—some through a sense of honor—some through fear of infamy. Each of these motives is sufficient to prove the spirituality of the soul. If our soul were the sport of our organic system, Sodom and Gomorrah would have plenty of companions in infamy. It could not be otherwise. Why should we differ in our actions from the brutes of the field, if the principle of action within us be swayed necessarily by our sense? And if it be not necessarily swayed by the sense, is it not, in some things at least, independent of it? Most certainly, unless you wish to maintain the absurdity that it is both independent in some things, and absolutely dependent in all. Therefore whether we consider the actions of our intelligence, or of our will, we find that these faculties can be exercised independently of corporeal organs. Hence our soul is a spiritual being. It is outside of the physical order; it is, in fact, what its longings and noble aspirations suggest it to be—the heir to a great kingdom. We do not deny but that in sensitive operations our soul is dependent on corporeal organs and sensible things; but this admission does not affect the truth of our argument. It only proves that our soul and body are intimately united; we will speak hereafter of that union. For the present we are content to place in a clear light the spirituality of our soul. This truth is impugned by many who do not understand what it means; the slightest consideration is sufficient to learn its existence. Some deny it through baser motives, viz: to excuse their wickedness, or to vindicate the " free love " theory. Each denial of metaphysical truth ends by debasing man; it cannot be otherwise. If we recede from metaphysics we must approach physics, or rather physical things. The passions and their gratification become the field of speculation, and the gross camp of practice. From this we can gather the connection between scientific truth and divine revelation. He who ceases to be a christian, must likewise, cease to be a metaphysician.

CHAPTER IV.

ESSENCE AND ORIGIN OF THE SOUL.

IT is strange, but nevertheless true, that some who, at times, over-estimate the power and capacity of reason, are the first to debase it, when its conclusions tell against their pet theories. It is nothing for them to bound, with one graceful somersault, from one pole of error to the other. The reason, perhaps, is, that since no great brain power is required to propound ridiculous propositions, they find the mental leap quite feasible. Probably it is pleasant; truth never cloys; it is never a stale subject of meditation; but error, in order to be agreeable, must be novel. Hence the evident self-satisfaction with which modern theorizers view their contradictory statements. To-day, reason knows all; no God is necessary—no revelation is to be thought of: to-morrow, because reason proves the existence of God and of an immortal soul, it is only a sickly ray incapable of having a clear idea of what the soul is. Thus these "will-o'-the-wisp" philosophers give a pale gleam here; vanish, and show a shadowy flickering in the opposite direction. God help the 'nighted youth that follows such phantoms of light. He will soon flop into Tyndall's "stagnant pool," if he does not previously sink beyond his depth in the mire.

Now we maintain that we have a clear idea of the soul. When we know its chief properties, and distinguish accurately between it and other objects, we certainly have a clear idea of it. We do not know all about it; neither do we know all about a grain of wheat, still we have no doubt but what our idea of wheat is sufficiently clear and distinct. We know the soul to be a simple substance, endowed with intelligence and will; we know what these faculties import, and how the soul exercises them by a self-determining power. Knowing all this we would never confound the soul with anything else. Hence our idea of it is clear and distinct. The controversy as to whether actual, or only potential thought and will, are essential to the soul, can be easily decided; aye, to a mathematical nicety. Every substance necessarily acts, as before shown; moreover, every substance acts in accordance with its nature; the nature of a spiritual substance is to think and will: the soul is spiritual; therefore it necessarily, or essentially, thinks and wills. Difficulties may here present themselves about innate ideas: we may discuss that point hereafter: but whatever may be one's opinion regarding the existence of such ideas, one must admit the above conclusion. We are too apt to boast a victory before it is gained. Because our opponent is unable to solve some difficulty which arises from his conclusion, we call upon him to surrender. This is a sophistical method of winning the day. When a conclusion inevitably flows from true premises, no matter what difficulties are started, they cannot destroy the truth of the conclusion. If an objection goes to prove the absurdity of our reasoning, then we must dispose of it; if it merely tends to obtain a reconciliation of our conclusion with some theory of another, we are not held to take notice of it. Even if we confess our inability to give the required explanation, it does not invalidate our argument. We must always bear in mind that " truth is not opposed to truth." If our statement is shown to be metaphysically certain, we must never recede from it; no other truth can be opposed to it. There may be an apparent contradiction, but not a real one. If we cannot reconcile the two, a greater intellect can. Hence limitation of knowledge is no proof of its total absence. I place uncarded wool into one part of a machine, and rolls come forth from another part. I know the fact that the machinery produced the rolls, but perhaps I cannot explain how it was done. Am I, therefore, to say the machinery did not do it? Surely not. A sophism as dear to the shallow controversialist as to the would-be physico-metaphysician, is laid bare by the above observations. Let the reader bear well in mind that once we *prove* a proposition we are not obliged to find a solution for any difficulty that may arise therefrom; we are in possession, and our opponent must prove the truth of his objection, not we its falsity.

The essence of the soul, then, is that it is an ever-active, simple and spiritual substance. The most profound meditation on it shows this and nought else; the most learned metaphysicians, if you divest their propositions of technicalities, assert this; our inner consciousness confirms it. When we speak of the union of the soul with the body we will explain some apparent difficulties.

Regarding the origin of the soul, some fanciful theories have been propounded. Pythagoras and some of the stoics affirmed that it was a part of the divinity: some "modern thinkers," who, by the way, are not modern in thought, profess the same absurdity. In fact all pantheists must hold some such opinion, for if there be but one substance, the soul must be that substance, or a part of it, or a modification of it. In order that the reader may clearly perceive the imposition of these "modern thinkers," who dress up in modern attire the stale and oft-refuted errors of antiquity, and seek to palm them off as original, as the latest outcome of modern thought, as the grand reward of modern progress, we will quote a few lines from St. Augustine. From them each one can see how that great doctor of the church, in a few pithy phrases, refutes fifteen centuries in advance, our modern pantheists. He says: " We see the soul sinful and in affliction, seeking truth, and requiring a deliverer. This changefulness shows me that the soul is not God; because if the soul were the substance of God, the substance of God would err, would be outraged, would be deceived, which is madness to say." (Contra Faustum Manichæum.) As we before observed the " current of modern thought," has evidently set up hill, and seems resolved to go out by the " gate of life, not death."

The Chaldeans, Egyptians, Socrates and Plato asserted that all the souls were created at once, in the beginning of time. According to some the souls were once blissful inhabitants of the stars, but owing to some crime, were cast out from their starry home, and doomed to expiation in these gross bodies. This poetic theory is, in all probability, a corruption of the primeval tradition regarding the fall of the rebellious angels, or the sin in paradise. It is another proof of the unity of the human family, and of biblic history. That our souls did not exist previously to their union with the body is easily shown. Memory is an essential attribute of our soul; if we existed in a former state we must necessarily have some recollection, however faint, of our previous life. But we have no such remembrance. The furthest stretch of our memory is to the days when we tumbled on the floor, or heard sweet lullaby on our mother's knee. We are more oblivious of that previous state, than was the Tichborne claimant of his Latin and French. Again; if our souls are united to our bodies as a punishment, we ought to long for a separation. But we naturally desire to live; we naturally shudder at the thought of a separation between soul and body. Therefore the union must be natural; it is no punishment. Metempsychosis, or transmigration of souls, is so ridiculous as not to need comment. It is another sad instance of the wanderings of the human mind.

It is not very difficult to trace the origin of the soul to its true source, if we only listen to our reason. It is created immediately by God, when it is to be infused into the body. The soul, being a simple and spiritual substance, cannot be a a part of matter; it cannot be a part of another simple substance; there remains, therefore, but the one way by which it can come into existence, viz: creation. But only God can create; therefore our soul is created immediately by Him. It did not exist in a previous state, as shown above; moreover, since its union with the body is natural it is evident that their union is coeval with their existence. Finally, since our memory is bounded by the fair horizon of childhood's dawn, there is no philosophic reason to say that our soul was created previously to its union with the body: if it were, it must have been otiose and unconscious, or a self-contradictory being. Therefore the soul is created when it is to be infused into the body. When that precise time is, we do not undertake to prove. In all likelihood it is the very moment of conception.

CHAPTER V.

FACULTIES OF THE SOUL.

WE have shown that the soul is a simple and spiritual substance: it has no physical parts; we cannot distinguish in it a right and a left, an up and a down. It belongs to an order of things entirely different to the physical one in which we move. It is a force brought into existence by the wish of the Supreme Force—God. It is not a blind unfeeling force like attraction; it imitates more fully the Infinite Essence; it is endowed with intelligence, memory, will, and various other faculties. This multiplicity of faculties does not argue multiplicity of parts in the soul; on the contrary, it serves to confirm its simplicity. It is the one same principle that thinks, wills, and remembers. Now we say that there are two grand faculties of the soul, intelligence and will; all the others spring from one or other of these two, or partly from both. At first sight memory seems to be a distinct faculty, and is generally held to be such; but a little reflection will show that it is only the intelligence concentrating its power on itself, instead of directing it to the consideration of something outside of itself. When we are asked, do we remember such an occurrence, our mind passes in rapid review the various ideas garnered up in its well-regulated store-house, until it lights upon the one it seeks. Imagination differs from memory inasmuch as it is partly a sensitive, and partly an intellectual operation, whilst memory is purely intellectual. Imagination aids the memory, because by recalling the circumstances of place, position of objects, &c., the concatenation of ideas will be more perfect. A delicacy of organization occasions a liveliness of imagination, being more sensitive to impressions than a coarser one. It seems too near an approach to materialism to make memory consist in resuscitating in the nervous fibres, or in the brain, the sensations had at a former period. Something like this happens in imagination; but we can remember purely intellectual ideas—what we thought about God, justice, truth. From this it is apparent that memory is the intelligence scanning itself. Hence memory remains after the separation of the soul from the body.

Now we say that the two grand faculties of the soul, viz: intelligence and will, are the soul itself: they are not a part of the soul, or anything in it distinct from itself. Intelligence is the soul considered inasmuch as it thinks, compares, analyzes, &c: will is the soul assenting to something, or determining itself to present or future action. This is evident from the fact that the soul is a simple and spiritual force. The one agent may act under various conditions and seem to be many different agents. Thus positive and negative electricity are the one agent; light, heat, and electricity are, according to some, the self-same agent though acting so differently. We shall here treat of the Intelligence.

Each one understands what is meant by perceiving, by knowing: no explanation could give us a clearer idea of this operation than we already have. We might, possibly, mystify some and cause them to think us learned by entering into an obscure treatise on this simple operation of the soul: we prefer, however, to make metaphysics, what it really is, clear and concise, even at the risk of being considered superficial. One thing is very certain to our minds and it is that many philosophers have gone too deep; in fact they have lost themselves in the profundity of their excogitations. A desire to appear a deep and original thinker will sometimes take possession even of the cool brain of a metaphysician, and cause him to write pages of unintelligible matter, on the most intelligible subject. Each one is fully cognizant of what it is to know. This operation of knowing is an act of intelligence, or it is, in other words, the soul perceiving. Truth and good are the two objects of the soul; inasmuch as the soul is seeking, or contemplating truth, it is the intelligence; inasmuch as it pursues good, it is the will. To know is the great and natural desire of the soul; we perceive many things; we know a great deal, still we fain would add to our store. Each new truth we learn gives pleasure to the soul. When we perceive a thing we are said to acquire an idea of it. Hence an idea is a representation of a thing in the mind; not a sensible, but an intellectual representation. A great deal has been written about the nature of ideas, and the manner of acquiring them. If we consider attentively the nature of truth, and the nature of the soul, we will not find great difficulty on this point. Whatever is, inasmuch as it is, is true. As before explained, all things which exist, or which are possible in themselves considered, imitate in a certain degree the Divine Essence. In it they have the reason of their intelligibility; in it they intelligibly shine. Abstract from that essence and reality ceases, and, as a consequence, truth. Objectively considered, all truth is in God. As regards the soul, we are to bear in mind that it is a spiritual force of limited power: one of its objects is truth; hence essentially it has an aptitude to acquire it. The Supreme Intelligence sees all truth in itself once, always, and altogether; but a created intelligence, like the soul, acquires its cognitions by the exercise of its power. All natural knowledge which we acquire, is but the outcome of the action of the soul, in its pursuit after truth. Now since there are visible and invisible things, it follows that truth may be referred to a double order, the sensible and the intellectual. Our soul being intimately united to our body perceives some things through the instrumentality of the senses, others purely through the idea itself. The knowledge of historic facts (by this we mean all sensible facts past or present) is acquired through the instrumentality of our senses: we read them; see them; hear them narrated; feel their existence. All knowledge derived from reasoning, comparing, analogy, analysis, sythesis, or any kindred operation, is acquired through the idea, and is intellectual. When we listen to the reasoning of another we acquire a new cognition; but it has not been transfused into us from the reasoner: his words merely served to call our attention to some manner of considering a question in which we never before looked at it. Our own soul turned its inborn power in the direction indicated and acquired the truth. Masters or books, in the strict sense of the word, never teach us intellectual truth; they only admonish our soul to fix its attention on such a chain of reasoning; the evidence of the argument is seen by both souls, but how? Let St. Augustine answer: "If we both see to be true what thou sayest, and what I say, where, I would say, do we see it? I certainly do not see it in thee, nor thou in me, but we both see it in the unchangeable truth which is above our minds," (L. xii. Conf. cap. 25.) By the acquisition of knowledge no new being is added to the soul; its latent power is developed, or brought into play. By study we place our souls in relation with a variety of objects, and thus increase its field of action: we ransack history to glean a knowledge of the reasoning of the ancients; or we read the writings of our contemporaries. In each case the soul develops its power; study is to the soul what gymnastic exercises are to the body; or it is like the breath of air which, while adding nothing to the essence of a live coal, still, makes it glow more brightly. While, then, we acquire a cognition of many facts through means of the senses, all knowledge, properly so called, is the effect of the internal action of the soul. Hence it follows that the soul, if separated from the body, could, by internal action, acquire knowledge. It would be conscious of its own existence, and from that it could prove the existence of God, and his great perfections. It could then speculate on justice, truth, goodness, and innumerable other subjects fraught with intellectual ideas.

There is a difference between an idea and the perception of it. Perception is the consciousness which the soul has that it is contemplating a truth; the idea is the object of contemplation. Perception is, then, a modification of the soul; the intelligibility of a thing, or its idea, is not a modification of the soul; neither does it pertain to the soul, for even if my soul never existed, the intelligibility of, say a triangle, would still be.

Cause and Origin of Ideas.

THAT we have various ideas no one denies; but regarding the cause and origin of them much has been written. Materialists and all those whose minds are of a gross mould, pretend that in some way or other, all our ideas arise from the senses. We have already said enough to show the absurdity of this baseless theory. Purely intellectual ideas, whose existence no one can deny, are altogether beyond the sphere of the senses, and completely independent of them. But let us take a soul fresh from the creating hand of God, and see how it acquires its ideas. Some have looked upon the newly created soul as altogether devoid of ideas; others have maintained that it has direct and innate ones; others, again, that after a sufficient evolution of the organization, primordial ideas, such as truth, justice, &c., are produced in it. Here again we think there is a large amount of philosophic confusion, and an unnecessary quantity of mental writhing. The nature of the soul, as often repeated, is a substantial spirituality; a force the very essence of which is that it should think, understand, know, will. You can as easily conceive fire without heat, as a soul without action. An intelligent being must know something; a force must essentially act; and it must act in accordance with its nature. Hence, the soul being intelligent; being a spiritual force, must from its first instant of existence have knowledge. It will be conscious that it is, and that it desires happiness. But to desire supposes an idea. Therefore we must either admit some ideas which are essentially coeval with the soul, or we must make the soul a self-contradictory being, both intelligent naturally, and knowing nothing; essentially active, but still not acting. This would be about the *ne plus ultra* of metaphysical blindness. Truth, or the acquisition of ideas, being the object of the intellect, it has from its creator an aptitude for this purpose, and the power to prosecute its object. The soul being linked to the body has its action modified by this latter; its innate power cannot be developed until certain organic conditions are verified in the body. Thus, perhaps, the soul, for some time, has only two ideas; when at length the requisite organization of the individual is verified, the soul develops its power and acquires other ideas. It does not follow from this that our ideas are all acquired through the senses; the two first were gained by a purely intellectual act of the soul necessarily conscious of existence and of its desire; many others cannot be acquired without a certain organic condition; but a condition is something very different from a cause. A perfection of organization is an essential condition for the full development of the power of the soul: this we grant, but we have already proved, that verified this condition, the soul, by its intrinsic action of reflection, reasoning, &c., can, and does acquire numerous truths. When the child has grown to be a youth, the soul begins more freely its play. Reflecting on its own existence, it will soon acquire an idea of effect and cause, and will rise to a knowledge of the existence of God. Many external circumstances accelerate, and render more complete our mental development, such as study, conversation and teachers.

Our conclusion, then, is this; the soul must necessarily know its own existence and something about happiness; therefore it has two ideas which are called innate, but not correctly; they are coeval with the soul. Actually these ideas and the soul are synchronous; logically the soul is first, for the ideas are had by the action of the soul. The soul is a spiritual force capable of acquiring truth; naturally joined to a body its action is modified by this latter; its power cannot be fully developed until certain organic conditions are fulfilled: once these are verified it begins to develop, both by reason of its inward actions of reflection, comparison, reasoning, &c., and by outward circumstances of study and teaching. This conclusion inevitably flows from the nature of the soul, and its union with the body.

Whether there be more than two coeval ideas we are not prepared to prove. Many have thought that the first principles of the moral order are innate. We find them constant, uniform and universal. This is strong presumption in favor of their being essentially connected with the soul. Some might possibly be acquired; from its own existence the soul could prove the existence of God, and his infinite perfection; knowing him to be its cause the soul would see the necessity of acknowledging its dependence and of respecting him. Knowing that there are beings like to ourselves, and knowing that we would not wish certain things to be done to us, we could infer that we ought not to do them to others. Still, since a knowledge of the first principles of the natural law seems to be prior to all consideration or reflection of this sort, it appears more philosophic to say that there is, essentially, in the soul a habit, or tendency, infused by the creator, by which the soul, at once, perceives the evidence of the general principles of the natural law, so soon as a given perfection of the physical organism is verified. Hence the universal idea of right and wrong. We think that the nature, cause, and origin of ideas, as well as the modes of acquiring them, have been made sufficiently clear.

CHAPTER VI.

THE WILL.

WE now come to the consideration of the second grand faculty—the will. As before observed, the will is the soul considered in its pursuit after good. Relatively, good is, *whatever is consentaneous to the nature of a being;* in general, whatever is, inasmuch as it is, is good. Everything has a tendency to that which can nourish, preserve and perfect it; or it naturally tends to its special good. In the lower creation this tendency is a blind force of their nature; it is part of a providential plan for the preservation of finite things. In man there is a two-fold tendency, by reason of his two-fold nature: the body has its animal tendency, and the soul its intellectual, or spiritual. Each one is conscious of this; we crave food and warmth for our bodies, and we long for truth, knowledge and a rest of spirit. Now we are not to consider the two constituent parts of man disjointedly; we are to take them as they are in nature, linked together, and forming one individual; and we are not to consider the relative good of each part in the abstract, but the good of the person in the concrete. The nature of man being rational, it follows, that although certain things might be good for the body were it unconnected with a reasonable soul, we must reject them as a good of the individual man, if they are contrary to the dictates of reason. This point should always be kept in view. It is a common sophism of the sensualist to reason about the body, and our sensual appetites, as if they were disjoined from a rational soul. Our animal tendencies to food, drink, &c., are good, in themselves considered; their indulgence, however, is to be regulated by reason. There may be obligations imposed on the individual, which are known to reason : these obligations may require certain checks to the sensible appetites ; if these restraints be disregarded there is a revolution in man ; reason is dethroned, and a rational being acts in an irrational manner. Each one can see that this would be an evil to the individual man, although it might be a good to the body considered in the abstract. In a word, being reasonable beings, all our actions should be in accordance with the dictates of reason. We need say no more about our tendency to sensible things.

The soul naturally tends to spiritual good. We all intimately experience this fact; we all desire happiness. Now perfect happiness consists in a complete satisfaction of that tendency by which we are borne towards good. As before observed, the will is the soul considered in its pursuit after good ; we essentially seek good, and hence the will, inasmuch as it is a tendency to good in general, acts by a necessity of nature. It cannot desire unhappiness ; it never chooses a thing because it is bad, but because it apprehends it, under some respect, as good for it. When one casts away, in a fit of spite, one's money, the will apprehends this act as a satisfaction of its spleen : in reality the action is hurtful to the individual, but the soul chooses to look at it under a respect in which there is an apparent good in it, and decides to act. Now our soul has a self-determining power; we can, at pleasure, direct our attention to this or that object; we can think on this, or that. The question arises : is the tendency to good free? is the self-determining power of the soul subject to some metaphysical law, to some blind fate, to a necessity of any kind? This is a most important question: on it hangs the whole weight of the moral law, all virtue, duty and responsibility. We say at once, that as regards the tendency to good in general, the will is not free; it must seek either real, or apparent good: but we maintain that as regards the choice of this or that particular good, or their rejection,—as regards the doing or leaving undone, or doing in this way or that way, a particular action, the will is entirely free; it is not subject to any intrinsic or extrinsic necessity; but the soul freely elects what it decides on performing in all these cases.

This is what is meant by "liberty of the will;" this is physical, not moral liberty. Physically we are free to plunge the dagger into a sleeper's heart; morally we are not free to do it. We here speak of physical liberty. The ability of doing evil is not necessary to true liberty: evil being an imperfection, the power of deflecting from good does not add to the nobility and perfection of a nature, but detracts from it. Hence our power of erring, of doing wrong, is an imperfection; it is unnecessary to true liberty. The power of choosing this good, or that, in this way, or that, now or hereafter, is all that is included in the idea of true liberty of the will. An infinitely perfect being cannot deflect from good; it would be a contradiction; still God is, in the true sense of the word, free.

The action of a reasonable being supposes a knowledge of the thing sought to be obtained—nothing is desired unless previously known. In all deliberate actions, then, there is an act of intelligence perceiving the object and its real or apparent good, and an act of the will determining itself to the pursuit of that object. Freedom of the will consists in an *active power of the soul by which the soul can, of itself, act, or not act, choose this, or that, provided all the conditions requisite for acting be verified.* A choice may be made in one of three ways: 1st.—We may choose one of two contradictories, love, or not love. 2d.—One of two contraries, love, or hate. 3d.—One of many different things, study, ride, walk.

Although no metaphysical truth, after the certainty of our own existence, is more evident to one who reflects for an instant, than is the liberty of the will, still many seek to deny it, either altogether, or in part. Fate, chance, physical laws and various visionary old tyrants are conjured up to explain our actions without admitting that noblest attribute of man, liberty of will. Like a nurse who calls a hobgoblin to devour a naughty child, and then personates the dread ghoul by making unearthly howlings, the opponents of human liberty summon their dark monsters of fate, and straightway, without proving their existence, yell as if refractory humanity were being devoured and led off by these spirits of the " vasty deep." In theology we exposed the humbug of fate and chance: we showed them to be simply nothing. The question is narrowed down to this: our actions are the effects of an active force; not being contemporary, either one produces the other, or the soul produces each one. Nothing outside of the soul could force it to will this or that, because in that supposition it would both will, and not will the same thing at the same time. This logic might do for men of fate, but not for us. Neither does one action produce another; the soul freely determines all its deliberate actions.

CHAPTER VII.

LIBERTY OF THE WILL.

THIS important metaphysical and moral truth must now be fully proved. Above we explained what the will is, and in what way it is free; now we will evolve some arguments to confirm our proposition.

1st.—*From our inner consciousness:* as seen above, by inner consciousness, or our intimate sense, is meant the soul affected in a certain way, and conscious of being so affected. It is an infallible means of truth regarding the present affections of the soul; for it is the soul itself testifying to its present modifications. Deny this and the soul becomes a contradiction, it feels, for instance, pain, and does not feel it; loves, and does not love the same object at the same time. Now our inner consciousness testifies that we are free; therefore our will enjoys immunity from all co-action and necessity in its choice of finite goods. Liberty is certainly an affection of the soul; hence it is directly the object of intimate sense; when then this sense testifies to the existence of this affection, it must, infallibly, exist. That our intimate sense testifies to the existence of freedom of choice is evident. Each one is intimately conscious that when various objects are presented to one's consideration, there is no force which compels one to choose this or that; each one, in such a case, recognizes only in the activity of one's soul, the reason of one's choice; each one, after choosing, is self-complacent if the thing proves a success, and self-condemnatory if a failure: each one, taught by one's past experience, resolves to act in a similar, or different manner in the same circumstances. Now all this proves that we are daily and hourly intimately conscious that our actions are subject to no necessity from within, or without, but are entirely dependent on the activity of the soul, which determines itself at pleasure. Therefore, in fact, we are free.

2d.—*From the nature of finite goods:* our soul desires good: it has almost an unlimited capacity for good. Imagine all the riches and pleasures of this world; the most delightful gardens and bowers; the most entertaining company, and luxurious feasts—everything that we can imagine of earthly good, and ask yourself, would I be happy if I had all these? The inevitable answer is, no, there is still something to be desired. Hence the capacity of the soul for good is greater than can be filled by created things. Now if an accumulation of earthly delights cannot fill the soul, much less can one particular one do it: but if our will were necessitated in its choice by the good apprehended in an object, that good ought to be equal, at least, to the capacity of the soul. Since no created good is equal to this capacity, it follows that it cannot necessitate the choice of the soul. It would be as sensible to say that it could, as what it would be to maintain that a donkey engine could draw a train of cars which ten large ones could not keep in motion.

3d.—*From the notion of reason:* A great doctor has said —man is reasonable; therefore he is free. This noble argument of St. Thomas is unanswerable. That man is reasonable, no one, I suppose, will deny. Now the connection between reason and liberty of action is this: everything acts according to its nature; consequently a rational being must act in a reasonable manner. To act in a reasonable manner supposes perception of the object, a reflection on its suitableness to the perceiver, and a rejection or choice of it. But this supposes freedom of will. In other words: the measure of our desire is our perception of the real, or apparent good in an object: in all earthly goods there is some defect, some aspect under which they may be considered as not good, or even hurtful. Now the intellect may consider them either under one aspect, or another; it will apprehend, at most, a limited amount of good; it will clearly perceive that that good cannot satisfy the capacity of the soul; it will apprehend that this one is preferable to that, or that none of them is desirable. Therefore the will will choose this one in preference to that, or reject them all. A little boy goes up to an apple stall: each apple has some good in it, and so his reason says; he turns them over looking for a nice ripe one; he almost decides on taking this one, but catches sight of a better one, and, perhaps, is taking out his pence to pay for it, when he resolves to try some other stalls before purchasing. He goes to the next one and suits himself; was he not free all along in his choice? When he returns home his little sister asks for one; he has two, one much better than the other; he longs to eat the better one, all his sensitive appetites demand that he keep it, but the generous little fellow says, no, and gives the better one to his sister, although, perhaps, his eye, aye, even his tooth, sheds a tear at the moment. Could any sane person pretend that such a boy did not possess liberty of will? The inborn activity of his soul determined each of his actions.

4th.—*From the manner of acting of all mankind:* when we wish one to do, or to leave undone, something we entreat, persuade or threaten. People make agreements about meeting at a certain time and place; they often pay in advance for labor to be performed; nations form alliances; leaders of armies hold consultations; parliaments enact laws; transgressors are punished; the well-deserving of the commonwealth are rewarded. All this goes to prove that all men, at all times, have been intimately convinced that the soul, by its own activity, determines itself to action. Of what avail would agreements be if we were not sure that we were free? Why hold consultations on the mode of attack, if all be subject to a blind inexorable fate? Prudential precautions would be idle observances; laws to punish would be sheer cruelty, if the will is destitute of liberty. If our actions be determined by physical laws, or physiological phenomena, how can we be certain that we can cease writing in five, ten, fifteen minutes hence? Yet we have no doubt but what we can read, write, rise, sit down or walk at any stated time. If our actions be subject to fate, we can subject fate to our fancy; if they be determined by physiological causes, we can determine, at pleasure, these causes. This looks so much like liberty that mankind is disposed to believe itself free. No court of justice would listen to the culprit, were he to enter the plea, that he was forced by a necessity of nature to commit the crime. Yet he would be justified in so doing were his will not free. Therefore the incidents of daily life, the history of all nations, teach us that all men have at all times been convinced of the liberty of the will: this universal and constant effect requires a universal and constant cause. This cause is the inner consciousness of each individual; or this effect arises from the evidence of truth; each soul being adapted to acquire truth.

5th.—*From the absurdities which would follow in the contrary sentence.* It must be well borne in mind that without real liberty of action, there can be no responsibility. Unless my rational principle can, by its active force, determine my actions, I cannot be accountable for them. Again, if the will be not really free, there can be no difference between what are called good and bad actions. Hence, unless our will is free there is no such thing as a moral order; virtue and vice are empty names; thanksgivings to benefactors, nonsense; duty towards God, an idle assertion; hate of iniquity, and punishment of transgressors, unjust. The coward who fled from his post, or the traitor who sold his country to the enemy, is worthy of the same praise as the hero who fronted the invader and repelled his attack. This is no poetic exaggeration; in sober fact all this would be true if the determination of our actions did not depend on the untrammeled activity of our souls. It is useless to seek to find a third term; either our will is under no necessity from within or without in its choice, or it is. If the first, then it is free, and we are responsible for our actions: if the second, then all these absurdities necessarily follow; the whole human race has been for ages under a huge delusion, in a matter, too, which nearly concerns each one. We do not think that any one can seriously deny the liberty of the will; no one, surely, is prepared to say that I may just as well raise my arm and smite him to the ground as not. Yet, if I am not free, what harm in doing it? Some deny, with their lips, free will, but they would scarcely accept the above enumerated absurdities. Still, such is the itch of some to be considered eccentric, or to fight against the truths of christianity, that they defend a theory from the inevitable consequences of which, their better nature recoils. It would be more creditable to their intellects to defend no principle whose consequences they must repudiate. Some seek to ease their troubled conscience by invoking fate; but in vain. They cannot succeed even in deceiving themselves; when some enterprise has proved a failure they bitterly reproach their hasty action; in seeking to gratify those passions, for the sake of which they deny liberty of will, they plot and plan the most efficacious means. In a word, no sane man can seriously believe that his actions are subject to any fatal necessity. Let each one, then, thank God, for the noble attribute of liberty, and use it in such a manner that he need never wish that it could be denied.

CHAPTER VIII.

UNION OF THE SOUL AND BODY.

IF we wish to know as much of man as reason can teach, we must consider the whole individual. We have proved beyond a doubt that there is in man a simple, spiritual substance, called the soul; this soul is the principle of thought, will, and feeling; truth and good are its objects: in its pursuit after the former it can acquire certainty, and in its choice of finite goods it is under no intrinsic or extrinsic necessity, that is, the will enjoys liberty, But there is more than this in man; there is a material part, an exceedingly beautiful piece of mechanism, provided with delicate organic apparatus, called the body. In life, neither of these, taken by itself, constitutes the individual man; the person arises from an intimate union of these two distinct and diverse substances. Each, considered separately, has properties peculiar to itself; considered in their union, they have properties and actions which could not pertain to either of them if they were disunited. Man perceives a house, for instance: this could not be done by the body alone, because as proved, a compound substance cannot be the subject of perception; neither could it be done by the soul alone, naturally speaking, because to see a material thing it requires material organs, the eyes. From this, and many similar properties of man, it is clear that man is a being composed of a spiritual and corporeal part, physically and substantially united. Their union is not accidental; neither is the soul in the body like a man on a velocipede : but they are so united that from their union arises a rational individual, having properties diverse from those of either substances, separately considered. Such is man ; such we must consider him if we wish to arrive at a reasonable explanation of ourselves, our thoughts and our daily actions. Hitherto we treated only of the more noble part of man ; now we will view him in his entirety. It is not our intention to prove the existence of the body ; we take it for granted ; neither will we speak of its anatomical structure ; we will merely consider its union with the soul. It may be objected by some, that hitherto we have spent a great deal of time on a dry metaphysical question. Now the question about our soul was surely a metaphysical one, but it was neither dry, nor uninteresting. It is replete with great social and religious principles. If the soul were not simple and spiritual, the will would not be free, and consequently, there would be no difference between acts of virtue and vice : it would not be immortal, and consequently, there would be no punishment to fear, no reward to merit ; our final end would be in this life. We would be creatures of a brief span, doomed to flutter a moth-like existence amid the garish trappings of life, and then to sink into nothing, like the veriest mote that sports a one-day life in the sunbeam. Dreary, unlovable, desolating doctrine of materialism—that chills the warm yearnings of future bliss—that checks the generous impulses of heroism, and restrains the lofty flight of intellect,—is all that would remain. We pity the blindness, the debasement, of those who bow in servile fear before a sculptured god ; but is not the intellectual darkness of the materialist as great, perhaps greater? And there are men who pretend to be cultivated

—who lay pretensions to literary acquirements—who sneer at the "ignorance of the middle ages," who do not blush to assert that there is nought in man except the gross material body, which is palpable and visible. Hence we have deemed it well to prove the soul to be simple and spiritual, endowed with intelligence and free will; that it can exercise these without the aid of corporeal organs; and, consequently, when its tabernacle of clay will have been dissolved it can still live and act; can receive merited reward, or condign punishment. But, unhappily, in our age we are in too great a hurry: even as you will see men drawing on their coats as they are rushing from the house, so, too, you may see them quitting educational establishments, before their mind has been mailed with the armor of truth. Dollars and cents are the objects in view; if boys can read, without stammering, trashy novels, and sickening love tales, and calculate interest with tolerable ease, they fancy themselves educated, and straightway begin life. If they have not received a good moral training they give way, at once, to debasing passions; the light of intellect becomes clouded; faith has either never been possessed, or has been renounced. Like dumb animals, they are content with animal pleasures; finally, either to banish the fear that haunts them, or because their intelligence has become almost darkened, they admit nothing in man except flesh and bones, fibres and muscles. Others, again, considering the wonderful structure of the human body; seeing its net-work of delicate fibres all tending to the brain, are lost in amaze at its harmony of design, and disposition of parts, and think it sufficient to explain all the thoughts and affections of man. Had such persons studied metaphysics they would have learned that it is impossible for compound substances, how delicate soever they may be, to think, feel, or reason. Since truth can never be opposed to truth, that which metaphysics evidently demonstrates cannot, by any possibility, be opposed to any fact made known by anatomy or physiology. There may be an apparent contradiction, but it cannot be real.

Now there are certain physiological facts which seem to be opposed to what we have said about the soul. Insanity, for instance, may arise from a compression of the skull on the brain, from a diseased organ, or from other causes. Since we say the soul is the principle of reason, it might appear difficult to see how reason could be affected by a vitiated organ. A right idea of the union of soul and body explains it. We have two undoubted facts: 1st, the soul is the principle of reason; 2d, insanity may be occasioned by a physical disorder. They appear to clash; what is to be done? A sensible man would not deny either; he would seek to reconcile them; if he could not succeed he would humbly profess his ignorance, and recognize the limitation of his intellect. But an unlearned and proud person, not wishing us to think that there was anything beyond his comprehension, would deny the existence of the soul, and, Alexander like, would untie the knot by ignoring it. We can, however, easily reconcile these two facts, the one of psychology, the other of physiology. God, in creating man, ordained that he should be a being composed of a material body and an immaterial soul so united, that from their union there should arise an individual endowed with reason and free will. This individual would have a tendency both to sensible, and intellectual good, by reason of his two parts: his reason, being the nobler, should guide and moderate, within due limits, the tendency to earthly things. The soul was, thus, pre-ordained to a union with the body, and the body was pre-disposed for this union. A mutual commerce, or reciprocity of action, naturally exists, between body and soul in the individual. Of itself the body is a beautiful piece of mechanism; symmetrically proportioned; artistically fashioned. But it is without motion—an inert mass. Imagine the body of Adam, fresh from the hand of God that fashioned it, stretched on its kindred clay: you may admire its noble brow, its well-cut lip, its chiselled parian cheek, its delicate nostril, its raven locks. 'Tis a beautiful, yet a sad sight: for the brow is cold, the lips are motionless, the cheeks are ashy, the eyes are vacant. Now imagine that you are watching the Almighty breathing into it the spirit of life, that is, infusing into it a soul. How sudden, how glorious the change! Warmth comes to the brow, motion to the lips, color to the cheeks; the nostrils dilate with the play of emotions; intelligence gleams in the eyes. Life and motion are seen where before there were only stillness and death: the mechanism of the body is set in motion; the muscles contract, the form rises from the earth, and Adam walks forth the lord of creation. The soul is thus the vivifier of the body, the principle of life and action. It makes the body move at pleasure, and thus acts upon it; the body receives on its organs of sense impressions from external objects, and transmits them to the soul. In this consists the commerce of soul and body, or reciprocity of action of which we have spoken. In order, however, that this mutual action may continue, the organs of the body must remain in a healthy, or normal state. If they become impaired to a certain degree, or in a certain way, the soul can no longer act on them as usual, and insanity may result. The soul will not be diseased, but owing to the vitiated state of the organic parts of the body, it receives from them disordered impressions, and unreal representations. The totterings of the drunkard, the phantoms which haunt the victim of *delirium tremens*, are explained by the liquor having acted so on the nerves, and on the organs of sight, as to have thrown them out of their normal state; the soul still acts on them, but not as formerly. The fingers may fly as usual over the chords of an untuned harp, but the music, instead of being sweet and harmonious, will grate harshly on the ear; so the soul may endeavor to move the body with firm tread, but the locomotive organs being vitiated, a stumbling gait is the result. An unnatural trembling of the visual nerves, will convey a false impression of external objects, causing one candle to appear in half-a-dozen different places, and transforming beautiful designs on the wall, into hideous monsters. In a word, soul and body being intimately united, certain organic conditions are necessary in order that the soul may rightly exercise its power. Organic sanity is a *condition* necessary for healthy intellectual action, not the *cause* of it; hence the explanation of insanity, and the inability to study when suffering from headache. All physiological facts which appear to clash with the spirituality of the soul, can be thus explained, and only serve as confirmations of our conclusion that the union between soul and body is physical and substantial.

Sleep is a partial cessation of the commerce between body and soul; rest is needful for the fatigued muscles and sinews, and for the harassed fibres of the brain, but it is not necessary for a soul. The activity of the soul is seen even during sleep; we are often conscious of pain in our slumber; it is a dull and confused sensation, because the sensitive organs are more or less relaxed, and less obnoxious to impressions. Again, dreams prove that the mind is ever active, although, by reason of the abnormal condition of the organic system, its action is often fantastic. The body, being composite, tends to dissolution; this is the inexorable enemy of all compound substances. The various forms of disease arise from a dissolution setting in in some particular part of the system. The whole art of medicine consists in giving such drugs as tend to stay the dissolution, or to restore the waste which has already taken place. If this be not done the process of decay goes on; sometimes quickly, sometimes slowly, according as the producing cause is more or less virulent. One by one the organs may become so affected that the soul can no longer make use of them; at length the vital ones give way; the pulse beats no more, the action of the heart is stilled, the commerce between the soul and body is rendered impossible; the individual dies. The body moulders in dust, because physically compound; the soul being simple and spiritual, cannot corrupt. A dispassionate consideration of the nature of compound, and simple substances, and a rational survey of man's actions and thoughts, easily effect a reconciliation between the facts of psychology and those of physiology. A knowledge of both these sciences is necessary, if we wish to learn all that can be learnt of ourselves. Some metaphysicians have ignored too much the reciprocal action of soul and body; they have, apparently, been stricken with a dread of materialism, and have almost flown to the opposite pole. A great many physiologists have never learnt metaphysics; enamored of their own branch of study, they neglect, or despise, other branches; they develop their intellect only in one way, viz: through the senses; hence they begin to think that nought is to be admitted except what falls under the sense. In their anatomical investigations, they do not see, or feel, the soul; upon this they conclude, it does not exist. A very illogical consequence, but one too commonly deduced. If they used their reason a little, they could prove satisfactorily, that notwithstanding the beauty and adaptation of the body, it is merely a machine without a motive power. Its parts, however delicate, could never be a principle of thought and will; its subtle fluids, and net-work of nerves and fibres, can be only *conditions*, not *causes*, of communication with other things. The miserable sophisms that are flaunted in our face as facts, the grotesque theories regarding man which many delve from their uncultivated brains, could never mislead the medical student who had made a good course of metaphysics.

We have now established the fact of a reciprocity of action between the soul and body: it might still be asked: "but *how* does the soul act on the body, and vice-versa?" We know the fact, can we know its *how?* It must be borne in mind that even if we cannot answer this question, the truth of what has been proved above remains intact. There are innumerable facts which science, in its present state, at least, cannot explain. Materialists would profit nothing by our ignorance, because we would ask them to explain how any one force acts on another. We can answer our question equally as well as they can that. It is a fact that at the will of the soul our muscles contract and expand. Why so? The soul is a force; the body is an aggregate of forces; the former is of a superior nature and domineers over the inferior ones. Volition acts on the subtle, but inferior forces, of which the brain fluid is composed; these act upon the fibres and muscles and thus set the whole machinery in motion. Volition is something like the discharge of an electric battery; the electricity discharged will act upon an object and be carried over it to a distance; so the self-determining force of the soul, being naturally ordained to act on the un-self-determining forces of the body with which it is united, sets them in motion, and guides their course. Since our soul is a finite being it can only have immediate relation with a limited number of inferior forces; hence it can only act immediately on our bodies; through means of the body it can place itself in mediate relation with other objects, and act on them mediately.

Perfectibility of our Intellectual Powers.

THERE are some facts known to all which might here be examined: 1st, Some persons are naturally more apt to acquire science than others; 2d, Cultivation perfects the intellect. The explanation of the first is this: man is to acquire knowledge, naturally, by the exercise of the powers of his soul. While in life we are not to view the soul separately, we must consider it united to a body. Although, as shown above, the soul can, by abstraction, have intellectual ideas, such as could never fall under the sense, and is consequently, spiritual, still the matter, we may call it, of most of its ideas, is derived through the senses. We use our eyes to read, our ears to listen to the professor, our phantasy to represent ideas. Hence it follows that our impressions will partake of the nature of the organs, through which they are conveyed to the soul. An organic change will produce a corresponding change in the matter of our ideas. A fine, delicate organization will be more sensitive to the impressions of external things, and will convey them more faithfully than a coarser one. Lively, subtle fluids will be quicker in their operation than sluggish ones. The difference of organization, then, is the reason of the difference of natural aptitude for learning. It is a consequence of the intimate union of soul and body. Regarding the second fact, that cultivation perfects our intellectual powers, the explanation is obvious. The object of the intellect is truth; it has, coevally with its existence, a certain amount of truth, and the power and aptitude of acquiring more. By the exercise of this power it increases its store of knowledge. Cultivation of the intellect is but a bringing into play its power; an opening up for it of a wider range of action, and, as a consequence, an adding to its ideas. As before observed, it is the gymnasium of the soul. This perfectibility of the intellect is another proof of its spirituality. Were we nought but well-regulated machines, kept in motion by some force akin to electricity—were our thoughts and affections only organic phenomena, there would be no possibility of advancing in science. A power to analyze, to judge, to compare various facts or impressions, and a power to recall former ones, are necessary in order to increase in knowledge. Now no one who has not abdicated one's reason, will pretend that such a power could, by any possibility, belong to mere sensations, or nervous affections, or any other of the materialistic substitutes for a spiritual soul. One affection, or phenomenon, would have no connection with the others; it would come, and pass away forever, like the trembling of a lute. Without a permanent principle of life and intelligence, there could be no perception, or remembrance of an affection.

This explanation of the difference of intellectual power in individuals, is more satisfactory, and more in accordance with anatomical observations, than that of relative weight of brain; or anterior and posterior development; or facial angle. Each of these theories is contradicted by actual fact. No doubt certain forms of head, certain developments of physiognomy, are often found associated with great, or poor talents in the person. It only follows from this that a system well or ill adapted to receive impressions, shows certain characteristic marks; it does not follow that these marks are causes. Again, we believe that, to a certain extent, the natural tendency of a person may be known from anatomical, or physiognomic observations; but, since the will is free, we can never conclude that the person is addicted to the passions towards which, naturally, he is inclined. A proneness to any vice, or virtue may be checked, and altogether overcome by the will. Hence phrenology, or the reading of character from the development of certain bumps, may, perhaps, tell the natural tendency of an individual; but it can never tell what his conduct really is, because of his liberty of will.

CHAPTER IX.

IMMORTALITY OF THE SOUL.

IN a social and moral point of view, what has hitherto been proved, would be of little avail could we not, likewise, prove that our soul is immortal. If our soul were to perish with its earthly companion, our final end would be in this world; no hope of a life beyond the grave would cheer the gloom of the just man in affliction; no fear of a stern judge would deter the impious. Our life here would be the greatest boon of existence, because without it we could not enjoy anything; hence its preservation would be at once our chief good, and primary duty. He who would expose it to danger would be a fool; he who would not remorselessly break down and trample upon all ties of friendship and blood, in order not to endanger it, would be the laughing stock of a community. What social chaos would result from this. The mother would cast the diseased babe from her breast, lest she might become affected thereby; the husband would shun the house in which lay stretched the wasted form of his wife, smitten by some contagious disease. The soldier would desert his post, and leave the city to perish, if thus he could prolong his life. Our final end being, in this supposition, in this world, all the pleasures we could cull would be our chief pursuit. If a man were an obstacle to the attainment of some gratification, to strike him down relentlessly would be our inalienable right. Darwin's process of selection would go on beautifully in such a state of society. Now let it not be objected, that a moral sense, or natural love, or reason, would be sufficient to prevent such consequences. These stimulants to civilized life exist only because the soul is immortal. If we were to end with death our moral sense, our love, our reason, would all cry out :—take all you can ; enjoy yourself as much as possible ; " eat, drink, and be merry, for to-morrow we die." This would, necessarily, be the promptings of a nature doomed to only a brief existence. Did reason tell me to consider another before myself, in the supposition of our souls being mortal, it would be *unreasonable*. Life is the greatest temporal boon, since it is the foundation of all others ; hence it would be madness to expose it for the sake of another, unless there were an hereafter. From this it can be seen what a degrading, selfish, anti-social doctrine materialism is ; what a misshapen brood of social evils it would engender ; it can, likewise, be seen what services the Catholic church has rendered to humanity ; by ordering all teachers of philosophy in universities, to refute the errors of an author read, regarding the immortality and unity of the soul, and similar errors, since, so the words run,—these are all soluble—(Act. Conc. Labbaei Tom. xiv, p. 187.) Does anyone know whether the enemies of our church call this a degradation of reason?

The idea of immortality includes the idea of perpetual existence and life. Hence when we say the soul is immortal we mean that it will exist forever, and exercise vital actions. It is not the kind of immortality attributed to it by some physical scientists, who make it, after death, an unintelligent substance floating in the azure, like electricity ; our idea of immortality is at once more noble, and more philosophic ; the soul will exist, and will be, as in life, intelligent. We will proceed in our proof by steps: 1st, The soul can exist and act when separated from the body. 2d, No created force, no natural process can destroy the soul. 3d, God only could destroy it, but he will not, he wishes it to be immortal.

Regarding the first proposition, that the soul can exist and act when disunited from the body, we merely need recall that we proved the soul to be a substance distinct and diverse from the body; although united in life they are not merged in one, but each remains a distinct substance. Hence the dissolution of the body does not involve the necessity of the destruction of the soul, no more than the death of one person involves the death of his neighbor. The soul can, therefore, exist after the decay of the body. It can also act; it is a substance, or force; all substances necessarily act, and act according to their nature. Therefore the soul acts as long as it exists, and acts as a spiritual substance, viz: by exercising acts of intelligence and will. But it can exist separate from the body; therefore, also, it can act as an intelligent being. It will not want for ideas on which to exercise its power; apart from its remembrance of the ones acquired in life, it will always have the knowledge of its own existence, from which it could deduce the existence of God and his great perfections.

The second proposition says, that no created force, no natural process can destroy the soul. There are only two ways by which a thing can be destroyed, either by dissolution of its parts, or by annihilation. Now we proved the soul to be physically simple; hence it cannot perish by dissolution, for only compound substances can be dissolved. The only way, then, by which the soul can perish is by annihilation. But we showed in theology, that as only God can create, so only he can annihilate, for annihilation is a suspension of the creative act. Moreover, all scientists agree, that by no natural power can any particle of matter be made, or destroyed. Therefore the soul, which is a substance, cannot be destroyed by any created power. Its properties of thought and will cannot be destroyed, because they are essential. That which cannot destroy the essence of a simple being cannot destroy its essential properties.

There remains, then, but one way by which the soul can perish, viz: by the action of its creator. Now, absolutely speaking, God could annihilate the soul; but looking at things as they are constituted by him, and not at the manner in which they might have been created, we can prove that not only he will not destroy the soul, but that he positively wishes and intends it to be immortal. We proved that all things were created for the glory of God; he is the end of man; his external glory is the object of creation. Again, we proved man to be rational and free. Now since God is infinitely wise he must have provided means sufficient and suitable to the nature of each thing, to enable it to attain its end. These means, as regards a rational and free being, must be certain laws, or directions, according to which it should conform its actions. An intelligent being is not to be dragged to its end; its dignity requires that it be directed to it by laws in keeping with its nature. Thus we find *a priori* that God must have imposed certain laws on man: this conclusion is confirmed *a posteriori*. Every nation, each individual, has, at all times, held certain actions to be lawful and obligatory, such as to reverence parents, and to obey God; and have looked upon others as unlawful, as crimes. This constant universal fact can only be explained by saying that it arises from the evidence of reason. No other sufficient cause could be assigned. Education, superstition, social intercourse and any thing of that sort is changeable; not only is it different among different nations, but it varies among the same nation during the lapse of ages; while the judgment of men, regarding these actions, remains unchanged. Therefore it is from the evidence of reason: therefore naturally a law has been imposed on man. Now God must have affixed a sufficient sanction to that law, otherwise he would be a foolish legislator. He must have determined a reward sufficiently great, and must have threatened a punishment sufficiently severe, to warrant a rational being in observing it at any cost. His wisdom requires this. Now, if we abstract from a future life, there is no motive sufficient to induce a man to observe this law at all times. Were there any such motive it would have to be one of these three: 1st, the good and evil of this life: 2d, the love of virtue and hatred of vice: 3d, the congruity of the law with the light of reason. Now it is evident that the first is insufficient; for the goods and miseries of this world are indiscriminately enjoyed by the observers of the law and by its transgressors. Very often, indeed, the just have more of the miseries, and a smaller share of the goods of life. Again, in the case of killing a man and usurping his possessions, the breaking of the law would confer a temporal good. It could not be the love of virtue and hatred of vice; if we were to end with death virtue would lose its charm, and vice its horror. Again, our perception of the beauty of virtue is not so very keen, especially when our interest in life, and our passions, solicit us to pursue a contrary course. Vice at first sight is hateful, but alas! how soon does it lose its horror! Pope truly says:

"Vice is a monster of such hideous mein,
That to be hated needs but to be seen;
If seen too oft, grown familiar with its face,
We first endure, then pity, then embrace."

Finally, the congruity of the law with the light of reason would not suffice. Without an hereafter the final end of man would be in this life; consequently reason would tell him that the law was *not* to be observed whenever it clashed with his present enjoyment or gain. Therefore unless the soul is to exist and live after its separation from the body, God would not have affixed a sufficient sanction to the law imposed by him on man. But this would be absurd. Therefore the soul does not perish with the body.

But the justice of God, no less than his wisdom, demands that the soul should survive the wreck of the body. Being just he must wish and provide that the lot of the observers of his law be better than that of its breakers. Now it is abundantly evident that in this life the lot of the just is often worse than that of the wicked. Therefore there must be another life in which due portions will be meted out to all.

If we consider the nature of man, either in itself, or in its relation to society, we will see, with equal clearness, the necessity of admitting another life. Man naturally and invincibly desires perfect happiness; all his actions prove it; he never performs the slightest turn, he never determines himself to action, without seeking either present, or future happiness of some kind. This longing after felicity is common to all; it cannot be explained without admitting that it is inherent to, and inborn of our nature. Therefore it has God for its author. But that which has God for an author can never be useless, or vain; consequently this ardent desire of felicity can be satiated. Now it is clear that it never can be satisfied in this life; no one would pretend that man can ever have all the desires of his heart gratified in this world. Therefore there must be another life, in which this happiness, so ardently desired, can be obtained. Moreover, reason tells us that our happiness is linked to an observance of the moral law; now in order to observe that law we must often undergo great sufferings; we must often deprive ourselves of many worldly benefits. If, then, there be no other life, reason is a false guide; it is worse; it is a traitor; our conscience is a vain prejudice; our probity of life a weakness; God himself would be making us enemies to ourselves; he would be our heartless tyrant. Such a tissue of absurdities is repugnant to natural reason. Therefore another life must be admitted. Again, the brute creation have all their desires gratified in this world; they only seek sensible good, and they get it. Now since man can never, under any circumstances, obtain perfect satisfaction of his desires whilst here, it would follow that unless there be an hereafter, his lot would be much worse than that of the brute creation. It would be better for man to degenerate into a monkey, than to go on developing intellectuality. If Darwin seeks man's good, he ought to turn his attention to the finding of some process of " natural selection," by which the human family can, as soon as possible, become idiotic gorillas, to be happy like those that now chatter unintelligibly along the banks of the Nile. St. Augustine, as usual, in a few well-chosen words, proves our immortality: " If we were brute animals, we would love only a carnal life, and that which was sensible; this would be a sufficient good for us, and therefore, since it would be such, we would not seek anything else." (De. Civ. Dei L. cap. 28.)

Considering man relatively to society his nature demands an after life. Man is sociable by nature; society is an outcome of our natural tendency. The individual has duties towards the state of which he is a citizen. It is sometimes an imperative duty for the citizen to expose his life to certain danger for the good of the commonwealth. Now this duty necessarily supposes a future life; as often observed already, if we abstract from immortality, the present life would be our greatest good, the foundation of all other good. There would, then, be no duty so consonant to reason as the preservation of life: hence the individual could never find himself obliged, by the dictates of reason, to expose it to certain danger for the preservation of the state, or for any other purpose. Again, in society, only public offences can be punished. Without the thought of a future state there would be no restraint on the secret actions of the citizens. How long would society last in such a case? About as long as good-fellowship appears to exist between a pen of pigs, viz: until the appearance of the swill-tub; then it is each pig for himself, and woe to the weak.

A final and cumulative argument can be drawn from the universal belief of mankind. Every tribe and nation, ancient or modern, has believed in a future state of some sort or other. It may be the Elysian fields, and shady groves of the poetic Greeks; it may be the avernus of the stern Romans; it may be the sensual heaven of the Moslem; it may be the happy hunting ground of the Red-man; or it may be something more refined or coarser, but look where you will, you will always find in the history of nations the fundamental idea of a future life. "Non omnis moriar," was as common with the mass, as with the cultured. More than this, there was joined with this belief of after existence, a belief that different lots awaited the just and impious. In the case of each nation an observance of certain general principles of morality, was the condition necessary to ensure a happy seat. Now this constant universal belief, like all other facts of a similar nature, can only be explained by attributing it to the evidence of reason. Therefore nature is the author of this belief; therefore it is true.

Again, each individual feels within him that he is not doomed to perish; he recoils from the thought; why? because it is unnatural. Truly, as well as beautifully, Addison wrote:—

> " It must be so, Plato, thou reasonest well,
> Else whence this pleasing hope, this fond desire,
> This longing after Immortality?
> Or why this secret dread, this inward horror
> Of falling into nought? Why shrinks the soul
> Back on itself, and startles at destruction?
> 'Tis the Divinity that stirs within us;
> 'Tis Heaven itself that points out an hereafter
> And intimates eternity to man."

Briefly we can thus sum up the dreary lot of man, if there existed no future life. He would be a rational being, destined for an irrational end; his reason would be at once his polar star and his rock of certain shipwreck; his nature would have a longing that there would never be any hope of satisfying; his condition would be more miserable than that of the brute creation. Having an aptitude and tendency to social life, he should either do violence to himself and renounce it, or join it to his own sure detriment. All the ennobling instincts of his nature, such as courage, care of the afflicted, desire of intellectual perfection and generous promptings, would be so many inveterate domestic enemies, hounding him on to his own destruction. Unhappy here from a thousand unavoidable causes, certain that he would be so during life, and, cruellest of all his tortures, sure that in a few brief years his soul, more vilely used than a particle of clay, would be quenched in nothingness forever. It would be a gloomy prospect; but our consolation is that our soul is immortal.

CHAPTER X.

CAUSE OF EVIL IN THE WORLD.

NO lengthy argument is required to prove that there is much evil in the world. No very fine-drawn definition of it is required: each one is convinced that certain things are to be left undone; if they be done they are said to be evil, sinful. However, it may not be so generally understood that evil is a negation of good, a deflection from it. Just as cold is the negation of heat, so evil is of good. The action from which evil follows may be positive, but evil will always remain something negative; the object of the actor is always real, or apparent good; but inasmuch as his action deflects from the rule of rectitude, it is said to produce evil. There are three species of good: metaphysical, physical and moral; corresponding to these there are three species of evil so-called. A defect of greater perfection in a being is what is called metaphysical evil; but in reality it is no evil; it is the necessary consequence of a finite nature. Every created thing must be deficient of some higher perfection of essence, but this is, strictly, no evil. Physical evil is a defect of the normal physical good of a being; thus blindness, ill-health, &c., are physical evils. Moral evil is, as said, a defect of due moral good, a departure from the rule of rectitude. The question concerning the cause of evil is an ancient one; like many simple questions, it seems to have puzzled some wise heads. Perhaps the very simplicity of it may have been the reason of its apparent difficulty. Great minds, sometimes, overlook an easy explanation of a phenomenon, and become muddled, in seeking to render satisfactory their own wild conceits. It is singular that many who are by no means noted for their virtue and goodness, would wish to impress us with a lofty idea of their respect for God. Unfortunately for their purpose, their acuteness is not equal to their zeal. Unused to reflection on God, they awkwardly trip when they propound their sanctimonious theories. In order to deny the Providence of God, they piously exclaim: " there are many evils in the world; but a good God, if he had care of the world, would not permit these evils; therefore he cares nought about what we do here below." This is the sum total of the arguments deduced from the existence of evil in the world, against God's Providence. It affects a mighty reverence for the sanctity of the Creator, while, in fact, it denies him both sanctity and wisdom. The question regarding the origin of evil, is thus closely united with the Providence of God; to palliate their own impiety, to stifle, if possible, the voice of conscience, many do not hesitate to deny to God intelligence; and they cloak their wickedness under an appearance of profound respect, for what a personal God *ought*, according to them, to do. We now confine ourselves to the origin of moral evil.

The manichæans, who were a shade less impious than modern deists and pantheists, asserted that there were two supreme principles, one good, the other evil; from the former came all good, all evil from the latter. Although it is hard to restrain a burst of laughter when reading this silly explanation of the cause of evil, the reader must remember that Bayle, whose works are the treasury of modern unbelievers, actually defended the cause of the manichæans. What opinion can be formed of the philosophic worth of the writings of a man who maintains a patent absurdity, a proposition contradictory in two of its ideas? Two *supreme* principles is the apex of absurdity, unless, perchance, a principle *supremely evil*, may surmount even the giddy height of the former. It is quite evident that two things cannot be both supreme; supreme does not admit either a superior, or an equal; hence if two things be equal, neither is supreme; they are both contingent, and one superior to both exists. Any child knows that much. Again; evil being a privation of good, a being supremely evil, would be a supreme privation, a supreme nothing.

But not only is this system most absurd, it is also quite insufficient for the purpose. Either the bad principle is from itself, or from the good one; if the latter, then the same difficulty remains; if the former, then it must be infinitely perfect; but being perfect it could not commit evil. In a word, the system is too absurd to merit a moment's consideration.

What, then, is the cause of moral evil? The abuse of human liberty; the act of man who misuses the gift of God. God created man free; he wished him to follow the directions given for his guidance, but he does not force him to it. The physical power given to man, and the ability to direct that power, are, in themselves considered, good; these God gave to man, and, consequently, gave him something good. God preserves these gifts to man for a certain time, and in this his action has good, likewise, for its effect. The direction of the physical power of man to a bad end, is the effect of the misuse of liberty of will; and only man is to blame for this. When the murderer raises his hand to bury the knife in the heart of his victim, what part has God in the act? This; he gave the murderer physical power; he gave him ability to direct that power; in this only good appears; evil begins when that power is directed to a bad end, in this case, when it is directed to the taking away of a life: but this direction is purely the work of man; therefore God has no part in the malice of the act. The murderer might have directed his physical power to the preservation of his victim's life; but he chose otherwise. God, therefore, concurs in physical acts by supplying and preserving the necessary strength, and this is something good; in the evil of acts he does not concur at all; for evil results from the direction of the physical act, and this direction is purely the work of the human will.

But some will say: God could have prevented evil, why did he not do it? Now it is to be borne in mind that God is not held to create that which is best; his liberty would be destroyed. Moreover, all that can be exacted by God, when creating, is that the being created by him be so endowed as to be enabled to acquire the end for which it was created. His justice and wisdom require this; his sanctity requires that the effect of his action be good Now in the case of man, the creative action produced good, viz: the physical strength of body, the light of reason and the power of self-determination; this justified God's sanctity. Being free, man needs not do evil; God imposed on him a law by the observance of which he can attain his final end: God gave him sufficient means to observe it; therefore his justice and wisdom are justified. We cannot, therefore, exact any more of God; we ought rather to thank him for what he has already given. Out of his own pure goodness he gave us life, reason, freedom of will, many temporal benefits, and he has prepared for us an eternity of happiness which we can acquire, if we be faithful to his inspirations. For these innumerable favors we ought to be humbly thankful, instead of grumbling at his bounty for not bestowing more. God could have confirmed us so in good that we would never sin; had he done so, he would not have been any better in himself; he would only have been more bountiful towards us; he did not choose to do this, neither was he obliged to do it.

The question can be summed up thus: the manichæan system is absurd, and insufficient if admitted. Evil arises from an abuse of the liberty of will; liberty is, in itself, something good, but being misused it produces evil. God, in giving man liberty of will, bestowed upon him a favor; he is not obliged to impede man in misusing it, for he satisfied his goodness in conferring good on man; and he satisfied his justice and wisdom by giving him means sufficient to attain to his final end. From the fact that evil exists, and is caused by a misuse of human liberty, we can deduce a strong argument to prove that a stern retribution awaits the impious in another life. By how much they have been delinquents, by so much will they be punished.

CHAPTER XI.

KNOWLEDGE OF GOD, AND LIBERTY OF MAN'S WILL.

THE question to be considered in this chapter is a mixed one; it embraces some of the principles established in natural theology, and some psychological facts; hence we deferred its consideration until the present. God is a being infinite in all his perfections; therefore his knowledge has no limits; it is incapable of increase, or diminution. He knows no more to-day than he did when he said: " let there be light;" he will know no more when time will be past, than what he knows at present. The reason of this is evident; every reality, everything knowable has the sufficient reason of its reality and cognoscibility in his divine essence. Now God knows himself; consequently he knows every reality, whether it exists or not; he is cognizant of everything knowable because in his essence is the reason of all cognoscibility. From this it follows that for God there is no past, nor future; he is an infinite, simple act, once, always, and together, willing and knowing whatsoever he wills and knows. Everything that will come to pass, or that could take place, is a reality, and consequently, is knowable; the reason of its reality and cognoscibility is in the divine essence; therefore it is known to God. Man's knowledge, by reason of his limitation, is acquired by degrees; being finite, we can have that relation to things, through which our knowledge is chiefly obtained, only with a limited number of beings; according as we put ourselves, or are put, in that relation with other objects, we acquire a knowledge concerning them; thus it is that there is a future relatively to us; and thus it is that our knowledge is not all in one act, but is acquired by degrees. Some, judging of God's knowledge as they do of man's, fall into the grevious blunder of making his knowledge a piece of patch-work, instead of a whole and seamless robe. From what has been said, it is evident that God knows everything knowable, the future as well as the past.

On the other hand, we proved that man enjoyed liberty of will; we saw that he can, at pleasure, determine himself to action, or to rest; he can choose this or that finite good. The question arises: " does God know the future free actions of man? does he know what I will choose to-morrow?" Most certainly; these actions, although not yet exercised, are possibilities, or, in other words, realities, and consequently, knowable; in God's essence is the reason of their reality and cognoscibility; hence they must be known to him. This reasoning is metaphysically certain; but an apparent difficulty occurs. Put into form it is this: either God does not know the future free actions of man, or man is not free; for what God knows is about to be, must come to pass, as he cannot be deceived; therefore it necessarily happens; consequently, we must either deny God's knowledge, or man's free will. This difficulty, at first sight, has a formidable appearance. Cicero thought it so insoluble, that he denied God's knowledge of the future free actions of man; he was intimately convinced of the existence of liberty of the will, and, to quote St. Augustine, "he made us sacriligious, that he might make us free." Others have admitted God's knowledge, but denied our liberty. Now the true philosopher will never deny either of two conflicting facts; once that he has proved both to be facts, he is sure that there can be no real contradiction between them; he will seek to reconcile them if possible; if he cannot succeed in this, he will lay them by, and label them, "unreconciled facts;" he will put them in the same catalogue with innumerable facts of a similar nature. This is the mode of procedure of true science; the counterfeit article, conscious of its own worthlessness, is afraid to acknowledge ignorance of anything, lest its total absence of knowledge might be suspected. Hence it will boldly deny some well-established truth, or it will propound some ridiculous theory. Regarding the present question, a little metaphysical refinement will suffice to harmonize facts which seem discordant. God knows what choice Peter will make to-morrow, still that choice will be perfectly free. Peter will not do the action because God knows it; but God knows it because Peter will do it. The fore-knowledge of God, like any other cognition, supposes its object, it does not make it. It is merely a speculative knowledge, and has no influence whatsoever on the action. It has the same relation to Peter's actions, as my sense of hearing has to the noise he makes; each is speculative; each supposes its object. Physically speaking, God's foreknowledge is prior to human action, but logically it is not. Every action, being something real, must have existed representatively in the divine mind from all eternity, as an object of God's knowledge. There can be no knowledge without the knowable; hence logically the determination of the free agent to action, is prior to the foreknowledge of it; the action is, therefore, unaffected by this knowledge. Once that we master the idea that all reality has its reason in the divine essence, and that everything knowable must be known to an infinite intelligence, and that logically knowledge is posterior to the knowable, the difficulty disappears; because the various circumstances in which a created will would be placed, and its choice in each case, are realities, and consequently, known to God; but since the choice is something knowable it must be prior, logically, to the knowledge had of it; hence it is not caused by that knowledge.

From the foregoing it is obvious that as regards God, there is no such thing as chance. A chance event does not mean an effect without a cause, for that would be an absurdity; but it means an unforseen and an unlooked for one. Thus, two friends have been separated for years. Each, without acquainting the other, sets out for a certain spot, and both arrive at the same moment. The meeting is called a chance one; but it was not without its cause. The act of each friend determining himself to go to the particular spot, on a stated day, caused the meeting; but since this mutual determination was unknown, and unthought of, the encounter is called one of chance. Now since God knows the every future determination of free agents, no effect of their actions can be unforseen by him. Knowing the constitution of physical things, and their laws, he knows all their effects and future changes. The stream of life rolls onward, bringing daily new beings with its tide; these buffet with the waves, or idly float with the current; no one of them knows whether the other will keep the straight course, or decline to the left; he only, in whose infinite essence is the reason of all reality, knows the future plashings of one and all.

CHAPTER XII.

FUTURE PUNISHMENT.

SOME persons take a peculiar pleasure in pulling up the long fixed stakes of universal belief. A strange mental delusion causes them to see awry everthing of the past: densely ignorant themselves, they proclaim the vastness of their fancied knowledge, and deride what they jauntily term " superstition of the past." If one were to ask what is this " superstition of the past," one would find it embraced the leading truths of philosophy,— truths which human reason long ago conclusively established —truths which the most brilliant intellect of every age believed and demonstrated—truths which christianity, likewise, teaches and evolves. Now this intolerant and intolerable pride of a few untrained intellects, which despises all the learning of the past, and which endeavors to persuade mankind that it was in hopeless darkness until the effulgence of these vagrant intelligences burst forth, is both laughable and provoking. Can any one repress an amused smile when reading the lofty pretensions of these modern lights? Not only can they tell man what he ought to do, but they can, likewise, legislate for the supreme intelligence. They promulgate, in pompous phrase, the laws which the Almighty must observe in his actions: if he will not observe them, they threaten (awful punishment) to renounce him, to deny his existence, to mount his supposed throne, and reign as gods themselves! Were these mad vagaries not blasphemous they would be highly amusing. The most deplorable feature of this mental madness is, that it rarely has a lucid interval. It chiefly arises from a complete concentration of the mind on itself; the lunatic never looks out to the genial day around him; shut up in its own diseased prison-house the mind broods and mopes on self, self, until it becomes impressed with the idea that nought but self is worth considering. Unwary scribblers, wishing to be thought piquant, and unable to judge between the mutterings of selfism and the plain arguments of reasoning minds, adopt the latest theory, as ladies do the latest style of dress, without attending to its reasonableness. Hence newspapers and magazines, reviews and monthlies, teem with flippant gibes against the very axioms of reason. It is to be noted, however, that this intolerable selfism always attacks, as superstitions, the beliefs, or propositions, which tend to restrain the indulgence of the baser passions. It always advocates something which, if practised, would degrade, not ennoble man. Hence, perhaps, animalism, not selfism, would be the more correct term for this disease. We never find selfism propounding any system of ethics by the observance of which the nobler properties of man would be brought into play. It pretends to emancipate reason from the bondage of superstition, but it only rivets on it the shackles of sensuality: it assumes the championship of freedom, but it only sets up the debasing tyranny of materialism. This is sufficient to stamp it with lasting infamy.

In order that the reign of animalism may be brought about, its supporters are not particular what line of argument they pursue. Nothing, in the way of denial, comes amiss to these intellectual giants; in fact denial is their strong point. The envious might be tempted to say that they prefer denial because it is always easy; it requires no great mental endowments to fit a man for denial. As shown before, if you take away the belief of the existence of a personal God, or of an immaterial and immortal soul, or of future retribution, you give a clear track for the march of sensuality. Now we have to demonstrate that not only God exists, and that our will is free, and our souls immortal, but, likewise, that future punishment awaits the impious. We have proved all except the last named fact. For our basis, we take the established truth that our soul is immortal: therefore some kind of life awaits each soul after the dissolution of the body. It must be borne in mind that we do not attempt here to prove the existence of hell, as taught by christianity; that belongs to sacred theology; we only undertake to show, from reason, that the impious soul is not happy; it receives some kind of punishment. Any one who has not bidden adieu to reason must admit that a law has been imposed on man; some things are to be done, others are forbidden. " Do unto another as you would another do to you," is an axiom of reason; so is this other—" that which you would not wish to be done to yourself, do not do to another." Clearly then some things are commanded, others are prohibited. Therefore naturally a law has been imposed on man. But there can be no law without a lawgiver; consequently there exists a supreme lawgiver, infinite and intelligent who has imposed on man an unchangeable law. Moreover, reason tells us, that this legislator is not indifferent regarding the observance, or transgression of his commands. It was shown above that a sufficient penalty must have been threatened against transgressors; that penalty, it was also shown, was not in this world; therefore it must be paid in the next. Again, God is just; he must intend the lot of those who observe his law to be better than that of those who break it; but in this life the lot of the former is often worse than that of the latter: therefore in the next life due portions will be assigned to all. Let any rational being take into consideration the following case which often is verified. Here is a just man, observing at all times the law of God; he is in poverty, but he does not repine; he could acquire wealth by unlawful means, but would suffer cruel torments rather than obtain it by a transgression. He is ready to stretch out his hand to those more needy than himself; he is often found by the bedside of the suffering and afflicted. Here is his neighbor who has never set a limit to the indulgence of his passions; hard, cruel, dishonest, licentious, he is as indifferent to the misery of others as he is ready to inflict it for his own aggrandizement. A sudden death cuts down both these men at the same moment. One was surprised in the performance of an act of charity; the other was called away in the midst of a scheme of oppression. These two souls, so differently prepared, the one so conscious of good works performed, the other so polluted with iniquity, enter upon another life. Can any sane man pretend that the lot of both will be alike? If the just soul enters into a state of happiness, what will become of the impious one? Evidently it cannot be happy: more than this, the transgressions against the eternal law must be avenged; it must suffer.

Were one to inquire still further, and seek to find out in what that suffering would consist, it would be no difficult task to show that part of it, at least, would consist in being deprived of the enjoyment of the supreme good. It was shown that our will has an indefinite capacity for good; nothing that we can imagine in this world, no aggregate of earthly pleasures could ever satiate our longing for happiness. Since this longing has been ingrafted on our nature, it must have God for its author; hence there are means provided by

which it may be satisfied. Now only the enjoyment of the
supreme good, of God, can satisfy our craving after felicity:
therefore there are means provided, through the use of which
the human soul can arrive at this enjoyment. Reason tells
us that some of these means are the observance of the natural
law. It is clear that the soul which enters on the next life
in the friendship of God will have its longing after happiness
satisfied, by being put in enjoyment of the supreme good: on
the other hand, the soul which leaves this world in enmity
with God, cannot be placed in the enjoyment of that good;
for then it would be equally happy with God's friends. It
will, therefore, be deprived of that good, the only one which
can give it perfect happiness. That deprivation will cause
an indescribable suffering: the soul, freed from its union
with the body, will no longer have an appetite for sensible
pleasure; by an overpowering tendency of nature it will be
driven on to long and long for the enjoyment of the supreme
good. It will see that it could easily have been happy forever, but that for a few degrading pleasures of earth, it
foreswore its creator, and forfeited its felicity. Not even the
fleeting satisfactions of life will remain for it to enjoy; it
will be incapable of enjoying anything, save that which it
has lost forever. It will tend to God by an impulse of
nature, but stern justice, with uplifted sword, will banish it
from the presence of the only object on which it desires to
look. One sight of that object will be vouchsafed it, but not
as a pleasure; the remembrance of that sight will only bring
additional bitterness to the desolate soul, for it will then
understand how much it has lost, and how easily it could
have gained its happiness. An awful feeling of desolation
will come over it; never, never to have one moment's rest;
never, never to have even the shadow of a satisfaction, or
enjoyment; ever, ever to crave, and never, no, never to

obtain. Sullen gloom, and grim despair will be its cruel tormentors; its accomplices in sin will be its loathsome companions; curses on its own foolishness, and useless upbraidings of its friends in iniquity will be at once its occupation and its torment. That the impious will suffer, at least this much, reason clearly proves. No one who reflects on this could think it light, or easily borne. Were one to suffer all the miseries imaginable in this world, such as disease, cold, hunger, pains, &c., they would not be so insupportable as the loss of the impious; because, in life, we have always some little comfort, some enjoyments in the midst of our afflictions: and, above all, the certainty that they will end soon, and the hope of future happiness. But the soul, deprived in the next world of the enjoyment of the supreme good, will not have one solitary satisfaction, and it will have an invincible certainty that it never will have any.

It is not uncommon to hear the impious prate flippantly about God's goodness; without goodness themselves, and often very demons of cruelty in satisfying themselves, it is somewhat strange that they should attribute so much mercy to God. In fact they make him all mercy, and no justice. Now it should be remembered that God is infinite in all his perfections; his mercy is infinite, but so, also, is his justice. These two can never come in collision; the first is daily exercised towards his creatures by bestowing fresh blessings on them, even while they are insulting him; his justice will be exercised in punishing if in spite of all his favors and warnings, a soul will continue to outrage him. Mercy reigns over all his works in this world; but justice will preside in the next. You may as well deny the existence of God, as deny that he will punish the wicked: a God shorn of justice is no God; he who would impose a law and not reward its observers, and punish its transgressors, could not be an infinite being. Hence it is more logical, but not less impious, to deny God's existence, than to admit it and deny his justice. But some will exclaim: there is no punishment; God never made man to send him to hell. Quite true God did not make man for that purpose, nevertheless he will send many thither; because man, by abusing his liberty of will, will force God, by reason of his justice, to condemn him to eternal punishment. It is not, then, God who is to blame, but man himself. It will not do to invoke God's mercy as a reason for still further offending him. It is sometimes urged that we suffer in this world for our transgressions, by remorse of conscience. True, sin brings with itself bitterness; but only in the case of pretty good people is this bitterness much experienced. This punishment of sin decreases with the increase of vice, until the hardened wretch knows scarcely what conscience is. Were this the only punishment of sin, it would fall more lightly on the hoary sinner, than on the youth guilty of only one crime.

CHAPTER XIII.

PSYCHOLOGICAL PHENOMENA.

HE soul is evidently the principle of life and action in man; this has been fully established. We may go further, and postulate what will be hereafter demonstrated, viz: that in all sentient beings there is a simple substance, or principle of life, which is, likewise, the subject of sensation. There is, as will also be shown, an essential difference between the vital principle of the brute creation, and the human soul, although they have some things in common, such as physical simplicity and sensibility. A considerable amount of learned lore has been expended, from time to time, especially in England, on the question of "spontaneous generation." It has been maintained that certain sentient beings come into existence without generation; the germ of life was enclosed within, or rather, was a part of the putrid mass, and spontaneously burst forth into full life. The conclusion sought to be drawn by some is, that the vital principle of sentient beings is only matter, and, consequently, the human soul can be a particle of matter. Although we proved beyond all doubt that the human soul is physically simple and essentially diverse from matter, still a few words on the question of "spontaneous generation," may not be amiss. The works of the creator are innumerable and varied; turn where we will, we find everything teeming with life; the earth, air, water are vast conservatories of living beings. They differ in size, physical organization, and perfection, but all have one note, at least, in common, that is, life. In each there is a vital principle distinct and diverse from the material part which is seen by the eye, or discovered by the microscope. From age to age these innumerable species of living beings are preserved and propagated; the power and wisdom of the creator are manifested continually by their existence. Certain fixed laws establish the mode of their propagation. In the production of their physical parts heat is always an active agent; under its influence the relative position of the parts of the seed is changed; a new combination of elements results. Now the fixed law for the coming into existence of a sentient being is this; whenever certain elements are combined and grouped in a determinate manner, the vital principle is created and infused into that mass; it is then no longer a corrupted heap, it is a sentient being in embryo. Under suitable circumstances it will be developed; in the case of some beings, rapidly, in the case of others, slowly. It matters not how this combination of elements is brought about; the law is fixed; whenever the necessary grouping and combination are verified, the vital principle will be created and infused. The chicken will come forth from the egg heated artificially, equally as well as from the one warmed by the natural process of incubation. Now in the case of those beings which seem to come into existence by spontaneous generation, the explanation is simple enough. There is a heap of matter; in it are all the elements required for the organization of a certain class of beings, but they are not in proper relation to each other. By some natural process, such as the action of light, heat, or electricity, the mass of matter is decomposed; part is set free as gas; parts which have an affinity for one another are drawn more closely together; the former grouping of elementary particles is changed, and a new one succeeds. After various changes of position, and different combinations, the particles required for the organization of a certain sentient being are brought into proper relations; the condition for an exercising of the established law for the coming into existence of that being is verified; the vital principle is created, and vivifies the embryo organism. This explains the origin of life under any circumstances whatsoever. The only exception that can be taken to it is, that we suppose the vital principle to be created immediately by God, and infused into the organism. We do suppose this; but we will prove in the next chapter that this is really the case. In fact, what we said about the origin of the human soul would be sufficient.

This much will do on the question of life; it is not an abstruse one; to fully understand it, it is only necessary that the philosopher should have no prejudice against christian teaching when investigating it. If he set out with the fixed purpose of endeavoring to establish materialism, he will make many mental splurges, and propound many specious theories, and still will not master a very simple, though beautiful, law for the existence of sentient beings.

There are some phenomena observable in every-day life, which might here occupy a moment's consideration. We approach the subject with diffidence, rather seeking light than bearing it. The opinion about to be given regarding these phenomena, may be very wide of the mark, but we think there is something of truth in it. We will first take the old saying: "speak of the ——— and he is sure to appear." No one can have failed to observe that, often as he has been speaking about, or thinking very much about, a person, that person has appeared. Each one can remember scores of times when this circumstance happened. Now an event which, in every age, frequently happens in certain circumstances, must have some connection with these circumstances. It seems most anti-philosophic to entirely disconnect the two. Taking it for granted then, that there is some link between the event and the conditions, the philosopher ought to endeavor to discover what it is. The following explanation is suggested: the friend who appears intended to call on you; he thought about you, about calling on you; and probably, on the way thought often about you, and imagined himself speaking with you. This internal action of his, this deep consideration of the soul, acted somehow on your soul, and stirred up thoughts of him; and so you began to speak of him. The objection at once is: *how* could his soul act on mine? Even if the *how* cannot be shown it would not follow that it did not act. That the active substance, or force called the soul, acts on the force of which the body is composed, has been fully established; now we can see no valid reason for saying that one spiritual force, or soul, cannot act on another, to some extent, at least. Analogy would rather say that it could; and experience seems to confirm the argument from analogy. It may appear egotistic to appeal to personal experience: but the writer, from the time he first read psychology, thought that one soul could act on another even in life. He took note of the occurrence, or verification of the saw quoted above, and found some remarkable coincidences. Each one might, perhaps, be sufficiently explained by saying it was merely accidental, if it alone were considered; but it would appear to the mind of the writer, highly improbable, and most unphilosophic, to assign them all to the theory of chance coincidences. Again; if you look intently on the side-face, or head of a person, that person, unless engaged in conversation, or buried in deep thought, will turn towards you: nay, more; look intently on one asleep and that one will awake. Now something must have acted on these persons; it was not your body, because you were not in physical contact with them; it was soul acting on soul. A good many phenomena, such as those called "presentiments," and others which are often lightly relegated to the sphere of real superstitions, might thus find a rational explanation.

Finally, another psychologic phenomenon worthy of consideration, is a certain class of dreams,—not those fantastic notions that often pass through a sleeper's mind, and which are disjointed and mixed fragments of waking experiences—but those dreams in which you see places and persons never before seen, but which are at once recognized when afterwards viewed. That such dreams are not unfrequent is, it may be said, undoubted. How can they be explained? Sleep is a partial suspension of the commerce between soul and body. May it not be supposed that, in that state, the spirituality of the soul comes more fully into play? More fully disengaged than in its waking moments, from the trammels of the body, the operations of the soul may be more spiritualized; in its regard space will, for the time at least, be partially annihilated. The sleeper may be resting his weary form on the plains of central America, and his soul, though united to it, may be contemplating the Boulevards of Paris. How does it do this? The soul is not of the same order of beings as the body; we are not to exclaim impossible for soul, because impossible for the body. The soul is ever active, ever acting; the supposed invincible reasons of Locke to the contrary, cannot stand against syllogistic rigor: a substance necessarily acts, and acts in accordance with its nature; the soul is a spiritual substance; therefore it must always act by thought of some kind, and by will of happiness, at least. Now the soul disentangled, in part, from its grosser companion, may perceive created things without the help of corporeal organs, by their essence. This would explain how it happens that some perceptions during sleep are so vivid, photographed almost on the mind.

CHAPTER XIV.

PRINCIPLE OF LIFE IN THE BRUTE CREATION.

WERE the vagaries of "modern thought" of a noble turn, we would not have much need to dwell long on this subject. But it happens that our would-be emancipators from the "superstitions of the past," belong to an ignoble race. Unlike most weak mortals, they are not ashamed of the fact; they rather boast of it. Their genealogical tree, like the spruce and juniper, has its roots firm set in the ground. The first link of the heathen poet's chain was fixed to the foot of Jupiter; but the spongy roots of our great "thinkers'" parent tree has a more lowly fastening. True, their progenitors are an antique stock; but ancient blood is, with them, no stimulant to pride. Our "thinkers" are humble; they only imagine themselves better than those who have noble ideas of man; these they pity, or despise; while they fondle the chimpanzee, or ourang-outang, as an undeveloped brother. It is scarcely fair, however, for them to claim the whole human family as vassals of their house. Those barons of the middle ages, whom no doubt they heartily despise, only claimed, as vassals, a few families: our "thinkers," on the contrary, seek to subjugate all mankind. If they are themselves but cultured apes, why insist that we should profess ourselves their kinsmen? Is it because they have given themselves over to animalism, that they want to degrade all to their own level? Whether they differ much or little, practically, from the lower animals, should be best known to themselves; that essentially they are different and diverse we are prepared to substantiate.

No elaborate piece of reasoning is required to prove that the brute creation feel, see, hear, taste, and smell. They are subject to various sensations; they are not indifferent to the infliction of a wound. They exhibit all the outward and sensitive signs of pain, which are exhibited by man; hence, since we cannot transform ourselves into one of them, we judge of their sensations, just as we do of those of human beings, viz: by their actions. Brutes are not, then, mere insensitive pieces of machinery; they have a sentient principle which is the subject of their various sensations. Undoubtedly they perceive external bodies; they turn aside from the barrier that crosses their path, just as surely as a man would do it. Their perceptions cannot be mere confused representations, because they distinguish between an object seen before, and a strange one. We do not think it necessary to enter into a further proof of the proposition that brutes have *distinct sensible perceptions.* Any one who will give the subject a moment's thought will at once admit it. There is, then, in brutes a subject of perception. This subject must be physically simple. We use the same argument as was evolved in proving the simplicity of the human soul. If the perceiving subject were compound, either the whole perception would be in one of its parts, or a part in each part, or all in each part. If it were all in one part, and if that part be supposed simple, then the perceiving subject is simple; if if be compound, again we say that one of the three above hypotheses must be verified, and we would repeat the argument until it would have to be admitted that that part was simple. If a part of the perception be said to be in each part of the subject, no one part could have a full perception of anything; there would be no distinct perception, and no power of distinguishing between objects. Finally, if the whole perception be in each part, the brute would see not one, but a dozen or more objects instead of one. Now their action proves that they see only the one object, when there is only one. Neither, therefore, of the three suppositions can be admitted; we must, then, conclude that the subject of perception in brutes is physically simple. It is so evident that feeling and perception require a subject devoid of physical parts that Condillac arguing against Buffon said we must either deny brutes to have real sensations, or we must grant that their subject of sensation is immaterial. In fact, if this subject be made up of parts there would be in a lamb many subjects of sensation, or many individuals; because suppose each feeling part endowed with reason, it could say *I feel;* hence what is called one lamb would be, in reality, many lambs. The force of nonsense could not go much further.

There is, then, in brutes a principle of life and sensation which is physically simple; it is called, by analogy, their soul; but the reader must bear well in mind that it is essentially different from the human soul. It is now evident that, in the coming into existence of all sentient beings, a direct action of the creator concurs. The body may be formed in embryo by the action of finite causes; but the sentient principle, being immaterial, must come into existence by creation. It is not a part of any pre-existing matter, because essentially different from it; it is not from itself, because it is finite; therefore it is immediately created by God. When the Creator determined to create this visible world, and all that it contains, he gave to many creatures reproductive organs so that the species might be propagated; but only the material part can be thus produced: the immaterial, or sentient principle, must be, as shown above, the work of the creative hand. According to the law established by the creator, the sentient principle will be created whenever the material elements are duly combined and grouped. Thus from age to age, innumerable sentient beings come into existence, natural and finite causes concurring with the action of the Infinite.

The chief question, regarding the vital principle of brutes, is to determine in what, and how much, it is diverse from the human soul. Selfism, the harbinger of animalism, is here our opponent. This enlightened *ism*, as usual, is for degrading man; it only recognizes a difference in degree between our soul, and the vital principle of a brute. The " superstitions of the past," said that there was an essential difference—that by no length of time, by no process of culture could a brute be developed into a man. The learned " modern thinker " cuts a sorry figure when placed in juxtaposition with the monk of antiquity. Brutes exhibit many wonderful phenomena of sagacity; they act, at times, in such a manner as to appear almost endowed with reason: hereupon some erratic genius, fired by a noble zeal to vindicate the calumniated, exclaims: " explain this if you can; define for me the limits between reason and instinct." This is about the substance of all his arguments. He thinks them triumphant; and rejoices in the discovery of a kinsman. Now the defenders of true philosophy often, in charity, perhaps, or through inadvertence, endeavor to define the required limits. They attempt more than they are called upon to do—more than they can do. In order to define the precise difference between any two given objects, it is necessary to have an adequate idea of both. Now we have not an adequate idea either of reason, or of instinct; hence it is unfair and ridiculous, to require the exact difference between them. But we can show that there is an essential difference; the one has essential properties which are not found in the other; hence there is a diversity of essence, and not merely one of degree. Once this is demonstrated we can quietly rest on our oars; all the examples of sagacity adduced cannot affect our position. The essence of things is unchangeable; the diversity between the essence of two things may be more, or less; but be it little, or great, so long as there is a diversity, one is not of the same species as the other, and can never develop into it.

We freely admit that brutes have perception joined with a remembrance of former sensations; they recognize objects seen before, and in this manner providence has provided that, from experience, they may learn what things are to be avoided as hurtful to them. Hence too, they can remember, and perform the tricks taught them by man. They, likewise, have sensitive appetites, and spontaneous motion. Hence they seek the object of their appetites with great sagacity. When the dog scents the carrion he recognizes it as connected with an object pleasing to his appetite, and bounds away in the right direction. God wished the various species of beings created by him to be preserved and propagated; he, therefore, endowed each species with properties suitable for these purposes. It is no wonder, then, that brutes should have the above properties; they are means well adapted to the desired end. When the bee fills its cell with honey, it acts from instinct. By instinct we mean an impulse, or tendency of nature by which brutes are borne to avoid that which is destructive to them, and to provide that which is necessary for their preservation. All this we concede to brutes; all this is in man with other essential properties that are not in brutes. We will consider a few of these properties, in order that the essential difference between a human soul, and the vital principle of a brute, may be apparent.

1st, The power of reasoning. It is not necessary to stop to prove that essentially man has the power of reasoning; he can deduce the effect from a cause; he can assign the cause from the effect; from the more known, he can learn the less known. Now we assert that this property is not in brutes, neither actively, nor potentially. That it is not in them actively, few will deny. In all their works and actions an unvarying sameness is observed. They construct wonderfully skillful nests and lairs, but the last one is no better than the first; what sagacity they have is born full-blown. It never improves, it never grows less. Take an egg, and by artificial means supply the process of incubation; never let the young bird see one of its kind. When it is full-grown it will build a nest as neat and as commodious as the one constructed by the oldest of its kind. Its action is not the effect of example, for it saw none; it cannot be the effect of reasoning, for it could not reason about a thing entirely unknown. Either its action is the effect of an irresistible impulse of nature, or its genius is many degrees superior to that of man; for only by slow stages, through much labor and comparison, in the course of many years, can man arrive at such perfection in his works. None, I think, will give the bird more talent than what he will accord to man. Therefore the work of the bird is not the effect of reasoning, comparison and study; it is the effect of an impulse of nature. Reason, actively exercised, must always progress; new ideas and new modes of action must arise from comparison of various works: reflection on them will suggest improvements, and ornamentation. Take a nomadic tribe; they sleep at first on the ground; the shade of some tree is their only protection. After a time, from an observation of the boughs of trees covered with leaves, they drive stakes into the earth, and stretch over them the hides of wild beasts. A step in advance has been made in the matter of habitation. They rove less, owing to the proximity of a hostile tribe; they feel the want of something more lasting than the tent of goat skins. Tramping through a boggy soil they note its property of adhesion; they find it hardens by exposure to the sun. What if a pile of it were raised around the tent? They try an experiment, and rejoice to find a solid wall, impervious to rain and wind. This is an improvement on the tent. Their habits become more agricultural; the mud wall is found to be damp and gloomy; wood split and fastened together would be more airy and drier. They try it, and thus from year to year they go on, making experiments, comparing, culling here and there. A city springs up; neat wooden cottages are succeeded by substantial buildings of brick and stone; these are superseded by magnificent palaces of marble; the nomadic tribe has given birth to a mighty nation. Now anyone who would follow out, in his imagination, the progress of various tribes, and note their ever-advancing strides of improvement; and who would then turn his attention to the total want of progress in works, or form of society, amongst brutes; and who, after that, would assert that brutes actively reasoned, is unfit for argument. He is simply insane.

Another, and a more obvious proof of want of reasoning in brutes is this: Everyone who has travelled during the winter season, when the snow is very deep, has been annoyed by meeting cattle on the road. When you are within sight of a gate you see an intelligent looking cow coming forth; she stops, looks down the road, sees you, sees the deep snow, but, nevertheless, advances. She meets your horse; she cannot pass but must turn and retrace her steps until she arrives back at the gate, through which she bolts to escape. Now did she actively use reason, she would have waited at the gate until you passed; the smallest child would have done it. By reasoning she would have seen that she could not do better than remain. This fact, trifling and perhaps, little thought of, is quite sufficient to convince any sound intellect that brutes are devoid of the active use of reason.

Equally evident is it, that they have not got it potentially, or in the germ. If they had, it must, through time, become active, else why the power? Now it is certain that domestic animals, such as the horse, cow, sheep, and dog, live in the same manner as they did thousands of years ago Their society is no different; their actions are the same; a total want of progress marks all their descendants It would surely be unreasonable to say that they have reason potentially, and yet make no advancement in refinement. For centuries the horse has been the slave of man; with bit and halter he is led about by a little child; beaten, half-starved, ill-housed, he still remains docile as before. He never atttempts to stir up his fellows to a rebellion against man. Yet had he but an infinitesimal part of the intelligence of the most degraded human slave, he could soon free himself from his state of bondage; he could soon trample upon his cruel master, and dictate terms of peace to mankind. An uprising of the horses, dogs, mules, and oxen, which would be quite possible had they a spark of reason, would be something more dreadful than the rebellion of the slaves in ancient Rome. We may justly conclude that the existence, in brutes, of a faculty which for several thousand years has never been exercised, is as mythical as that of the ghosts which haunt lonely church-yards on dark nights.

2d, *Language:* Rational speech is an essential attribute of man; in a few rare cases, by reason of some physical defect, the use of this faculty may be impeded; still it is possessed potentially, even by the mute. With the rapidity of lightning, with unerring precision, we can make known our feelings, affections, and our most profound ideas. We are endowed with a mechanism so wonderful in construction that, at will, we can modify our voice; we can produce a variety of sounds; we can imitate strange ones; reproduce past ones, and express, by these means, thoughts and feelings in rapid succession. We make no excuse for translating from Balmes —(Elem. Phil.) the following beautiful passage: " The mechanism of the voice, the great facility with which it obeys the orders of the will, clothing thought with a sensible form, is one of the most wonderful things imaginable. Who can measure the time which passes between the conception of an idea and its outward expression? Consider the orator from whose lips there flows, like a golden stream, a discourse, with the impetuosity of a cataract; how many ideas of every kind, the physical, the metaphysical; the simple, the compound; judgments, reasonings, comparisons, analysis, synthesis,—he expresses them all with the same facility as he conceives them. A thought rises in the orator's mind, and at the same moment, with the rapidity of lightning, it flashes in the mind of the listener; still it was necessary that the thought should be conceived, that the will should prescribe a movement of the organs of speech, that the air should vibrate, that the vibration should reach the tympanum of the listener and be communicated to his brain, and that the sound should serve his intellect as a countersign to perceive the idea. . . . And what is most wonderful is, that this is not a privilege of the learned, it is the patrimony of humanity; the rudest boor, the most ignorant old woman can do that which is done by the most famous orator; the facility, the rapidity, the prodigy of expression are the same; when we treat of so wonderful a phenomenon, what do a little more, or less of polish in expression, and attention in pronunciation, signify? That which is admirable is in the language itself, not in these slight adjuncts. Let us recognize the wisdom and goodness of the Creator, and return him thanks for so great a benefit." No one will say that the mechanism of the voice could be so modulated without the use of reason. The untaught hand may sweep over the keys of an organ and produce some sounds, but there will be no harmony, nor melody in the strain; there will be no series of sound calling to one and another; no combination and succession of notes will enrapture the listener; so the organs of speech, unless guided in their movements by intelligence, will emit no intelligible sound. A monotonous bow-wow-wow, or a piteous m-a-a-a, may be produced without reason; but intelligence is required for articulate orations. Moreover, man can perfect language; he can add to his vocabulary; he can modify his inflections and emphasis. All these are the results of intelligence. Now, if we turn to the brute creation, we find in many of them organic vocular mechanisms like unto ours. Through them they emit certain sounds indicative of pleasure, pain, fear or other natural sensations, but that is all. Their vocabulary is limited indeed, and it never varies; the little bee when flying in search of flowers from which to extract honey, emitted the same unvarying bnzz centuries ago in Hymettus, as what its fellows do to-day in our gardens; the bleating of the flocks which Romulus tended on the Aventine, was similar to that which we hear on our hillsides. No increase of words, no change of tone, no variety of expression has taken place among the brute creation during the lapse of ages. A few rude sounds which indicate a limited number of natural sensations, constitute their language. They never make appointments; they never descant on the beauties of nature; they never attempt oratory. The domestic gander is the best specimen we have of a brute orator; his gabbling is the nearest approach we have to the vapid declamation of some bipeds, who advocate Darwinism. Now the absence of progress, or change in the language of brutes, can only be attributed to their want of reason. The faintest glimmer of intelligence would produce, in one day, a change. Nature has given them the means of expressing, instinctively, some natural feelings, for their preservation and propagation; hence the necessity of vocal organs. Again; man instinctively cries out when suffering pain; so will a brute; but there is this notable difference: man can restrain his cries because endowed with reason and free will; but the brute cannot, because its cries are an impulse of nature, and it lacks an intelligence to control them.

From the foregoing we can conclude that brutes are utterly devoid of intelligence either in act, or in power. Moreover, the characteristic of reason is progress, that of instinct, stagnation. The former, by an innate power of self-determination, develops and waxes wise; the latter, being a mere impulse of nature, is never changed, or modified. Therefore between instinct and reason there is a difference of kind; the former is no degree of the latter, otherwise it would inevitably advance. A quality which is essential to the subject of reason, is wanting in the subject of instinct; hence essentially they are distinct and diverse; one can never develop into the other, for the essence of things is immutable. The workings of instinct are, at times, wonderful, and should make us recognize the wisdom of the Creator who provided so well for the preservation of his creatures; but if we examine closely these workings we at once discover the absence of a reason which foresees danger, and provides against it. The ant will construct its store-house with great skill, because prompted by nature; but, because devoid of intelligence, it foresees no danger from man, and builds on the roadside, soon to be rudely disturbed. Untaught by this disaster it will rebuild in a similar spot and suffer a similar misfortune. The bee will store away its honey in well-contrived cells, disregarding the presence of man who will soon rob it of the fruits of its labor. Man constructs his habitations and store-houses with a foresight of danger, against which he provides. If he has unconsciously built in the vicinity of a hostile tribe, he either abandons the dangerous locality, or strongly fortifies his dwelling. He foresees danger from fire, flood and sword, and takes precautions, in as much as he can, against them. The work of instinct may be neat and skilful, but it will ever lack the provision, against fortuitous danger, observable in the rudest products of reason. This difference invincibly proves the absence of an intellectual faculty in brutes—a faculty which not merely notes present wants and conveniences, but which, also, speculates upon, and provides against, future contingencies.

Admire, then, if you will, the works of the industrious brute creation; praise their neatness and finish; be delighted with their adaptation for their necessary purposes. Your doing this ought to be but another motive to adore the infinite wisdom and goodness of God who has provided so wisely, and so well, for his dumb creatures. But as you value a reputation for common sense, do not confound the cause of these works with that of the wonderful achievements of man. The bee-hive, beavers'-dam and store-house of ants may be ingenious, but a natural impulse, or instinct, is sufficient to explain them; only, however, a power of comparing, analyzing, combining and foreseeing, can be a sufficient cause of the noble war-ships of England—of the pyramids of Egypt—of St. Peter's at Rome—of the bridges which span rapid streams—of the railways which intersect great countries, annihilating space—of the telegraphs which bring regions far remote into instant communication, annihilating time—of the thousand and one great works which are the issue and embodiment of human reason. It would be a childish weakness, after such considerations, to attribute one particle of reasoning power to brutes.

Cruelty to Brutes.

There are some natures prone to gross contradictions: to-day they show a cruel callousness to human misery, and, perhaps, to-morrow they will melt in morbid sympathy over a derelict cat. Here they turn with loathing from a scarred and suffering child; there they catch up and hug a limping dog, that has been worsted in a scuffle with a neighboring cur. The starving mother may plead in vain at their doors, for food for her starving babe; but the whine of a hungry spaniel is answered with the half of a six-penny loaf. They express no horror at the sight of human beings crowded into filthy huts—huddled together, ten in a room not large enough for two; but a cry of indignation, loud, long and deep, issues from their throats, at the sight of a car-load of swine, somewhat uncomfortably bestowed. They form associations to applaud and perpetuate, if possible, cruel laws; and they join societies to prevent cruelty to brutes. Is this an outcome of " modern thought?" Now we are far from wishing to sneer at a compassionate nature keenly alive to every form of suffering; but we confess to no sympathy with that maudlin sentiment, too common, alas! of withdrawing all pity from human misery to bestow it on the fancied ills of brutes. We may safely assert, as a general rule, to which, of course, there are exceptions, that those who parade most pity for suffering brutes, have least for suffering man. It was reported some years ago, we know not with what foundation in fact, that an old lady in London, bequeathed her estate for the foundation of an asylum for abandoned cats. It is to be hoped that the Judge of Probate declared her insane, and directed the property to be handed over to an orphanage. England seems to be the hot-bed of a sickly sentiment of charity to brutes; and England seems to be a country much in need of love for her suffering children. Even those in England who ought to know better, find it hard to divest themselves of the ludicrous idea in vogue, regarding the treatment of brutes. If we consider the relation in which the lower creation stands to man, we will easily arrive at a rational conclusion on this question.

1st—Brutes have no rights, properly so called; right is a " power morally inviolable ;" hence it supposes reason in its subject. There being no right in brutes, there can be no duty on the part of man, towards them.

2d—Brutes were created for the benefit of man ; hence man can use, and slay them when it conduces to his comfort, or legitimate convenience to do so.

3d—Brutes being a benefit conferred by God on man, it follows that man has duties towards God concerning the use of said benefit.

From these principles which are evident, it follows that no matter what man may do to a brute, he never infringes any right of the brute; if he wantonly destroy cattle, fish or fowls, he is misusing God's benefits. He who knowingly and unnecessarily ill-treats a dumb animal, manifests an evil disposition which it is well to curb, even by fines and imprisonment ; but it ought to be clearly proved that the ill-usage was conscious, deliberate, not in a moment of anger, and unnecessary, otherwise the real right of man is infringed to vindicate an imaginary one of a brute. It is quite within man's prerogatives to inflict pain on brutes, when any end, advantageous to himself, is to be obtained. Vivisection, for purposes of experiment, is licit, even when there is only a probability of its being useful. In a word, common sense tells us that since brutes were created for our use and benefit, we can destroy them if troublesome, or subject them to pain if advantageous. Hence few experience any qualms of conscience, in remorselessly crushing those proverbially nimble little creatures which skip over the sleeper's form, causing him to dream of pins, needles, and other sharp instruments. It would be well if societies for the "prevention of cruelty to animals," were to turn their attention to the sufferings of humanity, and alleviate a trifle of human wretchedness. We do not advocate free license for a brutal nature to vent its spleen on a poor dumb animal; but we would prefer charity to man first, and then prevention of cruelty to beasts. The suffering endured by brutes is not so great as, at first sight, it might seem to be. It is only physical, and only the pain of the moment. Devoid of reason, they can have no mental anguish, nor can they foresee and dread a future suffering.

CHAPTER XV.

DARWINISM.

THERE are various ways of arriving at the temple of fame, if by "fame" be meant a notoriety, whether enviable or not. True, the statues of but few find permanent niches in that temple; though many may, for a season, be exalted to the honors of its altars, and smothered, almost, in a cloud of incense raised by an admiring and unthinking crowd. The adulations of the moment are the ambition of many; hence the innumerable artifices to secure this fleeting satisfaction. The hill of science, on whose summit stands the temple of fame, is steep and high; it has a secure road hedged with firmly rooted trees, which yield not beneath the climber's grasp; but there are various other paths along a shelly ledge; one false step, one nervous movement of the body, is sufficient to precipitate the unwary toiler from these treacherous ways. A motley crowd of writers jostle against each other, on those insecure roads; the ascent, along them, is shorter than by the royal road; but amidst the confusion and rude pushing of author against author, many a daring adventurer slips downward into the dark gulf which yawns beneath; one by one they fall with sullen plash; a wavy motion of the dark surface succeeds, and the aspirant for popular adulation is buried in the black waters of oblivion. In the meantime, the pains-taking climber by the secure road mounts slowly, but surely, till he reaches the reward of true merit-enduring fame. Persons who seek for literary, or scientific notoriety, without any nobler object in view, are regardless of the intrinsic merits, or demerits, of their writings. They desire to make a display; to dazzle the common herd; to say something that has an air of originality, be it ever so old in substance, or absurd in itself. Hence the mania for founding " schools of thought ;" those who inveigh most against masters, are striving to become the great teachers of our age; possibly they imagine that never, until now, has there appeared one among men capable of being a master. In fact, one is inclined to think that modern unbelievers, if one give ear to their words, possess, embody and express the total of human wisdom. The great philosophers of antiquity, and the great writers of Christianity, are drivelling idiots in the estimation of these modest theorizers. Fiercely as did the Iconoclasts rush against the christian churches to break the images of the saints, do these aspirants assail the temple of fame, to cast down, smash and trample under foot the statues of great pagan and christian philosophers, which have so long adorned its niches. Their motive is easily understood: so long as these masters are honored, the vagaries, crude notions, illogical deductions of modern pagans can never come into repute. We do not say that all our contemporary theorizers are actuated by these motives; but we do think that a childish vanity of wishing to propound something startling, has led many a thinker from the right path.

But our object is not to ridicule silly aspirants to fame. They will soon be forgotten. Something must, however, be said respecting what is known as " Darwinism." We do not undertake to say by what motives Mr. Darwin was prompted to propound and defend his wild theory. This much, however, may be said of the theory itself,—it is subversive of the common consent of mankind, of morality, and of reason. Mankind has always placed an essential difference between man and the lower creation; it is difficult to imagine how morality can co-exist with belief in a system, which recognizes no essential difference between a human soul and the vital principle of brutes; and reason is at once subverted if it be made a degree of instinct. Reduced to its ultimate analysis " Darwinism " is a theory which supposes a natural progression, or development, from species of a lower, to species of a higher order. According to it, man is but an evolution of this physical progression; the chattering ape developed into the speaking man; the great wheel of nature's mill is whirling round, and each revolution turns out a new, and more finely pounded grist of animated clay. The beautiful doctrine of St. Thomas regarding the graduated scale of created things, on which is seen marked the various species of beings, rising in perfection from the inert clod, to man on whose brow is visible the impress of the creator, was dimly perceived, and greatly misapprehended by Mr. Darwin. Instead of seizing the golden links of creation's chain as a means of connecting man with God, he endeavored to twist it into a fetter wherewith to bind man to the baboon. In support of a theory so opposed to all pre-existing notions, one naturally expects its author to adduce arguments. But what is the fact? In his " Origin of Species," Mr. Darwin seeks to appal us, in the beginning, by citing a number of authors whom he calls " famed," &c., and who, he thinks, favor his views. Now in matters of science, considered apart from revelation, as Darwin considers the origin of species, the opinions of a man, and his " I think " and " it is probable," are not of any avail; no, even if the man be famed for his philosophic lore, a quality we by no means concede to Mr. Darwin's authorities. Their opinions will be worth just as much as the arguments they adduce to support them, and no more. This may seem scant reverence to these gentlemen; still it is all we can afford to show them in the present case. Most of them, probably, would laugh at the idea of admitting the authority of the most learned society on earth; we claim, therefore, the privilege of scouting their dicta, unless their arguments will stand a philosophic test. This is a fair fight against our adversaries on their own ground; they will have small reason to claim the championship in pure reasoning, ere this review be ended. Claiming then, the undoubted right of rejecting the *beliefs*, *thoughts*, and *opinions* of Mr. Darwin's densely arrayed band of authors, when not supported by convincing reasons, we approach the ranks drawn out to overawe us poor mortals. Not one solitary argument do we find; not one single reason adduced; nothing but assertions more or less explicit, which show that these men had some kind of a belief, in some kind of natural process of progression, gradation, or natural selection. This grand army, then, placed as outposts to frighten persons off from Mr. Darwin's airy castle, vanishes; the bronzed armor is turned to lead; the polished weapons become wooden spears. The cited authors are like pasteboard sentinels set up to scare the boys; from afar they look fierce; their brandished swords threaten destruction; but if the urchins evince a little courage, and advance a few paces, they shout with glee to see the fierce mustachios shrink into the upper lip; the upraised sword cleave to the arm; the stern eye vacant and unmeaning. The value of the citations made by Mr. Darwin is not equal to the value of the paper whereon they are written; because they contain no arguments; they show simply what the peculiar opinion of these gentlemen was. This unsupported opinion loses weight when we reflect on the saying of Cicero—that there is no absurdity so great but what has had some philosopher for its supporter.

So much for Mr. Darwin's famed authorities. But what says the man himself? Has he any argument to evolve in support of his theory? By no means. In the introduction we are told the causes of the publication of his "abstract." He kindly requests the reader to repose confidence in his accuracy, when he does not quote authorities. He affects great candor, and a total freedom from prejudices. It may be here observed, that when once a man has thrown down the gauntlet to the Catholic church, he immediately pretends that he is altogether untrammeled by vulgar prejudices ; in short, that he, and he only, is capable of pronouncing a dispassionate judgment. Unfortunately many are deceived by this quiet assumption of impartiality; they little think that no greater slave to prejudice can be imagined than the man who loftily rejects the authority and science of ages; and who acknowledges that he sets out with the conviction that the opposite of his theory is false. In fact, such persons have already pronounced judgment in their own favor; how then, can they lay claim to impartiality? But to return: the introduction is so written as to dispose the unreflecting to consider Mr. Darwin a laborious student of nature, and a most dispassionate judge. He, thus, enlists at once the sympathies of his readers, and disposes them to believe him very learned

In his first chapter, headed "Variation under Domestication," Darwin makes to his sympathetic readers a huge display of erudition. He discourses on "changed conditions," "organism," and "reproductive system," with such an amount of self-complacency, as would lead one to suppose that he was imparting much information. But what is the fact? *He tells us nothing that we did not know long ago.* He says that descendants from the same parent stock undergo variations! that variations may be more or less! that they depend on various causes. Now it may be safely asserted that any boy, or girl either, who has come to the use of reason, is fully aware of the fact that accidental variations are verified in the descendants of organic beings; and anyone who has merely skimmed with the tips of his lips the stream of chemical lore, will not be at a loss to explain the causes of these variations. The difference of hue in the feathers of domestic fowls, from the same stock, which seems to Mr. Darwin to be almost inexplicable to common mortals, unless we suppose, " natural selection," and a law of progress be admitted—and the difference of length in the horns of cattle,—which is no doubt an *argumentum cornutum*, although the horns be too soft to inflict an injury on the luckless wight who might fall on them—are readily explained by boys learning the rudiments of chemistry. A forward young urchin would reply to the great difficulty: " nothing easier of explanation. All bodies organic and inorganic, are composed of various elements: the proportion of these elements, and their relative grouping determine the nature of the body; the slightest change of proportion, or grouping, will cause a change more or less marked in the resulting body. Now since organic bodies receive their increment partly from internal, and partly from external stratification, it follows that the nature of the soil must exert an influence on plants in determining their size and accidental properties; and the nature of the food must do the same in the case of living beings; whilst the state of the atmosphere must have an influence on both. Sow wheat in poor soil, the growth will be slight; put lime on the same land and sow the same kind of wheat, the growth will be luxuriant; because lime contains an abundance of the elements of which the stalk is composed. Color, being only an affection of the soul caused by the reflection of light from an object,—and since light is reflected this way or that, according as the particles of the object have this or that relation, it follows that the slightest change of proportion, or position of elements will effect a change of color. Hence since each domestic fowl cannot, physically speaking, be ever subject to precisely the same conditions of life, a variation of size and plumage must be the result; this variation confirms the theory of elementary proportion and grouping." Thus would the boy solve the great Darwinian difficulty. Organic chemistry fully demonstrates the truth of his solution. We are well aware that the state of the reproductive system affects the descendants; but every breath of air, every morsel of food, every excitement, or depression of spirits—in a word, each of the thousand and one changes to which finite beings are necessarily subject, has a certain influence on the reproductive system; consequently the very essence and nature of things finite must cause a slight variation in their offspring. The striking similarity often noticeable in twins arises from the *ova* having a similar chemical combination; and the dissimilarity sometimes seen is explained by a difference of chemical nature in them. The color of hair, size and such like accidental variations, present no difficulty, and argue no gradation; they necessarily follow from the theory of grouping and proportion.

Mr. Darwin thinks it a poser to explain how a person will sometimes exhibit the peculiarities, not of his parents, but of some remote ancestor. The explanation is not far to be sought. The quality is inherited, that is, handed down by the reproductive system; it is in the whole line of descendants, but is latent in many; its manifestation being impeded by a variety of circumstances, such as the presence of a greater quantity of antagonistic elements. Some remote descendant comes into existence, under a change of conditions, which lessen these elements and, at once, the quality peculiar to the far off progenitor, being unimpeded, manifests itself. Here the remark made by Dr. Johnson about Pope's " Essay on Man," might be applied to Mr. Darwin's work so far. The great critic said that in the essay, where true, there was nothing but the commonest truths, but told in such melodious numbers that persons reading the work fancied they learnt what they did not previously know ; so with Darwin's work ; it treats in such mysterious terms the most obvious and easily explained variations, that one might almost think one read something new,—something to explain which nothing short of " natural selection," " gradation," and laws of progress would suffice.

It would be a useless task to follow him through his weary pages, in the hope of lighting on a logical argument, in proof of his theory. We find many facts, useful to be known, but useless as proofs of a system to which they are antagonistic. There is greater difficulty in confuting an author who merely rambles and relates, than one who closely reasons. Hence all modern teachers of error eschew syllogistic arguments, and waywardly rove between the poles, and often beyond them, of their subject. We must, therefore, take Mr. Darwin's conclusion, place it in a mental crucible, and see if it can stand a scientific test. He thinks that all living species may be from four or five ; he even inclines, by reason of analogy, to one. Now this is the conclusion of all his labors, watchings and studies. It is mature judgment, given at a mature age, after mature consideration. It will seem rash, in one unknown to fame, to contest the soundness of such a conclusion. The serious want of Mr. Darwin's theory, like all false systems, is the want of logical sequence. Because accidental variations are verified, and because we cannot explain the reason of certain physical parts, therefore it is serenely concluded, all species are from a few, very few, perhaps one, primordial type. To most people this will seem a *non sequitur*, an illogical conclusion. Yet, if we sift Mr Darwin's evidence, and pulverize his facts, we find that he has no stronger argument than the above. It is true he does not put it into such scholastic form, for that would be the death-blow of his system; but it is diffused over pages upon pages of his work. To be just, we must say that he does not always use surface arguments; he often dives into the disordered depths of fossil stratifications. He delves in these gloomy recesses, and extracts therefrom bones of various shapes and sizes; these he fits together with great nicety of design, and produces an elephantine monster, more terrible in its grim and bony outlines, and more fraught with destruction to biblic history, than was the wooden horse to fated Ilium. Our only consolation is that the race is extinct, and has left no authenticated genealogy. Hence Mr. Darwin can only surmise as to its descent. In sober truth we have had too much disjointed writing floated down the "current of modern thought." An intellectual chaos is the outcome, and punishment of the rejection of divine faith. Instead of premises firmly established, and conclusions logically drawn, we have polished phrases, and assertions, *praetereaque nihil*.

We can guage the value of Darwinism by what we have said regarding its pretended proofs. But we will now assume an aggressive attitude. The theory of evolution necessarily supposes a natural and irresistible tendency to progress in the scale of beings According to it the rude, primordial types contained a principle of progression, a tendency to selection, and were subject to a law of development. These qualities of the original species were inherent in their nature;

the germ of future greatness was implanted, but was to be developed by slow, but sure, degrees. Now, unless the maximum of perfection has been obtained, which Mr. Darwin cannot admit, these principles of progressive development must be still at work; not only in man, but, also, in all creation. Progressive development, being a natural effect of innate causes, must be manifested, in some slight degree at least, in each generation. It would be an evident absurdity for an evolutionist to say that the action of progression was suspended for many generations, and then made a giant stride. Nature does not go by jumps, but by equal paces: hence the law of development, if it exists, must be continually in force; and a slight progression must occur in each generation. This being the case, a notable change must be effected in the course of three hundred generations. Now if we suppose seventy-five generations in a thousand years, we speak of brutes, we will have three hundred in four thousand years. The treasures of ancient Egypt, in a scientific point of view, are still extant; they are four thousand years old. From them we can learn that the bee of to-day has no appreciable difference from his antique progenitor; the donkey of our time is as stupid as was his far off ancestors: there is no essential physical difference between the domestic animals of to-day and those of four thousand years ago; yet, at least, three hundred generations have intervened. Therefore the law of progressive development must be at a standstill. Perhaps it will make a leap some fine day, and we may find apes transformed into professors of natural science. The examiners of candidates for the civil service might make the following a test question: if during a space of four thousand years, no appreciable change has taken place, either in the organism, or in the instinctive powers of gorillas, how many years must have elapsed since the progenitors of Darwin chattered unintelligibly by the source of the Niger? It is imposing a little too much on human credulity to ask it to believe in progressive development of species, when it has, likewise, to believe that an innate, necessary law of progression *has not progressed* in three hundred generations.

The above argument shows that stern, stubborn facts are against Mr. Darwin. But there is more yet. The metaphysical education of the evolutionist has been cruelly neglected. He appears to know nothing about the simple principle of life, which we proved to be distinct and diverse from the physical part of sentient beings. We proved in the preceding chapter, that there is an essential difference between the soul of man, and the vital principle of brutes. Hence the latter cannot develop into the former. Even, then, if it were admitted, which we think can never be proved, that the physical organism of an ape could develop into that of a man, the vivifying and intellectual principle of man would be wanting. We would have the body of a man, with the vital principle of an ape. When one reads the vagaries of some " modern thinkers " one is almost inclined to believe that such is the fact. It was shown that our soul is a simple and spiritual substance, created by God. In the Darwinian theory we must either say the soul is created directly by God and infused into the body, or it is not. If the former, the development of intellectual power is from the act of God who creates each successive soul with a larger grasp of intellect; if the latter, we fall into gross materialism; for a principle produced by finite agencies must be something material. In a word, Mr. Darwin is, or is not, a materialist; if he be a materialist, what he ought logically to be, he has been abundantly confuted; if not, we would ask : does the soul come from God? If it does not, it must be something material; for only matter can be the production of chemical, or any finite action. If it is from God, then the whole theory of evolution falls. The father and son must be of the same species; but they would not be, were any essential property in the soul of the one, and not in the other. Evolution is self-destructive unless it supposes materialism; if it supposes materialism it becomes the vulgar error of vulgar minds, so often refuted. Mr. Darwin must have studied to small purpose, if this is to be his only emolument.

A vast amount of useless speculation would be spared, could naturalists but determine what really constitutes a specific difference. Of this much, at least, we are certain, from principles of rational evidence, that the human soul cannot be a development, or an evolution of an inferior being. It is simple; only by creation can a simple substance come into existence. Essentially it is endowed with intellect and will; these attributes are wanting in every other visible being. Hence there is an essential difference between the soul and every other vital principle in visible creation. But the essence of things is as unchangeable as God himself; therefore such as the human soul was, essentially, five thousand years ago, such it is to-day; such it will be forever. If we only keep in view that an essential property can never be superadded to a being after its creation, we will readily perceive the fallacy of supposing things essentially different, to be the descendants of one parent stock. It will not do to assert that reason is in apes in the germ: if it were, by force of the supposed law of progression, it should manifest signs of development in two generations; especially when brought up in the society of man. But no such sign is manifested: the various tricks, or acquirements, of a well-trained baboon excite astonishment; but they are not incompatible with pure instinct. That no amount of training can effect an intellectual development in these creatures is proved from the fact, that the offspring of *highly cultivated* apes are as stupid, as were their progenitors before they were trained.

Again, substance is force; the human soul is a substance: it is, therefore, a force. The action of a force may be modified, but it can never be annihilated; it would be a contradiction of ideas. The same holds for the vital principle in brutes. Now if the force of reasoning be in brutes, its action may, indeed, be modified, but not annihilated: hence some trace of it would be discovered immediately; by training it would quickly develop. But facts are in direct contradiction with this; therefore there is no reasoning force in brutes, even in the germ. But out of what does not exist, nothing can be evolved; therefore the reasoning power of man cannot be a development of a potential faculty in brutes. Enough has been said to prove the intense stupidity of Darwinism as a philosophic theory.

The plan and order of creation, which are such puzzles to some scientists, are difficult of understanding only to those who seek to establish ones of their own. We are not to speculate as to what might have been, or could be; we are to take creation as we find it, in the concrete, with its various classes of beings. We find some which have certain properties, clearly essential; and others wanting in those properties. The inevitable conclusion is: they are sprung from different ancestors. How did these ancestors come into existence? Not of themselves, because finite; not by chance, for that means nothing; by creation; the will of God ordained them to exist, and straightway they existed. He provided means of propagation; he provided sustenance. Between the inert clod which was to be the footstool and recepticle of sentient things, and man who was to be the lord of visible creation, innumerable species of beings were to exist, in harmonious gradation. The creative act was, in itself, considered one and undivided; relatively to us it is multiform. How many centuries may have run out their sands, since first these mundane elements were created, we can never tell. From the science of geology, one might conclude that they were very many. Alluvial deposits, fossil beds, and stratified rocks which seem to have been formed by slow processes, during many ages, would appear to point to a remote antiquity. The christian scientist who defends the accuracy of the history of the world recorded in Genesis, has no difficult task. He is not obliged to consider the *days*, mentioned by Moses, as identical in duration with what we call a day. The Hebrew word translated day, means a space of time. How long, or how short that space was, the inspired writer does not say. Hence we may accord millions of years to each, without violence to the sacred text. All we are concerned about is the antiquity of man; we must believe that mankind are the descendants of Adam, the noble work of the sixth day. Those geologists and naturalists who have an itch for contradicting biblic history, must, if they wish to convict it of falsehood, prove that man has been an inhabitant of this globe for more than about six thousand years. This they cannot do. The bones of various species of animals, some of which are extinct, have been discovered in fossil beds to which great length of years have been attributed; but no trace of human remains has been found in these fossiliferous strata. Truth can never be opposed to truth; what is true in geologic science cannot subvert the truths of revelation; in fact, it tends to confirm them. When we hear trumpeted abroad some wonderful discovery of a geologist, which appears to contradict revelation; we must first see if the fact be established on sure basis, or proved from sound principles; then we are to examine what revelation really teaches on the point. If this be done we will certainly find that there is no contradiction between the truths of science and revealed ones. We know what a shout of triumph was raised by infidel philosophers, when it was supposed that geology made the world older than the years allowed it by the bible. But their triumph was short-lived: they forgot that Genesis does not tell the age of the world; it is only man's age that is recorded. Fifteen centuries ago St. Augustine silenced them on this point, as on many others; he, living in what evolutionists must consider a very benighted age, told us that the days mentioned by Moses might be taken for epochs; he said the seventh day still continues. He appears to have been nearly as learned as our scientists, who fifteen centuries later, aided, also, by their law of development, have discovered and heralded abroad the same fact. Although, then, we may allow millions of years to the past of the world, we are far from admitting all the crude theories of geologists on this score. It has been shown too often that their calculations are untrustworthy; thousands of years assigned to certain deposits, have dwindled down to a few hundreds, on further investigation. What secrets of the past may be embedded in the earth, and may, hereafter, be dug up, we cannot tell; of this much we are certain, nothing will be found to prove the antiquity of our race to be greater than that assigned it by Moses. We may observe, likewise, that he who formed Adam in his maturity, without making him pass through the stages of infancy, childhood and youth, may have made the world with the traces of a gradual growth.

In his concluding remarks Mr. Darwin glances into futurity; he evidently sees the flickering of that glory which is to form a halo round his name. Although he may be derided now, he feels serenely content that posterity will recognize his genius; he has been, clearly, born before his age; the law of development has acted too quickly in his case. He feels that his contemporaries will not emancipate themselves from their prejudices at his bidding; but his modesty suggests, as a balm, that great men are always met with contradiction. He, as well as Newton, must suffer this: but hope points to a rising generation who will listen to his voice. Now, we will also act the prophet, and peer cautiously into the uncertain future. Our glance sees the twilight of Darwin's glory; he saw its dawn; this generation saw its noon-tide; its setting is not far off. A handful of physicists, ignorant of the elements of metaphysics, and an unthinking crowd charmed by novelty of theory, and grace of style, kindled the smoky torches of his short-lived glory. The scientific world was sliding, for some time, down an inclined plane; Darwin, Huxley and Tyndall gave the last push, and plopped it into the " stagnant pool." The plash and shock were the only warnings it would heed; those who were not intellectually killed are scrambling up and returning slowly, but surely, to the firm citadel built by St. Thomas.

PART THIRD.

QUESTIONS HAVING AN INTIMATE CONNECTION WITH ONTOLOGY.

THERE are various questions, very interesting to the cultivated, which, being of a mixed nature, we have not sought to place under distinct headings, but will group them all under the above title. Some of them are merely speculative, others practical; these will be of service in this age of fluctuating systems; those will enlarge the mind, and open up vast fields for thought. A well-disciplined mind enjoys pure delights in investigating such subjects: the ill-trained intellect is a torment to itself, and a source of laughter to others, when it treats of great truths. Its vague assertions, its aimless analysis, its piteous calls for light, with something of the desperation of Aeneas calling his lost Creusa, move to smiles 'mid our tears. Of all the race of untrained thinkers German transcendentalists are the most ludicrous. Their ignorance of self-evident truths is often intense; their intellectual pride, generally, stupendous. They stoutly denounce dogmatizing, and straightway begin to "evolve" all manner of dogmatic nonsense, from their "inner consciousness;" they sneer at the credulity of those who believe well-established truths, and then swallow unutterable absurdities. From the beginning of our race until the present day, the same fearful retribution has always swiftly followed the sin of intellectual pride. Mere conceit, or foolish vanity, regarding dress and personal appearance, although ineffably silly, is not of a kind with the pride of which we speak, nor is it subjected to such dire punishments. When a created intelligence disclaims all subjection to a higher power; when it sets up its own poor light in opposition to a divinely guided guardian of revealed truth; when it throws down the gauntlet to sixty generations of christians, and proclaims itself superior to them all, it is a master-stroke of retributive justice to leave it to itself, and to its ridiculous errors. Sooner or later it will discover, as did our mother Eve, that it has not become wise, but rather that it has been sadly duped. It may not make that discovery this side of the tomb; it may not make it until, startled from its dream of wisdom by the never ceasing cry of lost souls, it, too, will swell the infernal chorus of—" we fools! we thought their lives madness and their end without honor." Yes, intellectual pride, or that unreasonable preference of one's own opinions to the decisions of a divinely instituted guide, is a fitting passport to the gloomy regions of him who thought to be like unto the Most High. It is the murky vapor which has obscured the light of many a glowing star; it is the storm-cloud which has uprooted many an oak of the forest. It is often a consequence of a deficient, or ill-regulated education: sometimes it is the effect of an indulgence of evil passions. In every case it is punished by being left to its own helplessness. In the following scientific speculations the head-lights of revelation are steadily kept in view, while the mind, illumed by these, pushes vigorously on the search after philosophic truth.

CHAPTER I.

TIME, ETERNITY, SPACE.

WE all speak about time; we complain of its tardy passage, or sigh over its quick fleeing moments. Our promises, appointments, hopes, schemes of aggrandizement or pleasure, all have reference to time. Few stop to inquire in what it consists; few seek to have any definite idea of its import. Those who speculate on its nature are often perplexed; yet its comprehension is not very difficult. If we mark the order of events we say, such or such a time passed between their transpiration. John came an hour after Joseph; Peter lived five years. In these examples the succession of events is the measure of time, whilst the events themselves are its extremes. Between the transpiration of the two events, viz: the arrival of John and that of Joseph, an hour passed, or a pendulum oscillated sixty times sixty. From this we gather that our idea of time is engendered by the succession of events. Some phenomena, being of constant recurrence, are naturally taken as measures of time. The sun appears and disappears, then appears again, and so on, day after day. This is our great division of time—day whilst we perceive the rays of the sun,—night when they are withdrawn. Were the sun to shine uninterruptedly our idea of time would be vastly modified; there would be still a succession of other events, and consequently, time, but it would not be the problem it now is. Now since time necessarily imports the idea of succession, or the acquisition of new perceptions, it follows that time can only be something relative to finite beings. Because the infinite acquires no new ideas; because he is intimately present to everything, there can be no succession for him, and, in consequence, no time. We can understand this more clearly if we reflect, that because we are of limited capacity, we cannot have immediate relations to everything, we cannot know all things. According as we come into certain relations with objects, we perceive something which we did not see before; a succession is verified, an idea of time is engendered. The intellect acquires a knowledge not had previously; it experiences a succession; comparing its present, with its previous, state, it says: there was a time when I did not know this. Now since the infinite is a simple act, knowing all, being intimately present to all, he cannot acquire new knowledge, he cannot undergo any change, hence for him there is no time. We can have a faint idea of this by observing that when we keep our minds intently fixed on one subject, for example, on some mathematical problem, we are unconscious of time, and are surprised, when roused, to perceive what a succession of movements have taken place, in the meantime, in our watch. Perhaps, what appeared to us as a moment, was what others call two hours. The more our wants are few, and our minds at rest, the shorter does time appear; the fretful or impatient sufferer imagines it much longer. From this it can be gathered that, in Heaven, the blessed have a widely different notion of time from ours.

Eternity.

THE idea of Eternity can be gained from that of time; the latter is not a part of the former; eternity does not consist of an infinite series of years. It is continual existence without succession. Time is existence with succession. Now since only the infinite is without succession, because only he is unchangeable, it follows that eternity is relative to the infinite only. If we would seek to have an idea of eternity, we must divest ourselves of our material notion of things; we must imagine God, an infinite, simple act, once, always and together knowing and willing what he knows and wills. For him there is no rising, or setting sun to form a constant recurrence of phenomena; he is ever intimately present to the sun; there is no acquisition of ideas, for he knows everything knowable; there is no longing after anything, for he is supremely happy. Unchanging, and unchangeable in essence or wish, he exists, free from the limits of space, and ever without time.

Space.

WE approach a very knarled question: what is space? is it real? what is its extent? Whilst in life our vision is shrouded; we see appearances; our judgments are formed, naturally, from the impressions received. Each one knows what is understood by distance, in the popular mind. Bodies are said to be extended, that is, to have parts outside of parts, and, consequently, to occupy a portion of space. Space itself is said to be the capacity of containing bodies. At first sight this seems quite plain and correct; we, for all practical purposes, understand sufficient by this. Poets sing of the vastness of space: geometricians cut it up, and enclose portions of it with lines of various imaginary proportions: natural philosophers enumerate extension among the essential properties of bodies. It would seem from this, that our notion of space and extension was sufficiently satisfactory. Such, indeed, it is in a practical point of view. If, however, we raise our minds to speculate on what really constitutes extension, or to find in what it finally consists, the question becomes beset with greater difficulties. We hold, and have proved, the objective reality of bodies; no amount of sophistry can impose on mankind the absurdity that only the subject *I* exists as a substance. As seen, there are innumerable substances in creation, some visible and compound, such as wood and stone; others invisible and simple, such as the human soul. The objective reality of the corporeal world is not less firmly established in the following theory regarding extension, than what it is in the popular one.

It is to be observed that our ideas of extension are entirely relative, or more properly, extension is a relative property. We say an object is ten feet in length; that is, compared with a foot rule it is ten times longer than that measure. There is no absolute standard of measurement; all that the intellect can do is to compare the proportion an object bears to some conventional unit of comparison, as perceived through the senses. Hence if we suppose that on some night, whilst all are buried in sleep, the world should diminish to the size of a pea-nut, and we and all things else should decrease in the same proportion, on awaking no one would be aware of the change. Our usual standards of weight and measure when applied to objects, would retain the same proportion as on the previous day. In reality the yard measure would be incalculably less, but relatively to surrounding objects it would be the same. Peter was six feet high yesterday; he is six feet to-day; how could we know that the foot of yesterday was greater than it is to-day? The animalcula that exist in a drop of water, if we imagine them endowed with reason, would think the passing from one extreme of that drop to the other an achievement as great, as we the walking round our world. From these considerations we can acquire a tolerably correct notion of extension; it is a relation of one finite being to another. As was observed when speaking of time, by reason of our limitation we cannot be in immediate relation with every being. Those things which are more remotely related to us, are said to be distant; by various physical contortions we change our relation to those things, and we are said to approach, or to recede. That *vacuum*, which seems to intervene between us and those distant objects, is an absence of any sensible reality. Hence space is a nothing; it is the privation of perceptible reality, just as darkness is the privation of light. From this it follows that since God is the infinite reality, being intimately present to everything, there can be, for him, no extended plains, nor lofty mountains to explore. Again; since our soul is a simple, spiritual substance, its relation to corporeal things is not to be restricted by our ideas of relation between two visible objects. When we consider the union of soul with body, we must remember that the soul belongs to one order of beings, and the body to another; consequently no contradiction can be shown in the assertion that the soul, though simple and inextended, is present, or has immediate relation with every part of the compound body. Place and extension being terms relative only to sensible objects, we must guard against applying them to simple and spiritual ones.

That extension is but a phenomenon arising from our limitation of essence, can be demonstrated with mathematical rigor. All matter is composed of simple substances, or forces: a finite object must be exhausted by a finite number of divisions. Now a simple substance, or force, is evidently without extension; it has no parts, consequently no relation of distance. The question at once arises: how can you so connect, or dispose a certain number of inextended forces, so as to produce an extended one? Evidently, no way can be found except the one, viz: you must leave a space between them. But this supposes what is to be proved, viz: that extension is real; moreover what is that space? What is between the force *A* and the force *B*? Either a reality, or nothing; if nothing, then there is no distance between them; if a reality, what is it? is it extended? if not, still no distance; if it is, then what are between the component forces of which it is constituted? We cannot, in finite things, go on *ad infinitum;* hence we must sooner or later come to a stop; what is between the ultimate particles of the last intervening body? Nothing; then it must be inextended; but if it be inextended the particles of the penultimate body, between which it is supposed to intervene, cannot be really distant from one another; hence that body is, likewise, inextended. So must the anti-penultimate, for the same reason; so must each preceding one. The whole explanation of the phenomenon of extension is contained in this; we are finite; our relation to other objects must be of various degrees; a compound substance, such as a tree, has various components; to each of these we have a different relation; we express these various relations by saying the right and left, the bottom and top, and thus form extension.

From the above reflections it can be seen that the saying of the followers of Aristotle, that the soul is all in the whole body, and all in each part of it, though ridiculed by some, is in no way absurd. In fact, it is the only reasonable explanation of physiological phenomena. God, though eminently simple, is all in the whole world, and all in each part of it, still he is inextended. The soul, being finite, cannot be thus intimately present to everything, but it can be so to a limited number of things, such as are the various parts of the body.

St. Thomas saw the dawning of the theory expounded above. His mighty intellect outran many centuries, and participated in the light and development of future ages. In (prim. prim. quest. 76, ad. 8) he proves the soul to be all in the whole body, and all in each part of it; and in (Tertia quest. 76) explaining the real presence, he feels, rather than comprehends the truth of this system. Had he the advantage of the progress made in physical science since his day, he would have left us a luminous treatise on the dynamic theory, and a satisfactory explanation of all difficulties regarding extension.

There is a harmony and connection between all truths. Although it is not the duty of the philosopher to expound revealed truths, we may observe that the true idea of extension given above, beautifully harmonizes with the Catholic dogma of the real presence. Once that we master the idea that extension is a mere relation, the difficulties drawn from the apparent contradiction of placing Christ, whole and entire, under the appearance of a small host, vanish, like the "unsubstantial pageant of a dream." Thus as science goes on, developing and progressing, instead of coming in collision with the teachings of the Church, as demented scribblers howl it must, it but serves to confirm, if that were necessary, many of her doctrines, and to reveal the inner beauty of God's holy fane. Here just one question might be asked of "modern thinkers:" how does it come to pass that Catholic philosophers and theologians, centuries ago, propounded and defended a theory regarding extension, substantially the same, as that which you must now tardily admit to be true? They were not, then, grossly contradictory in their assertions; the "subtilities of the schools," against which many of your herd sneer, are here proved to be founded in right reason.

Time and Extension are, then, the inevitable phenomena of a limited nature; a succession of perceptions causes the former; a diversity of relation the latter. Both argue a want of ulterior perfection in us; for the infinite, in whom is the plenitude of perfection, they cannot exist. The soul, being of an order superior to that of the body, must approach more nearly the attributes of God. Hence, when separated from the body, its ideas of time and extension must be wonderfully modified. It will not have to fly upward, or downward, to meet its judge. Imagine a man immured in a cave; through the chinks some straggling rays enter; from these he judges that far, far off there is great light; an earthquake hurls down his prison walls; without having to move a step he is in the glorious sunlight. So too when death has torn aside our earthy veil which permits some rays to enter, the freed soul, without motion, will be in the presence of its maker; for in Him we live and move and have our being.

CHAPTER II.

CERTITUDE.

SCIENCE necessarily begets certitude; if we have the former, we must possess the latter. Again, as shown in the beginning, our minds are capable of attaining certainty; either we must say with the sceptic that science is impossible, and then follows the curious consequence that, whilst steadfastly denying the possibility of certainty, we are strenuously upholding its existence, by reiterating that we *are certain we know nothing*: or we must admit with sane humanity that there are many things of which we are certain. As a matter of fact, then, certitude exists; there is no contradiction between a limited intelligence and certain knowledge. The human mind has an aptitude for certainty. It is idle, then, to inquire, " is science possible?" The question is as childish as this other one: is it possible for the subject *I* to exist? The very questions contain their own answers; if you ask, is science possible? you suppose it is; for you will be satisfied with either yes or no; whichever you accept you confirm the possibility, nay the existence of one cognition, at least. It is a piece of hyper-transcendental foolery to speculate on the possibility of that, of the existence of which we are, and must necessarily be certain. A question may be raised as to *how* we know; but there can be no question about the fact that we know many things. Hence although one may not be able to explain by what process the intellect acquires knowledge, still, the sceptic would gain no victory. The reasoning: "you don't know how your soul apprehends such an idea; therefore it does not apprehend it at all," would scarcely pass unquestioned by the veriest tyro in logic. From this we can judge how sad are the aberrations of human intellect, in those conceited philosophizers who maintained that no science could be had unless we had first found and proved its base. Generally each of them placed a new base, and, consequently, it would follow that nothing was known till Mr. A. placed his foundation; people, then, thought they knew something, but Mr. B. arises, digs up A's base and lays a new one, loudly asserting that nothing could have been known until his time. Thus the comedy goes on; C. springs a mine under the foundation placed by B., and begins anew. One hardly knows whether to laugh at the folly of such German base-digging, or to be angry at the amazing conceit of those philosophic fledglings who imagine that there was no science until they came to place its base. No one human intellect has a monopoly of knowledge; the mighty men of the past knew many things; the mighty men of to-day know, perhaps, more; but a still greater number of things knowable are now unknown which the mighty men of the future will know. We are certain that there is a limit to human understanding, but whether there be many, or few undiscovered truths, as yet, within that limit, we know not; of this much we are sure, the limit has not yet been reached. Perhaps it never will, in life; but under the fostering and guiding care of holy church, in the future as in the past, the human intellect will go on developing; now an Augustine, now a Thomas, now a Raphael, now a Michael-Angelo will lead his age, and make advances on future ones. Each devoted student may add one small stone, at least, to the edifice of human science.

Having discarded, as useless, all question as to the possibility of certitude, we may inquire in what does the first principle of certitude consist. Since there is certitude for the intellect, there must be a primary criterion by which the mind may know with certainty the motives which determine it to pronounce judgment, and, also, the necessary connexion of these motives with the truth. This is what we mean by the first principle of certitude. Now it is evident that that principle must be one known without demonstration, and intrinsic to each individual. Since it is the first it cannot be demonstrated by any preceding one; and since each individual mind is capable of certitude, each must have, in itself, a rule, or criterion by which it expends all motives of credibility. Unless this principle be in each mind there could never be certainty among men; if you suppose the principle to be extrinsic, before a mind can be certain, it must first determine within itself—does that motive exist? is it credible? Therefore any extrinsic principle cannot be first, for it must be judged by an interior one; hence the first principle of certitude is intrinsic to each mind.

Individual reason, or the intellect perceiving, is that principle; the intellect cannot be ignorant of its existence, neither can it be ignorant of the objective reality of its acts; therefore it is certain of the existence of certainty, inasmuch as it is certain of these. St. Thomas (de. Verit. qs. 11 art. 1 ad. 13 an.) says:

"Certitude of science arises from certainty of principles. . . . . hence it is from the light of reason divinely bestowed *within*, by which God speaks in us, not from man teaching without, that a thing is known with certainty." And (Lib. 3 cont. gent. cap. 154). "By natural light the ntellect is made certain of the things which it knows by that light." St. Augustine, writing against the sceptics of his time, turned the tables on them with a vengeance; (de Vera. Rell. cap. 39 b 73) he writes: "He who perceives himself doubting, perceives what is true, and is *certain* of that which he perceives; therefore he is certain of what is true." Perhaps the whole range of philosophy does not afford a more trenchant argument than this. It proves two things: first, scepticism is impossible; secondly, the principle of certainty is intrinsic—it is the mind perceiving.

This doctrine is widely different from that taught by rationalists. It merely asserts that reason is the rule of truth in the natural order, and a requisite in the supernatural to know the motive of faith. It maintains the dignity of reason, while it recognizes its limitation. On the other hand, rationalists pretend that nothing should be believed except what can be demonstrated by reason. If this means anything, it means that human reason is infinite, or at least, that there exists no being superior to itself. For, if a superior nature exists, it cannot be fully grasped by an inferior one; there must be in it some reality outside the reach of its inferior. This reality will be a truth which may be known, with certainty, by some other means.

Again, this doctrine is truly philosophic. It asserts that nothing is to be considered as certain except that which reason either directly perceives, or that which it knows to have a motive of certainty. If the intellect were never to pronounce judgment until it perceived the essential relations of things, or some motive for their certainty, it would never fall into error; it would invariably acquire true science. Passions, preconceived notions, intellectual pride—all conspire to lead man astray. The world spins round and hustles men along; a craze to keep ahead of all, causes many to pronounce judgment ere they have examined the case in all its bearings. Hence the crude and absurd theories that confuse men's brains. Reason is invoked as the authoress of systems which involve mutual destruction; these systems do not exist because produced by reason, but because she was absent during their incubation. Were one just recovering from a severe illness to attempt to walk far one would fall by the way, not because of one's returning health, but because it had not fully returned; so, too, when one adheres to a proposition whose truth, or whose motive of certainty, is not perceived, one falls into error, not led by reason, but rather against its dictate.

Finally this doctrine is in harmony with sound theology. Those who have the inheritance of the faith can, by its application, give a reason for the faith that is in them, viz: because it has a motive of certainty; those who are without can, by its guidance, solve these two questions: has God spoken? is he to be believed? Were individual reason to thoroughly examine these two questions, it would find an affirmative answer to each. It would, thus, be led on towards faith, and better disposed for its reception.

CHAPTER III.

RELIGION.

INTELLECTUAL perfection consists in the acquisition of truth; the perfection of the will in embracing it. Our noble faculties have been given for noble purposes. To know is the natural desire of all; to grasp sublime truths is the delight of the cultured; to follow these truths is the joy of the virtuous. The true philosopher will never sit down and idly fold his hands, saying: " I have found out all truth—nothing more remains to be investigated." The stolid arrogance of even a German transcendentalist would hardly go so far in words, whatever it might do in actions. Hence whatever else a philosopher may want, he will never lack a subject of interesting investigation. His mind can always find something whereby its powers may be developed, and its happiness increased. Of a certainty, a theme not unworthy of the consideration of the learned, is that one which, since man first was, has occupied the attention of the wisest and most noble of our race. No one, therefore, needs wonder that we proceed to consider religion in its various significations. Here is a great psychological fact, or phenomenon, viz: our whole race has ever exhibited some religious tendency; it has ever occupied itself with speculations on matters which it called supernatural. The historic fact is there; no denial or evasion is possible. From the Bible to the latest tract issued in England, every page of our history or literature, bristles with its proof. In view of this, what would a profound thinker do? Would he, like Dickens' Podsnap, dismiss the whole subject with one majestic sweep of his hand, or would he endeavor to explore its hidden springs? In good sooth he would do the latter; none but a brainless coxcomb would treat, as undeserving of notice, so grave a question. When we find the intellectual giants of our race—Moses, Solomon, Socrates, Plato, Aristotle, Cicero, St. Paul, St. Augustine, St. Thomas, Liebnitz and Newton, and a host of others, all employing their eloquent tongues, or their more eloquent pens, in treating of religion in some way or other, we can afford to disregard the sneers of our lilliputian "modern thinkers" when writing on this subject. That science which best promotes all which men most prize, honor, truth, fidelity, justice, temperance, and above all, charity, is surely worthy of the greatest mind. Even in the absurd supposition that we are but moths of an hour, ripples on a trackless deep, religion would be a subject deserving of consideration, inasmuch as it would promote social happiness. But when we reflect that our souls are immortal, that after a few struggles here an endless after-state awaits us, that science which treats of that future life becomes one of primary importance.

We here assume religion in the sense of a collection of beliefs and duties pertaining to the worship of God. It may be asked: is this connected with metaphysics? Assuredly it is, and most intimately. By metaphysics we prove the existence of a supreme being, the source and origin of all reality, the author of our existence, our supreme Lord and Master. From this idea necessarily follows the obligation on our part, of recognizing and properly honoring him from whom we depend. Reason and every right sentiment of our nature dictate this. Thus we have, at once, a natural religion which prescribes internal, external and public worship. Internal, because we must recognize and acknowledge our dependence; external, because reason dictates that God is to be honored by acts of the *man*, that is, not merely by his soul, but, also, by those outward actions which are the natural signs and sequence of internal feelings. Moreover, experience teaches that our nature is so constituted that external worship foments internal; it is the breeze playing on the ever-increasing spark. It prescribes public worship, because reason teaches that God is the author, not only of individuals, but also of a whole community which, being as it were a moral unity, has its special actions and duties and its special obligation of honoring its author. The history of individuals as well as of nations prove that thus man always thought and acted. Prejudices, want of reflection, passions, often led men to mistake the true object of worship; still, every sacrifice offered from Abel's to the latest victim to the Juggernaut, are so many proofs of the firm conviction of mankind that there exists a supreme being who is to be worshipped both privately and publicly.

CHAPTER IV.

REVELATION.

WHAT was said in the preceding chapter will hardly be questioned by anyone; still it was required for a better understanding of the present all-important subject. That the supreme being should be honored, is a self-evident proposition; no less evident is this other— he should be honored in the way most pleasing to himself. We here suppose that which was proved in the first part, viz: that God exists; that he is personal, not a vague notion, nor yet a great unknowable. He is the first force, the primary cause, not blind and unreasoning like the attraction of gravitation, but infinitely wise and omniscient. Of his own free will he created finite beings, and he rules the world by his divine Providence. It is necessary to recall these truths before entering on our subject matter. Like a beautifully disposed but intricate web, the various sciences are linked together; each thread has its peculiar use and special charm; each thread, if carefully followed through its devious ways and various connecting links, will lead to the common source. If one thread be cut, the hapless explorer becomes involved in a clewless labyrinth; it is possible that he may strike again on the right path, but the chances are a thousand to one against him. The student is charmed with the beauties of each thread, but only when it will be given him to take in the whole at a glance, will he have an idea of the sublime beauty and harmony of the sciences. He will then see them like so many shining fibres of chaste colors, neatly interwoven and harmoniously matched, forming a veil of glory through which some rays of the eternal light within penetrate and sparkle. He will then, indeed, wonder why man should have ever dared to hack and hew and rend this veil by endeavoring to make one science contradict another. We bring back to our remembrance the truths learnt in natural theology and follow them up.

Since God is our creator he is the author of our intellect; through it we learn many truths; these, we say, we know naturally. By revelation we mean a special action of God by which he makes known to us truths, by other means than natural ones. Now the question is: can God make known truths to us by other than natural means? There are some who, strange as it may appear, deny that he can. This denial is equivalent to a negation of God; for one man can make known to another his ideas; if God cannot do this much he is less than man, or in other words, he is not God. Thus rationalism is atheism under a more specious cloak. Now there are two orders of truths which may be the matter of revelation, those which could be known naturally, and those which could not. Regarding the first order no one who apprehends God as a personal being, infinitely powerful and wise, can have a moment's doubt. Since God is the source and origin of all reality he must know these truths; knowing them he can make them known; surely no one will deny to God the power which one admits every old woman to have, viz: that of making known her ideas. "Modern thinkers" will talk vaguely of the "first motor," God and "nature," but what do they mean? Either they mean a personal being, or not. If the former, then that being can make known its knowledge, and revelation will be possible. If the latter, then they are simply atheists under false colors, and are to be confuted by first proving the existence of a personal God. It is to be borne in mind that when we assert that God can make known his ideas, we do not claim more for him than each one claims for oneself. We can make known our thoughts and wishes in various ways; and shall not he whom we call infinite, be able to do as much? If so, revelation of truths which man might learn naturally is evidently possible.

But can God reveal truths which could never be known by human reason? We answer yes, most certainly. In fact, God can do it, 1st, if there be such truths; 2d, if he knows them; 3d, if to reveal them be neither contrary to his nature, nor to right reason. Now these three things are verified. That there exist truths which human reason could never of itself know is clearly seen from a consideration of the human intellect and of God. Our intellect is limited; true, it is susceptible of development. Many things which once appeared beyond the grasp of reason, are now seen to be its toys; many which are now considered as impossible of demonstration by human reason, ages hence, may be the pastime of school-boys. We cannot fix the limits of reason; we cannot say, thus far and no further can it go. But all this being admitted the stubborn fact remains that it is limited, essentially, inexorably limited. We cannot, like the greedy farmers in the time of Horace, pull up the stakes which mark our boundaries; they are part and parcel of our nature. Were the intellect unlimited it would not be susceptible of development, for the infinite is perfect. No matter, then, how much we may boast of the progress of intellect, we must admit that there is a point beyond which it cannot go. This being established let us consider the nature of God. He is the infinite, unlimited reality. Now no matter how much our mind may learn of this great reality, there will be always a something of it beyond its grasp, because, as seen, the mind is limited. This unattainable something in the essence of God will be pregnant with truths. Hence there are, for a certainty, truths which reason, of itself, can never know.

2d, God knows them; as shown before, the infinite knows everything knowable. He comprehends his own infinite reality, in which is the reason of all other realities. He knows thus his own nature and attributes, and all the works of his hand. We see piecemeal and with limitation; he beholds everything in one comprehensive glance. There is no reality unconnected with him.

3d, It is neither contrary to the nature of God, nor to right reason, for God to reveal truths beyond our comprehension. First it is not contrary to the nature of God. God is essentially good; now the characteristic of goodness is a tendency to impart to others that which itself enjoys. Hence God lavishes on his creatures so many benefits and means of enjoyment. Now all will admit that the acquisition of truth is, in this life, a great source of pleasure to rational beings. Everyone strives to know; a man of cultured intellect will despise the pleasures of the cup, will forsake the society of friends, will strain his eyes by a dim light, will abandon all to pore over books, in order to acquire more knowledge. From this it will be seen how much in harmony with God's infinite goodness is revelation. By it he increases the means of enjoyment of rational beings.

Moreover, man owes to his creator the subjection of all his faculties. Will, intellect, memory, all that we have of good is from him, and ought to pay him due homage. We must, likewise, bear in mind that to the creator appertains the right of imposing the conditions of subjection. Now in what could our intellect more fully exhibit its homage, than in believing truths it did not comprehend, solely because they were revealed? What other homage could our intellect offer? It shows no special subjection by holding as certain truths which it can of itself demonstrate.

In the second place it is not contrary to right reason. It is self-evident that revelation would add a new perfection to human intelligence. It would increase its knowledge; enlarge the horizon of its view; open up to it a vast field for reverential investigation. It is not considered contrary to reason for the parent to teach the child—for the master to instruct the scholar; neither would it be so for God to teach his creatures.

It must not be argued that revelation would be a degradation of reason, inasmuch as it requires the assent of the intellect to truths which it does not comprehend. This is the pet argument of self-styled philosophers, but it has no more weight than the glittering gossamer. When we believe revealed truths we have a motive of credibility for our belief. This motive is the certainty of God's truthfulness. We know that he knows all; we know he is truthful; if, then, he should reveal anything, we are certain it must be true. Is not this a logical and reasonable belief? The greater part of our natural cognitions does not rest on so sure a basis. We believe many things because persons whom we think worthy of credence have told us so; no one questions the reasonableness of such beliefs. Much less should any one call irrational the belief in revealed truths. We thus see that there are truths which human intelligence could never of itself grasp; that God knows these truths; and that it is neither repugnant to his nature, nor to the nature of reason to reveal them. Therefore, revelation is possible.

Whoever impugns this conclusion, or the arguments which lead up to it has either a wrong idea of God, or of human reason, or of both. If a personal God be admitted he must be infinite in essence and in knowledge; human reason is essentially limited; hence it cannot know all that God knows. But God being infinite in power can make known to man some of the truths, unknown to man but known to him. Hence the possibility of revelation. The reader will find that those who deny the possibility of revelation have a most grotesque idea of God. His name may frequently appear in their writings; they may, even, profess great reverence for him; but they will, probably, take upon themselves the task of determining what he should do, and how he should comport himself. They will make him something like the sovereign of England; he may reign, but he must not govern. And those who do this are the very ones who prate so flippantly about " modern thought" and " progress of ideas." Verily, their absurdity and impiety have not even the charm of novelty; they are but echoes from many a pagan tomb.

CHAPTER V.

NECESSITY OF REVELATION.

THE most efficacious antidote for intellectual pride is, one would suppose, a reflection on the vagaries of human genius. Notwithstanding all the gabbling of our modern half-fledged philosophers, about their incomparable genius and learning, society, in the long run, tires of their nonsense, and learns their want of value. It soon discovers that anything ingenious in their theories has been raked from out the dust of departed heathens. It finds that these birds are brilliant, but that their plumage is only painted, and, what is still more degrading, that it is stolen. They have prowled, like ghouls, around the graves of Xenophanes, Zeno, Metrodorus and other ancient writers, and evoked, by necromanic art, their long silent spirits. Confiding in the superficial knowledge of modern society, they steal largely from those tombs, and come before the world decked out in the ill-gotten costumes. For a time the fraud is unperceived, and the greatest literary rogue is the greatest hero. But time, that relentless foe to imposters, brings about their detection and overthrow. What moderately educated person when reading Tyndall's vaunted outcomes of " modern thought," and " modern progress," would suspect that he was but reviving, clumsily enough, a theory exploded centuries before the coming of Christ? Or who would imagine that Huxley unearthed his errors in the dusty corner of a library? Or that the whole army of theorizers against the teachings of christianity contains not an officer, or a soldier stamped with the seal of originality? But so it is; and so the world sooner or later finds out. Hence it is that the educated part of society, while recognizing the value of modern inventions and progress, proclaims that in intellectual power Socrates, Plato, Aristotle, Cicero and many other ancients, were immensely superior to the geniuses of our own days. This assertion cannot be impugned. If, then, these mighty minds were only stumbling and groping their way to primary truths, and often sadly wandered from the right path, we have in them a striking evidence of our intellectual imperfection. When the strong oaks are riven, there is but small chance for the escape of the beech.

Now, our object is not to depreciate human intelligence; we have already vindicated its dignity. But to understand aright the human mind it must be viewed in its historic aspect. It is but a childish egotism to look upon ourselves as anything but an infinitesimal fraction of humanity. We discuss in this place the necessity of revelation; in doing this we are not to limit our consideration to this or that man, or nation; we must contemplate our race in its entirety. Moreover, the revelation of which we are going to treat is a clearer and fuller exposition of the natural law. We have proved that revelation is possible; we now purpose proving that, viewing man in his actual state, a revelation of the natural law was morally necessary, that is, without it men would have had the greatest difficulty in learning the truths of natural religion, and in knowing their obligations. It is true that by the light of reason alone the primary truths of the natural law may be acquired; but it is equally true that few thus acquired them. Why this was so theology tells us when it demonstrates the fall of man. Cicero when considering the perversity of man, felt that some change must have been effected in him; as St. Augustine says: he "saw the effect but not the cause, for, being ignorant of the scriptures, he knew not about original sin." It is not, however, the province of the philosopher to follow up this point. He can take man such as history paints him, and show from that picture the moral necessity of revelation in the sense explained.

A dreary sight is presented to the student of the history of man before the coming of Christ. If we except the Jewish nation, what ignorance of God, the human soul, and virtue holds our race degraded! Man bowed to works of his own hand! adored an onion, as did the Egyptians; burnt incense before grotesque statues which they venerated as gods; got drunk in honor of Bacchus; offered homage to Venus by filthy impurity; exalted these and various other vices by placing them under the guardianship of some god or goddess. Often human beings were sacrificed; parents were considered justified in exposing and leaving their deformed babes to perish. Deeds, which a christian pen refuses to name, were publicly applauded. It must be borne in mind that this perversity of morals was not confined to barbarous nations; much, very much of it, existed amongst the cultured Greeks and Romans. It was truly a gloomy time—a time to which the apostle refers when he says that men were "living without hope, and without God in the world." This moral perversity was not a passing cloud on the human race; it was, or would have been, an endless night deepening in darkness as ages rolled on, without the aid of revelation. The further man receded from the days of primitive revelation in Eden, the more obscure became the moral darkness that brooded over him. Early Grecian and Roman historians have more deeds of natural virtue and heroism to relate, than their successors. Reading the history of mankind, excepting always the Jews, we note a gradual degeneracy. Horace noted it in his day, and placed on record that:

" The age of our fathers, worse than that of our grandfathers, bore us who are about to leave a still more vicious progeny."

The fine arts flourished amongst these people ; they were skilled in war, but the moral sense was blunted and festering. Of themselves they could never free themselves; for very few, indeed, would seriously turn their attention, for a length of time, to the science of morals. Moreover, they were steeped in prejudice and infamy from their childhood. Cicero (Tuscul. L. 3 N. 1) says: " As soon as we are born we are in the midst of continual wickedness, and a very great perversity of opinions, so that we seem to imbibe error with our nurse's milk. When we are returned to our parents, we are handed over to teachers, and then we become imbued with so many errors, that truth yields to falsehood, and nature itself to prejudice." This is but too true a picture of the state of the gentiles in his day. It would be morally impossible for persons under such circumstances to emancipate themselves from their worse than Egyptian darkness.

Neither could they hope for redemption from their philosophers. No school of ancient philosophy was free from gross errors. Socrates, Aristotle and the divine Plato, although intellectually far in advance of Darwin, Tyndall, or Huxley, were stumbling and groping along, but never reached the full light. Their disciples instead of emerging still more into the day, turned back and plunged hopelessly into the Erebus from which their masters had partly escaped. When we remind our readers that Plato admitted the community of wives, the exposition of infants, and drunkenness at the feasts of Bacchus, we have surely said enough to prove that philosophy among the ancients was insufficient to teach men their duties. But more than this; like our modern theorizers and constitution tinkers, the ancient philosophers disagreed on questions of religion and morality. Worse still, Cicero [Quæst. Tuscul. L. 2, N. 12] informs us that their lives were sadly out of harmony with their teachings. He writes: "How many philosophers are found whose morals, whose manner of life is such as reason demands? How many who think that their doctrine ought to be a rule of life, and not an ostentation of knowledge? how many who obey themselves and observe their own decrees? We see some eager for money, others desirous of honor, many the slaves of impurity; so that their life is wonderfully different from their teaching." Can any reasonable man suppose that a populace, steeped in debasing vices, could be brought to even that much of goodness which the philosophers professed, whilst they saw these teachers leading lives such as Cicero describes? We think not.

Now unless we admit an evident improbability, viz: that man could of himself, or by the assistance of the ancient philosophers, acquire a knowledge of many of the fundamental truths of the natural law, we must confess that, taking man such as history paints him, revelation was morally necessary, From a consideration of the social, moral and political evils of Gentile nations, even the most polished, we have a convincing proof of the insufficiency of human reason to elevate mankind, or to form a right society. We have, likewise, an additional cause of thankfulness for the philosophy of the holy scriptures.

CHAPTER VI.

MIRACLES.

WERE any proof required to convince an intelligent person that our champions of "evolution" are not philosophers, it could easily be supplied by pointing out the unscientific way in which they dispose of the accumulated beliefs and testimonies of learned and conscientious men during many centuries. A philosopher is cautious in admitting, but he is equally cautious in denying. His golden rule is to distinguish and to investigate; he may not pause to inquire into the truth, or falsehood, of nursery tales, but he will assuredly pay respect to an alleged fact which is based upon the testimony of many witnesses. Now, if there be one fact that stands out sharply defined in the religious history of man, it is the belief in supernatural events, or miracles. The Bible, every ecclesiastical history, the writings of all the great doctors of the church, the books of nearly every modern scholar, whether Catholic or Protestant, and the firm belief of christendom, all with one voice proclaim that miracles have been wrought. In the eyes of any reasonable being this ought to be enough to make anyone hesitate before condemning the possibility of such events. But our "men of progress" pay no attention to such authorities; they deem the question unworthy of consideration, and merely ridicule its defenders. In justice it must be admitted that, at times, some one of these scientists condescends to argue the matter, and endeavors to give his reasons for rejecting miracles. In such cases one of two things is surely seen; either the writer does not understand what is meant by a miracle, or he denies, by implication, the existence of God. This may appear a harsh and ungenerous judgment, still, in any case that has fallen under our observation, we can prove it to be true.

It is necessary to fully and clearly understand what is meant by a miracle, or a miraculous event. Too often persons apply the term miracle to some extraordinary natural effect, the cause of which they cannot perceive. Hence the adversaries of christianity seize upon these popular miracles, show them to be natural effects, and exult as if the impossibility of miracles were demonstrated. They forget the saying of Rousseau (Lettres de la mont.) that he who resists to the reasoning which proves the possibility of miracles from the infinite power of God, is a fit subject for Bedlam. A miracle may be defined: *an effect produced by the extraordinary intervention of the creative power in the order of things.* Hence only the creator can, of himself, perform miracles. Any change from the usual course of events brought about by mere created force, is not a miracle. Still, God may use a human being as the instrument of his power; in that case we say such a one performed a miracle, but we do not mean that he did it by reason of his natural endowments. It is self-evident that an extraordinary intervention of God can do as much as an ordinary one; but the ordinary intervention produces various results; therefore an extraordinary one can produce other results; hence miracles are possible. In this reasoning, it is taken for granted that God can intervene in an extraordinary manner, in created things. Who can deny it? If you say he was exhausted by a passing manifestation of his power, you deny his infinity; if he be inexhausted and inexhaustible, he can manifest his power anew. Again, we proved that the natural law and order of creation is from God; to each particle he gave its special power of action, and combined them all with such infinite wisdom, as to produce the wonderful harmony of creation. The framer of that law, and its preserver, is infinitely superior to the law, and can obtain from it effects which overcome the ordinary ones.

The great argument, against the possibility of miracles, is taken from the stability of the laws of nature. It may be thus stated: a miracle would be destructive of the stability and universality of the physical, chemical and vital laws of nature; it was the divine wisdom that established these laws; therefore, it is concluded, a suspension, or destruction of these laws would be an act of contradiction on the part of the creator. This is the only real argument against the abstract possibility of miracles, and it must be admitted that it presents a formidable appearance. It is founded on the wisdom of God, who is the author of the laws which miracles are supposed to destroy or suspend. We are far from despising this objection when so stated; we are equally far from shrinking from its consideration. We are convinced of two things—the stability and universality of nature's laws, and the possibility of miracles. These two may appear contradictory, but their amicable conciliation is easy. The ground is cut from under our adversaries by admitting with them that no suspension, no destruction, no contradiction of the physical laws is ever verified. When a miracle is performed these laws are not suspended, much less destroyed, they are simply *intensified*, or, in other words, the creative power sublimates them. To render this quite clear we have only to reflect that the forces of matter, the operations of which constitute the laws of nature, were impressed on the various substances by the creator; if the magnet attracts the needle, it was God who gave it that force; if oxygen and hydrogen combine to form water, it was God who gave them that adaptability. In a word, the forces of matter are from God. Now it is a constant law of nature, that the effect is proportionate to the cause. A mass of matter of a certain size will have a greater power of attraction than half the same mass. If we suppose two balls of lead, equal in every respect, except in size, the mass of one being double that of the other, it is a known fact that the disturbing power of the larger is just double that of the smaller. But if we suppose the attractive force of the smaller ball to be intensified, or sublimated, so that it becomes double what it at first was, its disturbing power will be equal to that of the larger one. An extraordinary effect is produced by the smaller ball, but it is not destructive of any natural law; it is in perfect harmony with them all. The possibility of the intensification of natural forces is easily shown. The study of electricity supplies a well-known proof. Take two magnets equal in every respect; each will hold suspended a weight equal, let us suppose, to one pound. Now wind a few feet of isolated copper wire around one of them, and attach one end to an electric battery. Cause a current to flow through the wire; on trial it will be found that the magnet, around which the wire is wound, will hold suspended a far greater weight than one pound, so long as the current flows. The other magnet is unchanged; its power of attraction remains the same. This simple example proves that the attractive force of a magnet is intensified by an electric current passing around it. No one recognizes in this a suspension, or destruction of any natural law; the effect is *unusual*, but, relatively to the producing cause, it is quite natural. It is just what the operator expected, because he knows that, if the cause be sublimated, the effect will be, not *contradictory* to the cause before its sublimation, but *superior* to it, being proportioned to the increased power. Since God is the author of created forces, and since the intensification of these forces involves no contradiction, God can intensify, or sublimate them. Surely he can do what an electric current can. Now a miracle is nothing more than an effect produced by an extraordinary intervention of the creator, intensifying and sublimating the natural forces. The possibility of this extraordinary intervention cannot be denied; it is not opposed to any divine attribute, nor to any physical law; on the contrary, it is conformable to right-reason that the infinite power can act at pleasure, when, as in the case of intensifying physical forces, no contradiction is involved. Therefore the abstract possibility of miracles is as clearly demonstrable, as any proposition of Euclid.

The above explanation of the nature of miracles may not, at first sight, appear satisfactory; still, it is substantially the same as that given by St. Thomas and all Catholic philosophers. According to them a miracle is an *effect that exceeds the order and force of created powers.* Its author must be God, either immediately, or through some created agency. There is no defect in the definition; but too often there is a defect in the explanation. Many, when defending the possibility of miracles, explain them as effects, contrary to the natural order of things, produced by the intervention of God who suspends the physical laws, or acts in opposition to them. Such an explanation is erroneous, and gives strength to our adversaries. The definition proposed by us, whilst it proclaims that only God is the first cause of miracles, recognizes the constant and universal stability of nature's laws. No suspension, or destruction of them is verified when God works a miracle; he who gave the forces sublimates them, for some reason worthy of himself; and the effect of this sublimation, or the miracle, relatively to God, is just as natural an effect, as those produced by the forces before their sublimation. Thus the power of the infinite is unchecked; his wisdom in not disturbing laws made by himself is manifested; no violence is done to natural forces, or laws; nevertheless this beautiful and sublime way of showing his glory to his creatures is left open. Truly the depths of the wisdom of God are great. Let us consider one or two examples of miracles to show how they harmonize with this idea. A person suffering from a grevious malady is suddenly restored to health. Our scientists say, "impossible; such a fact would destroy, or disturb physiological laws." We answer: by no means; such a fact is in perfect keeping with these laws. In sooth; the vital, chemical and physiological forces are operating in the sick man, but not in their normal manner. All that is required to restore him to health is to make these forces act normally. This the physician endeavors to do by giving certain drugs that have an influence on this, or that force. Now God, who gave the medicinal virtue to that drug, can act at once on the forces, and elevate them in such a manner as to restore them instantly to their normal state. A miracle is the consequence; the sick man has been restored to health in a moment. No law has been suspended or disturbed; no force has been destroyed; relatively to the producing cause the effect is natural. If there be no contradiction of physical laws, when the attractive power of the magnet is increased, by the passing round it of an electric current, there is, assuredly, no contradiction of them, when the vital forces of a sick man are sublimated by the intervention of God.

Again; here is a dead body; perhaps corruption has set

in; perhaps for four days it has been in the sepulchre, and now is fetid. The blood is congealed; the mechanism of the heart is motionless; the spirit has flown. To recall that cold, loathsome mass to life and action, might appear a contradiction to all natural laws: still it is not. It would be contrary to what usually happens; it could only be done by an infinite power, but it could be done without suspending, in the least, the laws of nature. In fact; no particle of what was in life the man, has been destroyed; as a consequence, no force has been annihilated. Every species of force that existed and operated in the living being, still exists and operates, although in a modified manner. If then, by an extraordinary intervention, the power that created these forces were to intensify and sublimate them sufficiently, each stray particle would, at once, return to its former position; the vital part that gave way, and rendered the body incapable of continuing its commerce with the soul, would be healed; the soul which had been created to vivify that body, and to remain united to it as long as its vital parts were capable of sustaining their action, would, according to the law and secondary end of its creation, resume its commerce. In keeping with metaphysical, physical and physiological laws the decomposition could be arrested; the vitiated parts restored; the mutual commerce between soul and body resumed, and Lazarus could walk forth from his gloomy sepulchre. To split the rocks, and to rend the veil of the temple, it only required that their repulsive force should be intensified, and straightway, as a necessary consequence, the rocks were riven, and the veil rent. In short, every miracle can be shown, not only not to suspend, disturb, or contradict the laws of nature, but to be produced in accordance with them. Still it can only be performed by God; for only he, by an act of will, can intensify physical forces. When a man is said to work miracles, it is always to be borne in mind that he is merely the instrument employed by God for that purpose.

The possibility of miracles being demonstrated, a question, as to the reasons why they should be performed, may arise. We do not pretend to assign motives of action to the infinite, or to know why he should at any particular time intervene in an extraordinary manner. Still, we can establish the existence of a law intimately connected with the divine government of the world; a law little heeded, when not absolutely denied, by worldlings; a law exercised under given circumstances, from the creation of man till now; a law as natural and fixed in its effects as that of gravitation. This law is the law of the extraordinary intervention of the Creator. It must not be supposed that miracles were an after-thought on the part of God. Too often they are considered as such, and people will ask: " could not God have obtained the desired end without having now to interfere?" As well may we ask: could not God have brought about vegetation by a different process to that which at present takes place? Doubtless he could; but he chose the present law of vegetation; and his law of extraordinary intervention is just as natural, in regard to him, as is that which governs the growth of plants. His infinite wisdom had before its eye, like a vast panorama, the whole order and scope of creation. In these were included, not only material things and laws, but, likewise and chiefly, intellectual beings and laws of morality. The universe was to be a vast arena made up of physical matter combined, actuated and governed by firmly established laws; and of intelligent beings endowed with freedom of will, destined for a moral end, and subject to laws superior to physical ones. It did not escape the knowledge of the infinite that man, abusing his liberty of will, would break intellectual and moral laws, and mar the harmony of creation. He saw that many would endeavor to defraud him of the intended end, and seek to erase from the human mind a belief in his existence and providence. Seeing all this, and having in more esteem the moral end of creation than its physical one, was it not a design most consonant to reason, and worthy of the Almighty, to establish, side by side with physical and intellectual laws, a law of extraordinary intervention, not suspensive of the former, nor contradictory to them; but one by which he might give undeniable proof of his providence, and promote man's moral end? He saw the fall of Adam, and its misshapen brood of evils; he saw the fierce battle that would rage between justice and wickedness, from the dawn in Eden until the twilight in Jehosaphat. Why, seeing all this, he created man such as he did, is not for us to inquire. But since he did it, and since he desires our moral rectitude, and since he is so good in himself, the law of extraordinary intervention, or of miracles, enters as fittingly into the plan of creation as does that of molecular attraction. Miracles, then, are not performed to remedy an oversight of the creator; they are not the result of a sudden determination on the part of God to interfere here below in an unusual manner; they are wrought, in accordance with a law constituted from the beginning, whenever circumstances known to the supreme wisdom warrant its exercise. If this were well borne in mind the world would hear less about " violent disturbances of nature's laws;" and less unscientific declamation against the possibility of miracles.

When are verified the conditions for an exercise of the law of miracles? We do not know; God alone who established the law, is judge of the requisite conditions. This much is certain: such a law is in harmony with all physical, intellectual and moral order; evidently possible, and, in the present state of man and things, morally necessary. Also, it is certain that miracles are wrought for the moral benefit of man, and only in confirmation of the truth. Since miracles are the work of the right hand of the Most High, they can never be performed except for some end worthy of the creator. Such an end might be the confirmation of a divinely revealed religion; the vindication of some divine attribute; or to prove that God is wonderful in his holy ones. This chapter may be concluded with what was said in the beginning: he who denies the possibility of miracles, either does not understand their nature and law, or he denies the omnipotence of God, and, by implication, his existence. We may add, that although we maintain that miracles are no suspension of natural laws, still we freely believe and grant that God could, for reasons worthy of himself, suspend or abrogate every physical law. His omnipotence can abolish what his omnipotence constituted.

CHAPTER VII.

EXISTENCE OF MIRACLES.

AS indicated in the preceding chapter, mankind has always been persuaded, not only of the abstract possibility of miracles, but, also, of their actual performance. The holy scriptures record many. It may here be observed that in the bible, the Hebrew word for miracle is *gheburoth*, and the Greek one, *dunameis*, both signifying *force;* this meaning is closely followed in the explanation given above of the nature of miracles. In every age miracles have been looked upon as a test of a divine mission; they are the outward revelations of an extraordinary intervention of the supreme power; they are the eternal seal of truth. By them Moses proved to the Egyptian king that God was with him; by them the prophets convinced a stiff-necked people that their mission was from above. When Christ proclaimed his divinity the Jews asked what signs he did to confirm it. He appealed to the works, or miracles he had performed. In later ages the belief has ever been the same; miracles performed in confirmation of a doctrine alleged to be divine, must be held as invincible proof. Hence the enemies of christianity endeavor either to show the impossibility of miracles, or failing in this, to deny their performance. With surprising coolness, or rather impudence, they maintain that no miracle has been scientifically proved:

that the general crowd is an incompetent judge of such an
event; that the miracles of scripture are fables, or inventions
of an ignorant multitude, or the work of sleight of hand.
Now a scientific writer must, in his investigations, proceed
according to well-founded canons of criticism; he must
weigh the motives of certainty adduced, and decide by the
light of evidence, not by the obscurity of prejudice. It is a
very specious argument to say, that if a miracle be performed
it is brought about according to an occult law; consequently
an uneducated multitude is incapable of deciding such a
metaphysical point. But we must distinguish the *manner* in
which a miracle is performed, from the miracle itself. The
former may be hidden, and, if you will, undiscoverable; but
the latter is a *sensible fact;* consequently, in this respect, it
occupies the same category in history as the result of a battle,
or an eruption of Vesuvius. The transparent sophism of
confounding an event with its manner of production, can
mislead no one who gives a second thought to the subject.
The old woman who sees her cabbages daily increasing in
size, can testify to the fact of their having grown, although
she may be quite ignorant of the law which governs their
growth; so, too, the old woman who beheld a miracle can
testify to the fact of its existence, whilst in total ignorance
of its law. Old women are accounted good judges of death;
if three or four pronounce life extinct we cease to hope for
the recovery of our friend; no one dreams of doubting their
decision; they have looked too often on death to be deceived.
But if they wash and enshroud that lifeless mass, and carefully smooth its pillow in the coffin, and sit by it for days
and nights, and then follow it to the tomb, and then mourn
during four long days and nights, who so demented as to
doubt the reality of the death? The fact of the death is
beyond dispute; the more fully so when we add sorrowing

relatives and sympathizing friends to the other witnesses. But if at the end of four days, this same train of mourners should wend their way to the enclosed sepulchre of their lost friend, and behold, at the call of one who wept and raised his eyes to heaven and thanked his father that he had heard him, the dead man come forth and walk and speak, would not the fact of his restoration to life be equally as certain as had been his death? Assuredly so; both events were sensible facts witnessed by several persons. Again; a certain man has been known by hundreds to have been a cripple from his birth; every day, for years, he was seen sitting by the wayside begging. In the presence of those who knew him, at the voice of a great teacher, he at once leaped up and walked. The instantaneous cure is a sensible fact, perfectly cognizable by all who have eyes; it matters not that they do not understand the law that operated it. In a word, every miracle which affects the body is a visible fact; its existence can be determined by the canons which decide on the value of human testimony.

In general, miracles are not to be hastily admitted; being unusual facts, they must be proved by evidence. We here speak of the scientific proof of miracles, apart from a divine authority which may have decided on particular ones. When a man asserts that he saw a person walking on the waters, the first thought is that he was deceived. An optical delusion, a hallucination, a wilful falsehood, each in turn is suggested as the origin of the story. So unusual is the event narrated, that we say the chances are a hundred to one against its reality, and in favor of an optical delusion. Very true; but let us consider that the chances are a hundred to one that eyes which, for years, saw aright, and faithfully transferred the impressions of visible objects, saw aright, likewise, this particular time. If the event be extraordinary, extraordinary likewise, is the visual deception. One is as improbable as the other. Now if three or four persons be added to the first witness, each of whom avers that he saw the man walking on the waters, the probability in favor of what they state is four times greater, than the probability of an optical delusion. By adding more witnesses, what was at first sight improbable, then probable, becomes morally certain. It is a moral impossibility that a number of persons could, at the same moment, without an extraordinary intervention of the creator, lose the normal use of their eyes. Since walking on the waters does not imply a metaphysical contradiction, nor even a *physical* one, because it might be brought about by intensifying the repulsive force of the water, or by sublimating its force of cohesion, and since it is morally impossible that a number of persons could fall victims to an optical vagary, the scientific man would admit that the fact was clearly established ; and, if a christian, he would add : " the finger of God is here."

If the miraculous fact were the restoration of the dead to life, the proof would be even more easy than in the first case. The reason is evident : sight, touch, and reason combine to afford an invincible proof that a person, looked upon as dead, and lying for several days in a sepulchre, must be truly dead, and incapable of resuscitation by any ordinary means or power. If they who saw the person buried, should witness him coming forth from the tomb, sight, touch, hearing, and memory would combine to identify him with the friend they knew before. No sane man could seriously pretend that all the senses of several persons, had, at the same time, and respecting the same object, become subject to a strange hallucination. This trick of all the senses would be more inexplicable and unreasonable, than the resurrection of a score of dead. Yet, to such extravagant absurdities are the adversaries of miracles driven.

From what has been said, it is abundantly evident that all which is required, in order to discern a fact, even one which partakes of the miraculous, is the normal use of the senses. These are just as acute, and as strong in the ignorant, as in the educated. Hence, regarding the existence of a sensible fact, the testimony of the former is equally as good as that of the latter. They can attest that such a one died, and was entombed for some days; then, that at the command of one who proclaimed himself Son of God, the dead man came forth. They may not be able to explain how it was effected; they may not even think it miraculous; no matter; they establish the fact. Let infidels prove that it was effected by ordinary means, or by natural power. Now, since any human being, having the use of reason, and the use of his external senses, is a competent witness for establishing the existence of a miraculous fact, in as much as it is a sensible effect, we have only to apply the criterion of historic truth, in a scientific investigation of the existence of miracles. Can any historic truth be established beyond a doubt? Certainly; then so can the existence of miracles. The primary test of historic truth is this: that a number of persons, of different states, habits, and inclinations, unanimously consent in attesting to the performance of a sensible work, of which they were eye-witnesses. This testimony increases in weight when the fact is extraordinary, such as the raising of the dead, the cure of one born blind, the feeding of thousands with five small loaves and two fishes. Such events, being unusual, make a deeper impression on the witnesses, and are more faithfully remembered. The weight is still increased when enemies who hate, even to the death, the one who is alleged to have done such things, join with friends in bearing witness to their performance. Now this test of historic truth is verified in the history of the miracles attributed to Jesus

Christ. They were performed in the presence of crowds; people brought their sick as he passed along, and by a word he cured them. His enemies, those who finally put him to death, saw and admitted these wonderful facts. Apart from the gospels, the Jewish rabbi, the Jewish historian Josephus, the pagan Celsus and a host of others, have recorded for all posterity, that the miracles of Christ were accepted as undoubted facts, by enemies of his doctrine. It is beyond our present scope to give a critical dissertation on these miracles; we only indicate the manner by which their truth may be scientifically established.

Did miracles cease with the apostolic times? This is answered in the affirmative by some. We say no, nor have they yet ceased, nor will they cease, until the angel's trumpet shall sound the hour for the accomplishment of the last great miracle—the resurrection of the dead. To omit thousands of others who wrought miracles as God's instruments, we may cite St. Francis Xavier. No historic fact is more fully established, than are his numerous miracles. If pretended scientists would only peruse attentively the process for his canonization, and the documents connected therewith, they would either have to discredit the battle of Hastings, the war of the Roses, the American Revolution, or they would have to admit the reality of his miraculous performances. Since they are not likely to do this, let more recent events be brought to their notice. We are not prone to credit every old woman's tale of wonders wrought by an extraordinary intervention of God; but are the cures effected at Lourdes to be ignored? Let a disbeliever go thither: let him examine, with the aid of all his scientific lore, each diseased one that comes up, until he has satisfied himself that he has found one really sick. Let him watch this one drinking the water, and note what follows. If the person is evidently cured, what will he say? Will he admit that the "arm of God is not yet shortened;" or will he, like the Jews of old, refuse to acknowledge the doctrine of Christ, despite the wonders witnessed.

Prophecy.

PROPHECY is a miracle in the intellectual order, just as the instantaneous healing of a sick man is one in the physical. It consists in the certain manifestation of a future event which could not be foreseen naturally. Hence, prophecy, to be real, must be made prior to the event, and be a knowledge unattainable by any natural means. To have a scientific power the event must, likewise, have come to pass. After what has been said touching miracles, little is here required. Prophecy is possible; God knows the future, both those things which are the result of natural laws, and the free actions of man. This has already been proved. He can make known that knowledge to others, as demonstrated in the chapter on Revelation. Hence prophecy is possible. This species of miracle does not suspend, or disturb any intellectual order; it is in harmony with psychological laws. By the aid of the phantasy the soul represents many things to itself. In prophecy we can imagine that the soul of the prophet has its powers sublimated, and that the phantasy is quickened and refined. The mental vision is extended,—the light of intelligence intensified,—the powers of perception become more nearly akin to what they will hereafter be, and a divinely excited phantasm of the future is presented. This is not opposed to any metaphysical principle; and it is in keeping with the mode of intellectual perception. The very fact that christianity proclaimed and defended the possibility of miracles and prophecy, a possibility now evidently established, is a strong persuasive argument of its divine origin; and what has been argued on these two points, in those pages, proves the christian philosopher to be more thoroughly versed in metaphysical, physical and intellectual laws, than the empty braggarts who arrogate to themselves all scientific knowledge.

The existence of prophecy could be critically demonstrated. The foretelling of an event is a sensible fact, of the reality of which men are competent witnesses; again, the accomplishment of the event, according to the prediction, is another sensible fact. Hence, the uneducated can attest that a holy teacher foretold that he would be put to death, and that he would rise on a certain day, and that he really did rise. The criterions of the value of human evidence can be applied to the testimony, and a scientific conclusion attained. Thus the miracles and prophecies of the christian religion, far from contradicting the truths of any science, or being incapable of critical demonstration, are, in an eminent degree, scientifically demonstrable. They do not happen at hap-hazard; they are not unskilfully tacked on to the great web of truth; they are in accordance with an eternal law, and neatly interwoven in the grand design of creation. Against them half-learned professors may declaim; against them the impious may rail and rage; against them the wavering may offer doubts. But so long as true science finds a resting place in the souls of the upright, so long will their possibility and existence be proved. It cannot be too often repeated that nowhere is to be found such illogical reasoning, and such unmitigated nonsense, as in the writings of our pretended "scientific lights." The stale and long exploded theories, the unphilosophic twaddle, the shapeless crudities, of some self-styled philosopher, are repeated, as received axioms, by a later light. Thus the putrid stream of error has flowed with unvarying monotony, from its source and origin, him who falsely promised wisdom, as the price of disobedience, to the faltering Eve.

CHAPTER VIII.

A DIVINE REVELATION HAS BEEN MADE.

THE possibility of revelation, and its moral necessity were established, but its actual existence has not yet been proved in these pages. Not only have the precepts of the moral order been more fully revealed, but many positive commands, and ineffable mysteries, have been made known to man. It is beside the scope of a work like the present, to prove the authenticity of the scriptures; we take it here for granted, for no sane critic doubts, that the books of the old and new testament are worthy of, at least, historic faith. The former were the heritage of a nation, zealously guarded, religiously preserved. One striking proof of this is, that although the contents of these books are often condemnatory of that nation, still they were treasured as something most sacred. The new testament is the complement and perfection of the old, and destined for the good of mankind. Men the most eminent for piety and learning; and men eminent for learning alone, have exhausted criticism, and invincibly proved these books worthy of all credence. The odd voice of some critical vagrant raised, now and then, against the historic value of the scriptures, has done much toward strengthening, if that were possible, the evidence in their favor. So puerile are the objections against them; so evidently impossible are the systems of

A DIVINE REVELATION HAS BEEN MADE. 243

accounting for them, that one who before had doubts of their value, would, if possessed of ordinary powers of mind, reject these doubts at once, on seeing how rotten was their foundation. Just as the ludicrous assaults and feeble barking of ill-conditioned curs, as a carriage rolls past, serve only to draw attention to its passage, so the yelps of a Strauss, or a Renan, only promote a deeper attention to, and belief in, these letters from God to man.

From the bible we learn that the Jewish nation, at all times of its history, expected a deliverer and a law-giver. Gen. 3. 15. records a promise made by God to Adam on this point; to Abraham, Isaac and Jacob the promise is renewed; all through the books of the prophets the future Redeemer is the grand theme. So general was this expectation that it was a matter of fact well known to the heathens. Suetonius (Life of Vespas) says: " an old and constant opinion prevailed in the *whole East* that, at that time, persons from Judea should rule over all." This alludes to the idea of a Messiah, who was to be a great temporal ruler, according to the notion of many of the Jews. Tacitus (Hist. lib. V. cap. 13) has almost the same words as Suetonius; and Plutarch (De Iside et Osiride) has a similar passage which will be quoted in another part of this work. From all this we gather that there was prevalent, in the east, a constant and deeply rooted expectation of one who was to elevate mankind; to rescue it from its errors and its vices, and to rule over it by well established laws. As can be shown, this expectation arose from the promise of God made to Adam, and handed down, by tradition, to posterity. Now the four gospels tell us that a great teacher appeared in Galilee, and through the country of Judea, during the reign of Tiberius. He taught by the roadside, on the mountain tops, and in the synagogues. He attacked the false teachings of the Scribes and the Pharisees;

he expounded the books of the law and the prophets; he openly proclaimed himself as sent by God, aye, as the Son of God, and equal to his Father. His doctrine was sublime; it was directly opposed to the evil passions of man; it was consistent in all its parts. Unlike the vague speculations of Greek and Roman philosophers, the teachings of Christ were clear and practical. Read by the light of his doctrine the history of mankind was no longer a riddle; his origin and his end were distinctly shown; the cause of his deep degradation was pointed out. What Cicero had dimly suspected, viz: that man had not been always so degraded, was established. We were no longer creatures of chance, the sport and mockery of licentious gods; the world was no enigma now, even to the very child. The human intellect, by the doctrine of Christ, made one vast bound in scientific and supernatural knowledge, passing the dark ways where the great mass of philosophers fell, and clearing the dimly lighted limits where Socrates, Plato and Cicero stumbled. Out into the clear noon-day of truth the human reason burst; behind it, a dark abyss of crime, folly and error; before it, a well-illuminated road of virtue and truth. Christ urged it to follow that road and not to decline to the right hand, nor to the left. Think, for a moment, how much wiser is the christian child than the pagan philosopher. For the latter, the world, man and history were unintelligible books of fate: for the former, the world is a vast creation of the Almighty—man is a free agent in his actions, but responsible to God—his history is explained by the sin in Paradise and its direful effects. It is only by such reflections as these that man can form an estimate of what he has gained, in knowledge, by the doctrines of our Saviour. Now, Christ 'proclaimed his divinity, and performed many miracles in proof of it. He cured all manner of disease, and raised the dead to life. It is not necessary to cite chapter and verse ; the new testament is filled with an account of the wonders he wrought in direct confirmation of his divine mission. His miracles were witnessed by thousands ; his enemies examined them and admitted them as such ; there was no room for fraud or deception. Lazarus had been four days in his tomb, but Christ saying : " Father, I give thee thanks that thou hast heard me. And I knew that thou hearest me always ; but because of the people who stand about have I said it ; *that they may believe that thou hast sent me,*" and then crying with a loud voice : " Lazarus come forth," the dead man, obedient to the call, came forth from his charnel vault. Friends and enemies saw the miracle ; all admitted it, though all did not believe. Now our argument is this : this miracle was evidently the work of a divine power ; Christ did it in proof of his divine mission ; if he did it of his own power, he was a divine person ; if it were done by the power of the Almighty Father, it confirmed the divine mission of Christ, for God would not work a miracle to give color to a lie. But if Christ's mission were divine, his doctrine, which he taught as being that of his heavenly father, was divine and revealed. Hence the miracles of Christ prove that a divine revelation has, in fact, been made.

The rapid spread of this doctrine throughout the world, is another proof of its divine origin. Christ chose twelve poor, uninstructed fishermen as his apostles. He commanded them to preach the same truths as he had taught them. He foretold that they would have to encounter persecution and perhaps, death, for his sake ; but still they were not to be discouraged ; he would be with them always, to the end of time, and they would succeed. Now these ignorant fishermen went forth to a world hardened in crime ; with no earthly help they assaulted the strongholds of error ; they beat down the barriers of human passion and crime. No persecutions daunted them; whip them to-day, and to-morrow they appeared as resolute as before. The powers of this world, yes, and the powers of hell combined against them. The whole earth became a great battle-field whereon the new doctrine was pitted against superstition and vice. Humanly speaking the apostles had no chance of victory, but what was the result? In a short time thousands, yes, millions of every rank and state of life embraced the new creed. Honor, riches, pleasure were gladly abandoned, and poverty and oppression were joyfully borne by the converts to Christ's faith. It was no passing emotion; the tide of revelation swept over the world with a steadily increasing wave. Nineteen centuries have well nigh run out their sands, still the tide rolls majestically onward; to-day, as in the beginning, men are found ready to shed their blood in testimony to their belief. Where is the school of philosophy that survived unchanged, its founder, or that had pupils beyond the limits of its founder's country? Outside of christianity, none. Here, then, is a great historical fact. A person appears, proclaims himself sent by God, is himself God, and in witness thereof performs stupendous miracles. He directs his disciples to continue his mission of teaching, and without the remotest possibility of success, humanly speaking, that doctrine supersedes the superstitions of the past. It endures till now; is stronger than ever. It has softened the fierceness of mankind; it has ennobled his thoughts and affections; it has formed societies and governments which are immeasurably in advance of ancient ones. The primitive belief and tradition of the human race have been verified; the regenerator came. His works, both in themselves and in their expansion and duration, invincibly prove his divine mission. God has spoken to mankind; out of the infinite depths of his knowledge we have been taught; a divine revelation has been made.

CHAPTER IX.

RELIGIOUS INDIFFERENCE.

THERE is a certain class of individuals who, wishing to prove themselves superior to the common herd, manage to make themselves supremely ridiculous. The genus *Fop* is an animal known in the scientific, as well as in the fashionable world. His antics in the latter are rather amusing than otherwise. When he jauntily trips along the street, arrayed in garments cut in the very latest style, and with every hair brushed, twisted, greased into its particular place, and a mosaic of odors hovering around his person, the bystanders feel an almost irresistible desire to laugh; and ill-mannered urchins glance wistfully from the mud to his spotless linen, as if weighing the consequences of besmearing its whiteness. Not one expression of sympathy would be elicited, were he to stumble and lightly spatter his well-fashioned apparel. The scientific Fop is not always, though he is pretty often, amusing. He would like to be thought abreast of every modern theorizer; he would wish to adopt, as his own, every doctrine that happens to be fashionable. It must be remembered that reason does not always rule the learned; much less does it rule always the imitators. Just as many persons,.in most respects sensible and shrewd, will follow some ludicrous mode of dressing, merely because *it is the fashion;* so many will adopt systems, or ideas, simply because they imagine them to be in vogue among the educated. On every side are heard the words,— "modern thought"—"progressive speculation," and "free thought." The scientific fop at once moults, so to speak, intellectually, and jabbers wildly about these high-sounding terms. It counts for little that he is an entire stranger to thought of any kind; or that he has no capacity for speculation. Even as his brother of the fashionable world shines in garments, the making of which he understands not, so he, he thinks, may shine in literary spheres by an unknown and borrowed light. But alas! for him, he glimmers only for a moment, and falls from the firmament of literature like those unsubstantial bodies, popularly known as shooting stars. If by "modern thought" be meant the ever-expanding intellectual wave, that increases with the march of centuries, every sensible man must revere it; but it is too commonly used as a taking gloss to cover a misshapen error. Again; if by "free thought" be meant that play of mind which, in considering matters not revealed, is not confined to the well-worn grooves, and which does not blindly follow a master, then that is the kind of thought developed and encouraged in great catholic seats of learning, and nowhere more than at Rome. But too often by "free thought" is understood the right of thinking what you please, be it ever so absurd in philosophy, or impious in theology. It is in this latter sense that we combat "free thought." Just as man is not at liberty, in a moral sense, to do as he pleases, so, in a moral sense, he is not at liberty to think as he pleases. There is an internal, as well as an external order; an intellectual, as well as a physical one. Each order was established by God, and he exacts from us an observance of both. Our intellect is from him, and to him it must pay homage. That homage consists in receiving, at once, what we know to be true. God is the source and origin of truth; when a known truth is rejected we injure God by closing our eyes to his light, and we injure ourselves by hindering the perfection of our intelligence. It can never be too often repeated that the power of erring argues a defect, and that the mind is elevated, not degraded, by unhesitatingly assenting to truth. It is self-evident that if it be unlawful to kill an innocent person, it must be unlawful to wish to do it. From this it is apparent, that thought is hedged round by a code of laws, which must be observed. Nothing is gained by breaking them, for an increase of error is no gain. There is a divine over-shadowing around all the works of the creator, within which all their revolvings must be confined. Within that sphere all is clear and well-ordered; beyond it are confusion and darkness. Anterior to man there are principles which claim his subjection; which limit his sphere of lawful action and thought. It is, then, a metaphysical absurdity to proclaim the mind emancipated from all law; hence liberty of thought must never be construed into a permission to accept, or reject, at pleasure, an evident truth.

If, then, in metaphysical speculations the human reason be subject to laws, how much more will it not be governed by them in revealed truths? But it is the fashion, at present, to pretend to rise superior to the " narrow-mindedness " of the past, and to profess an indifference even in religious matters. This is a certain evidence of mental decay. We know that our doughty champions of " modern progress " proclaim this as an age of intellectual vigor, ever developing and gaining strength. Scientific popinjays swell the cry, and would-be large minded individuals take up the refrain. Still we assort there is no surer sign of mental decay than religious indifference. The mind that fails to appreciate the difference between clinging to what God has revealed, and in being indifferent thereto, must be sadly out of tune. Whatever God has revealed must be true. No healthy intellect can be indifferent to any truth; hence indifference to revelation denotes a sickly intelligence. But that which is of more account is, that this indifference exposes man to imminent danger of everlasting misery. God revealed truths in order that we might believe them; he revealed his will, on many points, in order that we might obey it: to our belief and our obedience he promised eternal happiness. Revealed truths are no scientific speculations; they are not mere intellectual pastimes; they are facts pregnant with practical guidances. Being subject to God, we are bound to serve him in the way he may think most suitable. That way has been revealed; those who know this, have no choice left. No greater insult could be offered to God than to reject what he has revealed; it is giving him the lie direct. Surely no one can suppose that God can look with equal favor on the man who strives to conform his actions to the rule laid down by himself, and him who is careless whether he observes or not, this rule. Men talk about a religion of the heart, and the moral order. It would be all very well, provided no revelation had been made. In a family or school, the members, so long as no rules have been promulgated, act as they judge best; but once a disciplinary code has been published all are expected to observe it. Just so it is with mankind. Had man been created in a purely natural state, and left entirely to the light of his reason, he would have been at liberty to serve God in the manner that seemed to him most fitting. But man was constituted in a supernatural state, and a revelation was made. Apart from the moral law, engraven on every intelligence, the Almighty judged well to give other positive laws to his creatures. It is folly, then, to expect to please him, if these laws be neglected. Of course we always suppose that a person knows this revelation, or that it has been sufficiently brought under his notice. In a land like ours, everyone, we think, who has arrived at maturity, knows that for more than eighteen hundred years there has existed a vast organized society, claiming to possess the deposit of revelation. We showed that Christ did reveal; his revelations are in the church founded and guided by himself. A man knowing this must feel that he is bound to accept those truths; he cannot say, " I will receive so many and no more." These revealed truths cannot be self-destructive; consequently a doctrine which asserts one thing, if it be revealed, must exclude a belief in its opposite.

Free thought, then, in as much as it means religious indifference, is unphilosophic and dangerous. It is abundantly evident that a revelation has been made. It is our duty to learn what has been revealed, and to make it the guide of our every action. We are not to patch up a religion for ourselves, clipping a piece here, and snatching a shred there. The garment of revelation is seamless throughout; its every part is consistent. In the whole cycle of revealed truths, no one is opposed to any other, or to any real scientific conclusion. The wilful rejection of one revealed truth is an enormous offence against God; indifference to them is base ingratitude, and mental madness. The one who acts according to one's lights is blameless; but the one who through pride, passion, or worldly interest quenches the lights vouchsafed by God, and closes one's eyes to the truth, will have a hard reckoning when the accounts will be finally closed.

CHAPTER X.

HOW TO SEEK REVELATION.

IT is not enough to point out the possibility of revelation, and to prove its existence; the subject, to be complete, requires that the method of seeking it be established. Very few have the effrontery to deny, openly, the existence of revelation; but many speak slightingly of it. They endeavor to mystify the subject; to make it a sort of German transcendental medley of metaphysics, chemistry, and laws of nature, with a slight leaven about the " great unknown." The faith of the true christian is derided; incautious youths are poisoned in principle ere they can reason aright. Faith is represented to them as a superstition of the " middle ages ;" a mental slavery unbearable to a man of modern thought. Monks and old women may chatter about it, but a rationalist is superior to this weakness. Still, it may be submitted, that the greatest intellects that tower majestically heavenward from the ocean of humanity, Solomon, Augustine, St. Thomas, Newton, Milton and a host of others, were not pigmies in mind; nevertheless, for them, revelation was no childish superstition; it was the truth and will of God made known to man. But a " modern thinker," whose sole feat of intelligence consists in writing a treatise, of questionable merit, on some physical subject, loftily waves aside these great names, and compassionates their blindness. It is hard to restrain what one feels, when reflecting on the stupid obtuseness and intolerable arrogance of these charlatans of science. To see the number who give too ready an ear to the jargon would lead a believer to imagine that the day is not far distant, when, if it were possible, even the elect would be seduced. Modern infidels show cunning in their stupidity; they know that it is a vital question for them to control the education of youth. They must instil their poison before the reasoning powers are properly developed. This is their secret of success. True christians often wonder how it is that rational beings can hold, and defend the absurdities of modern infidels. They will say: "my boy of twelve could solve their foolish objections." True; but it must be borne in mind that these infidels were nursed in an atmosphere of disbelief; they inhaled a similar atmosphere at school. The truths of religion were presented to them distorted, and through a distorting medium. Their reasoning powers received, so to speak, a twist in youth, and grew awry ever after. Hence the difficulty of making them aware of their intense stupidity; they have intelligence, but their intellectual lenses have too great a proportion of common sand. The various rays are not clearly discriminated; they are blended in one inharmonious jumble. Once let the faculties be fully developed, and no bad habits contracted, and the individual will have no difficulty in perceiving the truth.

In seeking after any truth a method in keeping with the seeker, and the truth sought, must be followed. Thus abstract principles and metaphysical speculations are pursued, not by experiment, but by logical induction; physical properties are ascertained, on the contrary, by experiment, and not by pure reasoning. Now revelation is a matter of fact, depending on the free will of God. Between the truths revealed and the speculations of our mind there is no connection. Clearly, then, logical induction is not the method to be followed. When it is asserted that Jones said Brown did the deed; we do not bring our logical powers to bear on the deed in order to see how it agrees with reason; we simply seek to discover whether there be any *motives* for believing that Jones really spoke, as reported. The case of revelation is parallel. It is asserted that God revealed such a truth.

We cannot bring any experiment to bear on it; if we attempt a metaphysical disquisition on it, we will fail, because the fact depended from the free will of the Almighty. We can only look around, and see if there be any *motives* of credibility sufficient to convince the mind that God has indeed, spoken. If he has really revealed this, it must be true, no matter though it be above our comprehension. Even were it possible, which it is not, for all revealed truths to be proved by reason, how few could prove them! If revelation could only be known by scientific arguments it would benefit only an infinitesimal proportion of mankind. True christians would form a kind of spiritual aristocracy, very limited, indeed, in numbers. The poor, the blind, the halt, the infirm—all those who had not received a thorough philosophic training, would be shut out from any participation in the gospel dispensation. Evidently, even on this account, logical induction is not the method for acquiring revealed truths. First, then, there is no connection between our speculations and facts depending from the free will of God; secondly, even if there was scarcely any could ever know these facts; therefore, revelation, which is for the benefit of mankind is cognizable, like all other facts, through its motives of credibility.

These motives may be many and various. In general miracles and prophecy are the grand touch-stones of revelation. These sensible effects of a divine interposition can, as shown, be known by all. No subtile powers of reasoning are required to bear witness to a miracle. Hence once a miracle has been performed in confirmation of the divine origin of a doctrine, no one, under whose notice it is brought, is deprived of an easy means to be certain of its truth. In this way the truths and benefits of the gospel revelation are not confined to a few, which they would certainly be if logical induction were the method of ascertaining them; they are as readily made evident to the unlearned as to the man of letters. True, free will is left to man, and he may abuse that precious gift; he may turn aside from the light of evidence and, like the Pharisees, though admitting the miracles of Christ, may refuse to bow to his doctrine. It is a strange contradiction, yet, one often meets it in a life-time. Now it is certain that the doctrine taught by Christ was confirmed by stupendous miracles, and, also, by prophecy. Hence that doctrine is divine. This is a simple and effective argument. No sophism can escape from its inexorable logic; no ordinary intelligence is incapable of grasping its force. It stands out before all, resplendent in the light of its own evidence. If you refuse belief in the miracles of Christ, you may as well burn every book of history from Herodotus to Lingard. Not one historic fact has such an overwhelming flood of light cast on it by history, as has each miracle of Christ, recorded by witnesses, whose simple truthfulness breathes in their writings, as evidently as it glows in their martyred blood. Starting, then, from this firm basis that Christ's doctrine is proved divine from his miracles, the seeker after truth may proceed another step. He may say: " can I find, in later years, a doctrine in favor of whose truth miracles were wrought? If I can, then that doctrine is identical with the one taught by Christ." We would merely point out to such a one the well-proved miracles of St. Francis Xavier, the Jesuit apostle of India. Let him peruse attentively the process for his canonization, and he will find his miracles as well attested as any historic fact can be. The inevitable conclusion would be,—his doctrine, his faith, were the same as those preached by Christ.

Again; unity combined with perpetuity is an attribute of truth. It is commonly said that a lie has a halt in its gait; sooner or later, it is detected by this peculiarity. A system which contradicts itself, even once, is not divine in its origin. It may have some, perhaps many, divine principles in its composition, but allied to these there is something human. A heaven-born system is ever in harmony with itself; in all its essential characteristics it is as unchangeable as its author. Length of time does not decrease its vigor; the attacks of the powers of hell, and persecutions by worldly princes do not dim its light, or make it foreswear its principles. Its sails are never trimmed to suit the shifting breezes of popular favor; its flag is never lowered at the bidding of a tyrant. Fearlessly it proclaims its mission, regardless alike of the threats of its enemies, and the dangers that human fear apprehends. As the hour-glass of centuries runs dry, its unity remains unbroken, and its youthful fire unquenched. It bred martyrs in the beginning, and it breeds them now; it animated many to renounce, for Christ, everything the senses hold dear, and it animates many to do the same now. In harmony with the development of the human intellect, and the discoveries of science, it unfolds more fully, and defines more sharply, its principles. Ever capable of satisfying the wants of man, in every stage of mental culture, and in every degree of social life, its language is modified while its principles remain unchanged. Like the delicate rosebud that, under the gentle warmth of the sun, unfolds gradually its leaves in unison with the approach of summer, until it glints, full-blown, in the dew of a midsummer morning, so this heaven-born system, breathed upon by the spirit of truth, expands and develops as the activity of the human mind is increased, until it will finally stand confessed in all its supernatural beauty, in the " fullness of the age of Christ." Who finds this system finds peace.

CHAPTER XI.

FAITH AND REASON.

HE who attentively notes how prejudice distorts the mental vision, acquires a great insight of human character. He will find how quickly and grossly an individual will contradict himself, and how serenely unconscious he will be of the fact. He will observe that a man will rail against faith to-day, and to-morrow will dogmatize with exceeding fierceness; woe betide the hapless wight that dares oppose his conclusion. In short, as a general rule, man's mode of action is a strange jumble of contradictions, enlivened by his ludicrous belief in his own consistency. In this respect, pretended scientists afford the keen observer of men and things, a greater amount of quiet enjoyment than any other class of individuals. The most credulous of men themselves, for they blindly follow some blind leader, they sneer at the faith of christians; the most ignorant of scholars, for they never dive below the surface of any science, they laugh at what they are pleased to term the "ignorance of the school-man." Could they but for one short moment realize the absurdity of their writings, some hope of their reformation might be entertained. But this they cannot do, although any ordinary catholic college has, in its class of philosophy, no boy incapable of convicting them of gross ignorance. Does this language appear too strong? Only to those who have paid little attention to their writings will it appear so. Few people are aware of the easy manner in which many acquire fame. Our age is restless, and men's minds are restless too. Those who are cut adrift from the faith worry their intellect with unceasing speculation. Rarely adopting a correct principle ; rarely acquiring a metaphysical truth, it is no wonder that their minds are unquiet. This intellectual unrest breeds a craving for novelties ; hence as soon as any new theory is propounded it is eagerly seized upon by these starving intellects. It pleases for the moment ; its propounder is hailed as a genius of gigantic dimensions. Scribblers for the press, not wishing to be thought retrogrades, trumpet abroad the praises of the scientific star. Perhaps not twenty men have read the work which thousands praise. It requires great moral courage for a critic to come forward and to dispassionately review the work of such an author. But if one should " screw up his courage to the sticking point," he can easily tumble the airy castle of fame around the ears of the enthroned hero. It appears incomprehensible how any man, possessed of average talent, could look upon Stuart Mill as a great metaphysician, or Tyndall, Darwin, and Huxley as anything more than clever physicists. It is as if the human intellect were oppressed by a hideous nightmare, when we see men disregarding the heaped up testimony of generations, the clear light of ages, and the very instincts of our nature, to follow the glow-worm light of a few illogical theorizers.

Rationalists are never tired of repeating the stale falsehood that faith enslaves reason. In this they are either ignorant of the nature of faith, or they are malicious. If the first, they should peruse attentively an explanation of faith ; if the second, they are outside the lists of honorable controversy. What is faith? It is a firm assent given to a revealed truth on account of the authority of God who has revealed it. There are two ways distinct in principle and object of acquiring knowledge; in the one we acquire it by the natural power of reason; in the other, by divine faith. They differ in object because, by faith, there are proposed to our belief mysteries which could never be known to us through reason alone. Our soul is endowed with the faculty of reason by which it acquires a knowledge limited, and at times, uncertain, of natural facts and phenomena. In the process of reasoning from cause to effect, and from effect to cause, we are liable to err; consequently our deductions are not always true. Moreover, to draw a conclusion we must have a principle which is either admitted, or which can be proved. Hence, since reason, of itself, is unable to know the intimate nature of things, it follows that it cannot, of itself, know scientifically the effects that depend thereon. On this account we are unable to show *how* the soul acts on the body, and the body on the soul. We know, and can prove that there is a reciprocal action, but *how* it is, is to us unknown. How much more, then, in the supernatural order will our reason be at a loss? But there is a being from whom nothing is hidden—there is a wisdom that knows no limits—there is a truth absolute, eternal, unfailing. If now that being should deign to speak to us some hidden words; if it should reveal some mysteries of the supernatural order; if it should make known to us something of that unexplored country to which the passage is through the tomb, our mind which longs after truth, and which is perfected by its acquisition, would be ennobled and made more like to its first principle. Now this has been done in revelation; and it is that firm assent to revealed truths, on account of the authority of God who has revealed them, which is called faith. Since God is truth eternal, absolute, necessary, that which he reveals must be true to-day, to-morrow, forever. Faith in the soul is, as it were, the image of God imprinted on the intellect of man; and since God is one, faith, his image, can be but one. Moreover, since God is the author of reason as of faith, it follows that right reason can never be at variance with faith, for truth cannot contradict truth. The object of the reason is truth; the object of faith is truth; but between reason and faith there is this difference, that may err, this cannot. Ignorance may darken the intellect; passions may corrupt the heart; self-interest may bias our judgment; hence our conclusions, from reason, are often erroneous. In the teachings of faith this cannot happen; once we know a thing has been revealed we are certain of its absolute truth. Whenever, therefore, a conclusion from reason, or science is found to be opposed to revealed truth, we may be certain that an error has been committed in our train of deduction, and that it can be detected by our own, or by some superior intellect. Faith makes known this error, even as a teacher points out the blunder in an intricate calculation which the scholar was unable to discover after hours of patient search. Let this point be well understood. We accept every demonstrated conclusion of any science; we are certain they can never clash with revelation; but we are not going to receive as axioms, nor even as probable conclusions, the crude and illogical deductions of any man, or body of men. If the dogmas of faith be viewed in the sense in which they are understood by our church, they will never be at variance with the logical outcomes of any science. The apparent contradiction arises either from a misunderstanding of revelation, or from some hasty conclusion from false premises. As an example of the former, take the cry raised against the truth of Genesis, when geologists proved that our earth could not have been formed in six of our days, but that it passed through stages, or epochs of great duration. A shout of victory went up from infidels; they thought they had caught Moses napping. Their exultation only showed their ignorance of the sense of revelation; our church never taught that the days of creation were to be understood as of the same length as a natural day. St. Augustine had expressly taught that these days could be taken for *epochs;* and to prove his assertion he added, that the *seventh day still endures.* Hence it turned out that the infidels, not Moses, had been under the influence of the drowsy god. The examples of hasty and false conclusions are innumerable. Alluvial deposits said to be many thousand of years in process of formation, turned out to be able to boast of only two hundred years of existence. Skulls found in caves, and asserted to be at least ten thousand years old, were proved to have been the head-pieces of some dashing Gauls in the time of Julius Cæsar. Perverse human ingenuity has set out with the fixed purpose of disproving revelation; being thus blinded by prejudice it eagerly seizes on anything which appears in contradiction with God's word. Without examination, without scientific demonstration it launches forth a wild conclusion, and claims a victory. But its dream of success soon has a rude awaking. Some cool, logical, unimpassioned devotee of science takes up the question, and roughly shakes the baseless theory. Thus will it ever happen, for the truth of God will stand all tests.

Just now a strange paragraph is going the rounds of the newspapers. It is said a German professor has, by the aid of electricity, composed an egg, and artificially hatched therefrom a bird. This may astound some, and delight others. If it be true, materialists will, in all probability, hail it as a confirmation of their crazy theory. "Here," they may say, "is life produced from, and by material." Not so fast with your conclusion. Recall what was said in the chapter on Life, written months before the writer heard of this German egg. We said that in sentient beings the vital principle was simple, and created by God; but the law of production was, whenever by the usual process, or by the chemical action of light, heat, or electricity, a certain disposition and grouping of material particles were brought about, the vital principle was infused. This explains the production of worms in corrupting meat, or cheese; and, also, that of minute insects from some metallic salts when subjected to the influence of electricity. The light and heat acting on the meat, or cheese, disarrange the former grouping of particles, and a new disposition is the result; the conditions for the operating of the law of life becomes verified; the creator supplies the vital principle. In the same way electricity verifies the conditions for the law of life by its actions on the silicate. These chemical agents are not the authors of life; they are secondary causes which prepare the conditions necessary before God gives effect to the law of life. Before materialists can bring their case into court, they must prove that the *vital principle* is produced by natural means. This they can never do. We can always prove a sentient principle to be a simple substance; such a substance can only arise by creation. If this story about the artificially produced egg be true, it will prove the professor to be an ingenious and patient student of nature; he will be entitled to a niche in the temple of fame; but it will not affect revelation. We are well aware that all the component parts of an egg are in matter, round about us. An exact analysis of an egg would reveal the nature and grouping of its parts; we can discover no impossibility in bringing about this disposition by chemical agency. In fact, it is always brought about in this way. Skill, patience, and care would be required for a man to assimilate and group the parts, but we cannot see an impossibility of success. If he should succeed, what follows? Simply that he has brought into play on matter a secretive power, similar to the one at work in the animal economy of a bird. The bird is not the creator of the vital principle that animates the young chick; its action is limited to a secretion of material parts which, under the process of incubation, assume a disposition suitable for animation. This is just what has been done by the electric current, so neatly manipulated by the German professor. We say this in the supposition of the truth of the story. Perhaps it is only an egg from a mare's nest. Even so, we say again we can see no impossibility in such a thing being done: and if it were done, it would not clash with revelation. The words of Moses, when speaking of the creation of the lower animals, seem to imply that secondary causes, probably heat and electricity, acting on the water, and on the land, prepared the bodies of fishes, birds, and beasts, into which God infused the principle of life. Thus it would hold good that the water and land *produced* them, and that God *created* them according to their species.

Although the christian intellect bows to faith, its assent is not a blind motion; it is a most reasonable act. Supernatural faith is not born of a scientific demonstration; it is a gift from on high; still, the assent given to revealed truths is in accordance with reason. It is a reasonable act to believe that for the truth of which we have ample evidence; but we have ample evidence of the truth of revelation, viz: the authority of God who has revealed it; therefore our assent to it is reasonable. Right reason can demonstrate the foundations of revelation; it can expend the motives of credibility; it can prove, from miracles and prophecy, that such a doctrine is divine; finally it can prove that a divine doctrine is absolutely and eternally true. It matters not that the truth in question be a mystery, beyond the comprehension of the human intellect. Reason can show that God has revealed it; that is enough to give us an invincible motive of certainty in its regard. It may be said; but if the reason does not comprehend a truth, can its assent thereto be reasonable? Assuredly it can; how many persons can comprehend why a stone falls to the ground? why friction produces heat? why water bubbles when boiling? Every one knows and believes these things, and their belief is never called irrational; simply because they have sufficient evidence to know the *fact*, although they know not its cause, or rather its *how*. If, then, we can prove that God has revealed the mystery of the Holy Trinity, our belief in that truth is most reasonable, although we do not comprehend its *how*. It is strange that so evident a vindication of the reasonableness of our faith does not occur to rationalists. Naturally there are two ways of acquiring truth, by evidence and by authority. We are daily called upon to believe facts of which we have no evidence direct; we have the authority of some man, or body of men. A poor unlearned hewer of wood who would say, "I do not believe that the angles at the base of an isosceles triangle are equal to one another, because I do not comprehend it," would not be praised as reasonable in his disbelief; he would, probably, be called an idiot. All authority is against him; he stands alone; a thousand on one side,—zero on the other. Just in the same way the man why says, "I do not believe such a mystery, because I do not comprehend it," should be classed. The authority of God who has revealed it, is against him; it is more than a thousand against zero. A man to whom the gospel revelation has never been sufficiently proposed, may doubt that it is the word of God; but once that you prove to him that Christ was a divine person, which can be done from his miracles and prophecies, he can no longer doubt his doctrine, unless he wishes to be numbered among the insane. Thus it is that those who boast most about their rationality are, when cornered up, the greatest murderers of reason. They force their intelligence to become a suicide, by using it to deny truths which are surrounded by a halo of evidence.

Reason is not cramped, or enslaved by faith; on the contrary, its flight is extended, its base of operations enlarged, and its freedom made more secure. Consent to error is a slavery from which faith protects reason; each is a help to the other; and the ideal of intellectual perfection in life, is realized when sound reason, enlightened by faith, cultivates soberly and piously the science of divine things. Faith is *above* reason, but not *opposed* to it; it is above it, because what it makes known is more sublime, and it is absolutely certain; it is not opposed to reason, because the object of both is truth. They walk the same road, but when reason, on account of its limitation and its defects, begins to fail, faith raises it up, and tenderly carries it along a path which it, indeed, sees, but whose windings it knows not. It is as when a father lifts up and carries his child that can proceed no further; the child sees the road, and trees, and houses, but knows them not, for never before had it been by that way; it is pleased with the fair prospect, although it understands but in part the explanation of its father. The teachings of faith being absolutely true, it follows that it must be intolerant of error. Intolerance of error is, essentially, an attribute of truth. The enemies of the catholic church upbraid her with intolerance of doctrinal differences. This is an involuntary homage to her never failing truth. Were she a mere human institution, she would have accepted, at some time in her long career, a compromise of doctrine to save her from the many fierce attacks which she has endured.

But no; she changes not; she is as intolerant of a doctrinal difference to-day as what she was when St. Paul (Gal. 1-8) wrote: "But though we, or an angel from heaven, preach a gospel to you beside that which we have preached to you, let him be anathema;" or when St. John (2 Ep. 1-10) said: "if any man come to you, and bring not this doctrine, receive him not into the house, nor say to him, God save you." Being absolutely certain of the truth of her doctrine, because it was revealed by God, she must be absolutely certain of the falsity of anything which contradicts it. It is only when there is a possibility of one's being in error, that one can admit the possibility of the truth of the opposite. But in the teachings of faith there is no possibility of error—for God cannot err—hence true faith can never hesitate; it rejects with horror that which is contradictory to it. However, although faith must hate error, it does not hate the erring. In this lies our vindication; we hate doctrinal error because it is an insult to God; we love the erring, because in them we recognize fellow creatures, made to the image of God and redeemed by the blood of the Saviour. Were these points properly understood we would hear less about "cramping reason," and "intolerance."

Another difference between faith and reason is the perfectability of the latter and the unchangeability of the former. Reason can be trained and rendered more expeditious in its operations; being finite, yet having a great latent capacity, it can be wonderfully developed. So can all its inventions. The first attempts at telegraphy in France, more than one hundred years ago, were clumsy and imperfect. See now to what a high state of perfection it has advanced. Thus it was with the beginning of every human art. But the doctrine of faith has not been proposed as a speculation of the mind, which can be perfected; it is a divine deposit, perfect already, because it is the work of a God. It can have no essential development; its meaning and scope may be more fully explained, and its terminology more sharply defined; but its sense and essence are always one and the same. God knew when revealing it all the changes which would be wrought by steam and electricity; he was as wise then as now. He revealed then what he would to-day, or centuries hence, for he revealed what was eternally true. The sense of his revelation is never modified or affected by the development of human science. Let all sciences progress; let them use their own methods in their own spheres; but let them keep within their proper limits, and accept only logical conclusions from true premises. If this were done, all their advancement would only tend to throw additional light, if that were possible, on the teachings of faith. Centuries ago the doctors of the catholic church called reason the "preamble of faith;" centuries ago that church solemnly asserted that "truth cannot contradict truth." In our own day the Vatican Council said, that the church, "far from throwing obstacles in the way of the cultivation of human arts and sciences, rather assists and promotes their cultivation in various ways." We accept every proved conclusion of every science, and every revealed truth, with an absolute certainty that between them there is no contradiction, no collision, no repugnance.

CHAPTER XII.

FAITH IN ITS RELATIONS TO THE BODY POLITIC.

CIVIL society is the result of man's social tendencies. God did not intend man to be a rude and untamed creature; he did not create him in a state of savagery; nor did he implant in him a warlike feeling against his kind. He gave him a nature nobler, far, than that of any other visible creature, yet a nature more helpless, in its early stages, than is that of the vilest insect. Both its nobility, and its helplessness in infancy, evidently prove that man was not intended to lead a nomadic life, but that civil society entered into the scheme of creation, as a natural outcome of man's requirements, and his social qualities. Evidently domestic society, of, at least, many years duration, is necessary for the preservation of the human race. The young of birds and beasts can soon fly, or run as swiftly as their dams; but not so with the infant. Months of tender nursing must be followed by years of watchful care, before a human being can, of itself, procure its livelihood. It requires no length of argument to show that the Creator never intended all the anxiety, care, and labor of providing for the wants of the child, to devolve on the mother. Father and mother were to share the task; but to do this properly a domestic society is required. But not alone during infancy has man many wants; in his mature years his requirements are numerous, and his capacity to supply all is often inadequate. He may grow his corn and thresh it too; he may pasture his sheep, and secure their wool; he may feed his oxen, slay them, and procure their hides; but can he grind his corn, bake his bread, spin and weave his wool, tan and make his ox hides into shoes? Whilst he would be engaged in these, and fifty other necessary offices, the seed time would pass, and his land would lie untilled. To supply more effectually his wants, and to satisfy, likewise, his craving for intercourse with kindred spirits, man would naturally seek to form a society in which a division of labor, mutually advantageous, might be effected. Thus, by a disposition of divine providence, civil society arises; in it, if properly constituted, man can perfect his noble faculties, and acquire a large share of temporal happiness. Now no society can exist without an authority which will render its members secure in the enjoyment of their rights. Consequently since God wishes civil society, and since the essence of civil society requires authority, God must wish such authority to exist. As often, then, as a multitude of men form a civil society, there is in that society, independent of the will of men, by divine ordination, a civil power which is to provide for the temporal good of the whole community. "All power is from God:" he alone is the source and origin of all legislative power, just as he alone is the source and origin of all being. The subject in which that power resides may be one person, or many persons so united as to form, morally speaking, one subject. Hence there are various forms of legitimate authority, such as monarchy, aristocracy, democratic and mixed forms; still, the power is in each case the same, although the form under which it is exercised be manifold. A great deal has been said about the "divine right of kings," and much nonsense has been let loose on the current of literature, through an ignorance of the proper sense of these words. We know that certain persons were specially selected by God to rule certain states; but the civil power which they exercised was identical, in origin and essence, with that exercised by any other king, or president. The meaning, then, of the "divine right" of kings is, that the civil power exercised by the supreme civil and legitimate authority of the land, be it king, president, or assembly, is from God. Legitimate civil power is *always* from God; the subject in which that power resides is *sometimes*, but not *always*, specially chosen by the Almighty. Queen Victoria wields a power which is from God, yet we do not say that God specially selected her to rule; President Grant, though chosen by the voice of the people, wields a power which is from God. Presidents have a "divine right" in the same sense as have kings, that is, that their power is from God. It is wild to talk about a "power from the people;" the people may determine the subject in which the power is to reside, but they cannot give the power. "No one can give what he has not got," is a trite axiom; but no man has the right, of himself, of governing others, nor of prescribing civil laws for himself; therefore he cannot give any such power to another. Only God has the right of governing all; hence only he can give to an earthly ruler that power. A distinction must be made between *conferring* power, and *determining* its organ. Only God can do the former; in certain cases the people can do the latter. In short, only God has power, of himself, to rule; he wished civil society, and, as a consequence, wished a power to be in it; sometimes he determined directly the subject of that power; more often the subject was determined by some human fact. In every case the legitimate subject, howsoever determined, exercises a power which is from God.

A pre-existing right often determined the organ of civil

power. A father, settling in some hitherto uninhabited country, takes possession of a tract of land; he gives a part of this to each of his sons, but imposes certain conditions for the peace and well-being of the community. His prior right of possession determines him as the organ of power. His son who succeeds to his estate, succeeds, likewise, to the rights inherent to the property, and becomes in his turn a lawgiver. He is the instrument divine providence uses to provide for the social good of that society; the power which resides in him is divine, being from God, while the fact which determines him as the organ thereof is human. Again, suppose many persons occupying simultaneously certain tracts of a new country, and drawn together by social tendencies, and for their mutual welfare. An authority is necessary to decide the disputes which may arise, and to protect each one in his rights. Since, however, no one has a pre-existing right, the members of the community agree to choose by vote a ruler. The ruler thus elected becomes the organ of a divine power, whilst the fact by which he was determined is human. The vote did not *create* the power or right of making laws; it merely determined the one who was to be the subject of a power given by God, for the good of that society.

The supreme civil ruler of a state (of course we always mean if he be legitimate) is, then, a delegate of God for the temporal good of man. Hence the honor ever shown by the greatest and best of mankind to kings and princes. It is not the purple garment, nor the golden sceptre, nor the crown of jewels, that inspires a feeling of awe and reverence in a well-balanced mind, when in the presence of royalty; it is the recognition of the prince's sublime office of vice-gerent, in temporal things, of the Almighty. Disrespect for the organ of the civil power increases in a direct ratio to the decrease of religious feeling. Contempt for legitimate authority is a pretty sure index of a shipwrecked faith. Every firm supporter of the king, or president, may not be a religious man; but every despiser of their office may be safely classed with the irreligious. But if civil rulers have such an important office, it is self-evident that their responsibilities are very great. Power has not been conferred upon them for their personal advantage; it has been given for the good of their subjects. They should be a reflection on earth of what God is in heaven; the vindicator of the wronged; the dispenser of justice; the avenger of crimes. They should be the fathers, not the oppressors, of their people. They stand on a giddy height, and weak human nature may easily lose its balance. Pride, ambition, anger,—all the evil passions of our nature will rise up within them, to work, if possible, their ruin. Their position is fraught with danger, still they can triumph. On almost every throne of Europe great, wise, and just kings have sat; monsters of vice have afterwards occupied the same thrones; at the last day the former will bear witness to God's justice in condemning these who could have been better. Now since a king is the vice-gerent of the Almighty, in temporal things, it follows that if he grossly misuse his power he may forfeit his right to rule. We do not undertake to specify the crimes which might bring about a forfeiture of right; but it is evident that God does not give power unconditionally to man; consequently, there must be actions which incur a deprivation of power. Now the question arises: is there any tribunal on earth competent to decide when, if ever, a king forfeits his right to rule? We who believe in Bible revelation know that God stripped various kings of their royal powers on account of their bad actions. By the preaching of Christ both the civil and religious order of things were modified. Previous to Christ God interfered more directly in temporal and spiritual matters than what he afterwards did. Christ withdrew from the province of kings spiritual matters, and placed them under the guardianship of his church. Cæsar had what belonged to him, and the church had her rights assigned. The latter was to represent Christ to the end of time; it was to take up and continue his mission of teacher, guide, and judge. The old law received its complement and perfection when the new one was promulgated. God was henceforth to reign on earth in and through his spiritual kingdom. The power of Cæsar was left intact in temporal concerns, but all spiritual jurisdiction passed away from him forever. A new revelation was made; a new dispensation was preached; a new order of things began its course. When human society was thus radically renovated and changed by the Saviour, can we suppose that he left aught incomplete? Surely not; he came to provide our eternal good in an effectual manner; and, also, to inaugurate an era of justice and peace. But if we assume that there is no tribunal to pronounce on the conduct of kings, not only in their spiritual actions, for every christian must admit such a tribunal in the church, but, likewise, in their official duties, could we say that everything was complete? Would the temporal happiness of society be sufficiently safeguarded? By no means; it is clear that kings may grossly misuse their power; they may become pests and scourges of kingdoms, instead of being their joy and comfort. There must be a tribunal on earth before which they can be summoned; and which can judge their conduct. That tribunal must be one invested with divine prerogatives, for it has to try the organ of a divine power. It cannot be the subjects of the king, for they are one of the party to the suit, and it would be a mockery of justice to make a man judge in his own cause. It cannot be other kings, for each is independent in his own state; and no one of them has jurisdiction over the other. It can only be that divinely instituted society which was appointed supreme judge on earth, of all morality. We know that this conclusion will be scouted by state-worshippers; but the reasoning cannot be gainsaid. Reduced to a nutshell it may be thus stated: kings have their power from God subject to conditions; for the good of society there must be a judge to decide when these conditions have been violated; such a judge must have spiritual jurisdiction, because he has to pronounce on a question of morality; now the church is the supreme spiritual power on earth; therefore the church is the judge who is to declare when a king has forfeited his right to rule. Representative of Christ, who has supreme spiritual and temporal power, the church has a divine mission to fulfil. The eternal laws of justice and truth, together with the deposit of revelation, have been placed under her guardianship. To guard them effectually she must have power to judge *when* and *how* they are violated; otherwise God would have appointed a blind sentinel. It is by a violation of the things encharged to her vigilance, that the conditions, under which kings hold power, are transgressed. Consequently she is competent to judge the transgression. It seems strange that anyone believing in the divine mission of the church could doubt this. Protestants may not agree with Catholics as to which is the true church; but Protestants must surely agree with Catholics that the true church has supreme spiritual power; if it has this, it must have the power of declaring a forfeiture of right to rule incurred by a sovereign.

The existence of such a tribunal does not import a curtailment of the due action of the state. The civil ruler can only become amenable to this tribunal by the commission of flagrant outrages, which violate, at the same time, the eternal laws of justice, morality, and revelation, and the rights of his subjects. He has no right to do this; consequently liberty, in its proper sense, is not restricted by coercing his evil actions. Persons imbued with a hatred of christianity wildly declaim against this idea; they rave and tear their hair and shout all manner of blasphemies. But vapid declamation, and angry railing are not arguments; they only serve, like foam on a rock-broken wave, to mark the raging of a baffled force. Many of those selfsame men, who deny this evident concomitant of supreme spiritual jurisdiction, do not hesitate to arrogate to themselves, and to discontented cliques, the power of declaring that a king has forfeited his kingdom. Thus it ever is; the lawful authority of the church is only denied by those who are anxious to attribute to themselves her prerogatives.

There are, then, in the world two divinely constituted orders, the spiritual and the temporal; over each of these a divinely endowed representative presides. Each is supreme and independent in his own sphere; and the limits of each are sharply defined. The primary object of the civil ruler is to procure the temporal good of his subjects; that of the spiritual ruler their moral good; the ultimate end of both is the eternal happiness of their subjects. Now it is evident that our temporal good, properly understood, can never run counter to our spiritual, and vice versa. It is the same God who has established both orders, and linked them together by a golden chain. The first, or if you like, the last link of that chain is fastened to the footstool of the Godhead's throne, and runs thence, down the pathway of ages, to the last generation. It is only when the links of that chain are snapped, or rudely strained, that confusion, disorder, tyranny, and revolution distract nations. Political disorder breeds a spirit of irreligion, and religious torpor begets anarchy. A terrestrial Utopia is only possible in the supposition of a nation, people and king, acting according to the teachings of the gospel; giving to Cæsar his due, and rendering to the church her right. A king is not exempt from obedience to God; he is as strongly bound to hear the gospel, as is the lowest of his people. Now it is through the church that the gospel truths are preached and explained; hence it is to her that the king is to have recourse for his spiritual guidance. High and glorious as is his position; great as are the dignities of his office, still, he has not a particle, or shadow of spiritual power. Cæsar is no longer Emperor and Supreme Pontiff; Christ stripped him of that, and left him as poor, in that respect, as the trembling serf. He is, then, clearly bound to hear the church; he is subject to her spiritual jurisdiction; if not, he must be both a spiritual guide and lawgiver for himself. Although, then, he is supreme and independent in his own sphere, that is, in purely civil matters, he is subject, in spiritual things, to the church. So long as he confines his attention to the temporal good of his people, there can be no clash between him and the church. Once he oversteps his boundaries, and begins to fell trees in the domain of the church, he is met by the vigilant sentinels, that ever keep watch on the towers of Israel. This is the origin of every quarrel between the state and the church. Can the student of history point to a single instance in which a quarrel was brought about by an interference of the church in purely temporal concerns? Never, never, never,

It may be asked: how are explained the many disturbances between the church and kings, during the middle ages, when all Europe was of the one religion? In every case the answer is the same: Cæsar was not satisfied with full political power; he longed for what was unlawful. The great struggle between Gregory VII, and that monster of vice, Henry IV of Germany, was no personal conflict. It was a war of ideas; a fight of eternal principles against an odious political tyranny. Henry broke his solemn engagements with the nation; he trampled on her constitution; he ravaged Saxony, and mocked at her sufferings. But he did more than this; he endeavored to divorce his faithful wife; he impiously sold to impious buffoons, bishoprics and abbeys. His dark catalogue of crimes is written by Voigt, a German and a protestant. In such a crisis as this what was the duty of the Pope? Be it remembered that he was then the universally recognized head of christianity. The German Empire was a creation of his predecessors; he could not sit idly on his throne, and turn a deaf ear to the groans of a suffering people. He exhorted, reproved, advised, commanded, but all in vain. Henry would feign repentence, swear amendment, and in a few months begin his crimes again. The sacred rights and liberties of the people, as taught by the gospel, were cruelly outraged, if not almost destroyed. Human liberty was about to become the manacled slave of a most vicious monarch. Servile courtiers cheered him on; a dispirited nation offered but feeble resistence. But God still lived, and his church had not ceased to produce heroes. One of these was Gregory, the grandest picture in the panorama of church history. He became the fearless champion of the church's rights and the people's liberty. It was a renewal of the fight between Goliah and David, and the final issue was the same. It is true that Gregory died in exile, but he died a victor. His sublime idea of disenthralling the church from the usurpations of princes, and of securing the rights of subjects against the encroachments of tyranny, lived in his successors; developed under their fostering care, and laid the foundations of civil liberty in the christian world. In our day Gregory is maligned by those who never read his letters and his deeds.

He is traduced by those who boast most loudly about the civil rights for which he fought. It is the blackest of ingratitude to denounce one of the noblest champions of human rights, simply because he was pope. We do not mean by this to imply that protestants, as a body, are guilty of this. They cannot help the snarling and yelping of that small mongrel band of ignorant bigots who still breathe, unchoked, the pure air of heaven. This may seem an inappropriate digression in a work of this nature; yet, we fain hope that it is not. It serves to illustrate the proposition, that only when the state oversteps its rights, does a conflict arise between it and the church. The present struggle in Germany is one between conscience and tyranny. The state interferes with the spiritual functions of the church; it seeks to control the education of the clergy, and to regulate the conditions under which they shall discharge their priestly duties. Would any religious community consent to this? Certainly not, unless they foreswore the christian name, and set up a new form of idolatry, known as state worship. The catholic conscience refuses to recognize the right of the state to meddle in religious matters, and hence the relentless persecution, which tends to disintegrate Germany, and which casts a foul blot on the history of the new empire. Still, men who call themselves liberal, applaud the odious tyranny that tramples on the sacred rights of conscience, and confines to dreary prisons virtuous and learned citizens, accused of nothing save a refusal to subject their conscience to antichristian enactments. This is a fruit of the vaunted German progress! It is fast leading that unhappy country back to the degenerate days of the Roman Empire. If the idea of Henry IV lives in Bismarck and Emperor William, the indomitable spirit of Gregory still fires his venerable successor, and the future historian will have to chronicle another Canossa.

Every page of human history is blotted with the vices and ambition of men. The war against God began in Eden, and will last until the angel will declare time to be no more. There is no reason, then, for wondering at the unceasing strife between the world and the church. Lawless passions array themselves against the only power that opposes them effectively. But there is reason for wondering at the sympathy and applause too often given by persons calling themselves christians, to the persecutors of the catholic church. It may be asked: is it possible for harmony to exist between the church and every form of legitimate government? Undoubtedly it is; civil power has to do with temporal matters; faith with spiritual ones. If each keep within its own province they can work harmoniously for the common good. How are the limits of each power to be known? In general there can be no difficulty; all that pertains to divine worship, to the preaching of the word of God, to the administering of the sacraments, and to the regulation of ecclesiastic discipline, belongs evidently to the spiritual sphere. Roads, bridges, customs, post offices, railroads and all temporal concerns of this nature, clearly pertain to the civil sphere. There are, we think, only two subjects about which any difficulty could arise; and regarding even these, there needs be no struggle. The two questions are marriage and education. To prevent litigation, and for various civil reasons, the state may wish to have legal proof of marriage. To procure this it is not necessary to force civil marriage on its subjects. In every age and nation marriage has been looked upon as a religious action; under the gospel dispensation it was raised to the dignity of a sacrament. Hence matrimony, regarded in its essence, pertains to the spiritual sphere. To wrest it from the control of the church, and to place it entirely under the state would clearly be usurpation. But since civil consequences depend on matrimony, the state, if it be not satisfied with the register of the church, may demand that all marriages be, likewise, entered on the public registry. To this the church would offer no objection; the end desired by the state would be efficiently secured, and all fear of a conflict would be over. In our free Dominion we have no conflict on this point, and the legal proof of marriages is rendered certain.

The question of education is capable of a peaceful solution, if statesmen only wished to respect the rights of conscience. A believer in christianity must be educated in accordance with its principles. It is not enough for him to know merely the things of the world; he must, likewise, be taught the science of revealed truths. His intellect must develop in a christian atmosphere; be expanded by christian virtue; and be guided by christian motives. This is the only proper way to mould a true christian character, or to foster that deep religious feeling, without which life is a misspent season, and death a gloomy passage to eternal wail. Education, then, is evidently a matter of conscience and, as such, has been withdrawn from the civil sphere. The state has no more right to prescribe its nature, than what it has to superintend domestic cookery. If its interests require a knowledge of reading, writing, and arithmetic in its subjects, it can order them to acquire this knowledge; but it cannot set up so called "secular schools," and force parents to use them. To impose on a people this bastard system of fragmentary instruction, is to assault the inviolable castle of every English subject, and to storm the domestic hearth. Yet this is called progress; in good sooth it is different from what our fathers looked upon as progressive liberty, when they fought to maintain the immunities of the fireside. Now, two courses are open to the state, each one avoids a collision: either let it leave education severely alone, or come in under its proper form of an auxiliary, not as a principal. Let parents send their children to denominational schools, if they will, and let these schools draw a *pro rata* allowance for the average attendance, provided the inspector finds the pupils up to the required standard in *secular* knowledge. In this way parental rights are respected, and the state has a safeguard that its money is not given without due value being received. This course which common justice indicates, is not pleasing to men who call themselves liberal. The name of every virtue, almost, has been abused, at some time, by being usurped to further a wicked end; the sacred name of liberty is now assumed to rivet the shackles of religious oppression. These "liberal statesmen" tell the people: "you must take our system of education, for we want to give freedom to all." It is in vain for a great body of the people to protest; their sacred rights are sacrificed on this altar of counterfeit liberty, Men, lost to all sense of manhood, perform their rude war-dance around the accursed pile in which the violated liberties of thousands of their fellow-citizens are being consumed; they shout for joy because those who differ from them in religion are oppressed; they heap fuel on the flame, unconscious that, like the Chaldean officials who fed the furnace for the destruction of Sidrach, Misach, and Abdenego, they are only preparing the funeral pyre of their own freedom. For be sure that the state which infringes on the liberty of part of its citizens, will very soon attack that of all. History might teach them prudence, if religion has not taught them charity.

The true idea of life contains an element of the supernatural. Man is subject to a double order, but is destined for only one end. The two orders to which he owes allegiance are divinely instituted; they are the work of the hand of the Most High. God cannot impose on man contradictory obligations; hence man can fully, freely, faithfully discharge every obligation which he has towards the civil power, and towards the church. Just as truth cannot be opposed to truth, so one obligation cannot be opposed to another. There may seem, at times, to be a clash of obligations, but it is not so in reality. The question about "divided allegiance," so strangely raised by a great statesman, is the creation of an over-wrought brain. Allegiance is only due to the state within its own sphere; in matters beyond its jurisdiction it has no right to command; hence, in these, we have no obligation to obey. The refusal of obedience, in such case, is not a want of allegiance; it is a simple protest against a vain pretention. The christian is bound to give due allegiance to the state; but this obligation does not cause him to become a mere machine, to be worked at the pleasure of every constitution tinker. He remains a rational being, endowed with an immortal soul, gifted with a conscience, and responsible to God for his actions. Conscious of his dignity, and aware of his responsibilities, he will not become the tool of the state. He will bow to it within its own province, but will laugh at it when transgressing its limits. It is scarcely correct to say that there are some laws which we ought to disobey. A law can only be imposed by legitimate authority, in matters of its competence. Hence acts of parliament concerning spiritual matters are not laws; and although we disregard them, we are breaking no law. A law must be a reasonable ordinance; but the chatter of temporal rulers about spiritual affairs is so much unreasonable vaporing. Will any man of common sense assert that we must blindly accept every mandate from parliament, or king? No; but why? Simply because he is convinced that there is a limit to the power of the state. Who is to define this limit?. Not the state, surely, else man has no safeguard against tyranny. If the state can assign the limits of its power, it may pitch the stakes where it list, and every tyrant may justify his oppressive measures by deciding that he is acting within his right. Clearly the state is not a fitting surveyor. God, the author of the order, has fixed its boundaries: it ends where the higher order begins. This higher order, embodied in the church, has had its limits revealed; it must know them, for God indwells forever in his spiritual kingdom, vivifying its forces, rendering fruitful its labors, and guiding its actions. The church knowing thus positively its own limits, must know, at least negatively, the limits of the state. One of three things, either the limits of each power are not known, or they are assigned by the state, or by the church. If the first, nought but confusion could ensue; God could never have left such a disordered state of things. If the second, you have no safeguard against tyranny, and, moreover, the inferior order surpasses in dignity the superior. To accept either of the two first is a manifest absurdity. It remains, then, to say in conformity to reason, and to the christian spirit, that the church, guided by the Holy Ghost, defining its own limits, shows the bounds of state power.

The church and state are two divinely instituted orders; each is for the good of man; consequently, man's obligations to both can never clash. Each is independent in its own sphere: in this there is no contradiction. The territories of two independent states are not more clearly defined and distinct than are the provinces of church and state. Civil power, being for the good of man, may be forfeited by atrocious crimes; God has fully provided for man's temporal good; consequently he has established a tribunal that can decide when a forfeiture of power is incurred. This being a question of morality, is decided by the supreme guardian, on earth, of faith and morals, the church. Man can be a faithful subject of both orders; he does not divide, or minimize his allegiance by refusing to obey him who has no right to command. Any other view of these two powers is anti-philosophic and unchristian; barracks are not to supersede churches; nor are policemen the divinely appointed sentinels of Israel's watch-towers.

CHAPTER XIII.

RESURRECTION OF THE BODY.

A continual round of growth and decay is verified in the vegetable world. The seed is cast into the furrow; a partial corruption, caused by moisture and heat, sets in; the germ of vegetable life enclosed in the seed bursts forth, receives increment from the soil and the atmosphere and becomes a plant. This in its turn withers and mingles its particles with the earth, or disperses them through the air. Seasons come and go, and come again; things die but to be reborn; only out of corruption springs the material part of beings. Even during the lifetime of plants or animals there is an unceasing action going on in their systems; parts are being thrown off, and other parts assimilated. Activity, fecundity, regularity, shine in the vegetable order. The fall of the leaf does not bring an enduring sadness, because we know that ere long luxuriant foliage will again bedeck the trees; the decay of our flowers causes slight regret, because we know that in a short time they will bloom again. Hope of a renewal cheers us continually in the midst of vegetable decay. But there is something we love more dearly to look upon than the flowers, or the fruits; there is something more beautiful in our eyes than the lily or the rose; it is the face and form of loved friends. The mother watches her child growing up year by year; she notes with loving pride the development of her son's manly form, or the delicate grace of her daughter. Through the stages and vicissitudes of childhood she patiently cares for her offspring ; in the midst of her care and anxiety, a glance at the innocent face of her child so acts upon her maternal affections as to cause her to forget her weariness, and nerves her to undergo any hardship for its dear sake. But, at times, notwithstanding all her care the playful child or the blooming youth, may be stricken down by some disease, and waste slowly away like a withering flower. At length its frail tabernacle of clay becomes so weakened as to be no longer able to contain the immortal spirit that vivifies it, that spirit departs ; a shrunken, pale corpse alone remains. Deep is the mother's grief as she takes a last lingering look at her fading darling ; wildly she clings to it until friendly hands bear her away. When the graveyard is reached, and the first hollow rattle on the coffin, of clay saluting kindred clay, resounds, her pent up anguish bursts forth : she now fully realizes that her child is, indeed, dead, and about to be hidden from her eyes. In this dark hour of maternal woe is there no softening ray of hope ? is there no bright beam playing gently around the gloomy recesses of the grave, and lessening the horror of the charnel vault. Anti-christian teaching says no more ; everlasting gloom is all that remains. But sweetly on the ears of the afflicted christian mother fall the words of Holy Writ : " For I know that my Redeemer liveth, and that on the last day I shall rise again ; and in *my flesh* I shall see God my Saviour." Hope lights up the christian grave ; even as the flower fadeth and dies, and again springs up to new life, so the human body that moulders in corruption will one day arise to die no more. This is the consoling belief of christians ; this the thought which assuages the pain of the bereaved mother weeping by the tomb of her buried children. Like almost every other truth this one has had its opponents; against them it is to be proved, in the first place, that the resurrection of the dead is possible.

When we say that the dead shall arise we mean that each individual will come forth with all the essential parts, at least, of the self-same body in which he, or she, quitted this life. In every body, as in every material being, there are certain parts which are essential, others which are merely accidental, It is not necessary to determine what, or how many particles of matter constitute the essential parts of the body; one thing is certain, some parts enter essentially into its idea. By death and the subsequent corruption of the body not one single particle, not one atom is destroyed. The flesh corrupts, the bones moulder away, but nothing is annihilated: part of the body escapes as gas,—part mingles with the earth,—part floats in infinitesimal fractions through the air. The winds of heaven may waft to other climes the particles of the bodies of our dead; the waters of the ocean may cause stray bones to float to distant shores, there to bleach and slowly waste away; but what then? Every atom, whether in the east or the west, is garnered up in the vast storehouse of nature; the constituent elements of these bodies still exist: the same almighty power that first called them into existence, and adapted them to form a human body can, if it will, bring them together again to re-form that same body. Once that the idea is mastered that nothing perishes by corruption, that only the component parts of the body are separated, the possibility of the resurrection of the flesh is evident. A corrupted body is not unlike a watch taken to pieces; a wheel lies here, another there; on this side is the spring, on that the box. To a rude barbarian it would seem impossible to re-unite the various parts in such a way as to re-produce the ticking time-piece he so much admired. Relatively, to many it might be impossible; but the maker of it in a few moments, without one false attempt, re-adjusts the scattered wheels, puts each in its place, and the ticking once more is heard. So it will be with the body. Its component parts will be widely scattered; many of them will be invisible, but the creator by one act of his omnipotence will recall them to their places, and cause the soul to re-animate them.

It must be borne in mind that no law of nature is abrogated, suspended, or violated by this. Elements that once combined to form a body may surely combine again. All the elementary forces that acted in the body during life still exist; an act of the omnipotent can intensify or sublimate them; thus intensified they could instantaneously combine and be adapted to a union with the soul. What was said in the chapter on miracles may be here consulted.

Against the possibility of the resurrection only one objection of weight is brought, it is this: the particles of matter are continually undergoing a round of combination and dissolution; parts of plants are assimilated and become parts of sheep, which in turn are assimilated and become parts of men. Hence the generations of the past may have fed plants which fed sheep which our generation eats; consequently parts of the bodies of our ancestors may now be parts of us.

How then can each, at the resurrection, resume the part which was common to many? This difficulty, which is the only one of any importance that can be started, is negative rather than positive. We may freely admit that some of the accidental parts of Jones become parts of Brown: but in this there would be no difficulty; in the resurrection Jones does not require the accidental part, Brown may keep it. But our opponents, if they wish to make out a case, must prove that some essential part of Jones at death, was likewise an essential part of Brown at death; this they can never do: hence we stand in possession and cannot be disturbed. No amount of ingenuity can prove the resurrection impossible.

The sacred scriptures clearly prove that we shall all rise, but the philosopher asks, can reason alone prove it? Our reason suggests two strong arguments in its favor. During life, body and soul constitute one individual; the actions exercised are actions of the individual: hence, although the soul is the principle of life and action, it is the individual who is said to merit reward, or to deserve punishment. Therefore it seems fitting that the body should rise to share in the soul's bliss or misery, so that the individual may be rewarded or punished.

Again, the soul, naturally, has a propensity to a union with the body; their separation is violent: but that which is violent and unnatural cannot be of long duration; therefore the separation of soul and body will not be perpetual. Neither of two things which are naturally adapted to a union, in order to form one whole, can be perfect when separate; therefore in order that nothing might be wanting to the perfect happiness of the soul, the resurrection of the body would be required.

We love our friends in life and desire frequently to gaze upon their countenance; but when the cold touch of death has chilled their life-blood, and quenched the light of their eye, we are soon constrained to bear the stiffened corpse from our homes, and to consign it to a tomb. Burial in sepulchres and vaults was practised in the early days of our race. It was a natural consequence of their belief that death was but a temporary sleep. Just as the loving mother tenderly lays her sleeping infant in his cot, so did friends lay their loved dead in the tomb: the first expects an early rising of her child; the latter expect it only in the far future. As years rolled on some nations began to burn the bodies of the dead, and to collect the ashes into urns which were often preserved in the homes of the family. Christianity restored the primitive use of burial underground. In our day some few seek to revive the practice of cremation, whilst others look upon it as a flying in the face of the christian belief in the resurrection. Primitive man, ere yet idolatry had debased him, the Jews and the Christians all practised burial underground; hence cremation seems peculiarly a pagan custom. As regards the resurrection it makes no difference by what means a dissolution of the component elements of the body may be brought about. Cremation does not annihilate any more than does corruption; each is but a process of dissolution; the first is quick in in its operation, the last is more slow. The attempted revival of cremation may be undertaken—though of this we are not sure—as a protest against christian burial. Speaking under correction, we cannot see that this process of disposing of a corpse is incompatible with christianity; it is, certainly, against its present practice; but if it can ever, in future years, be proved that in large cities burial is highly noxious, and cremation safe, the church might alter her discipline, and after the funeral service consign the body to the glowing crucible. We think, however, that there is ground enough to entomb all generations, and enough of purifying elements to disinfect the atmosphere.

www.ingramcontent.com/pod-product-compliance
Lightning Source LLC
Chambersburg PA
CBHW022104230426
43672CB00008B/1274